A SMALL TOWN &
THE GREAT WAR

A SMALL TOWN &
THE GREAT WAR

HENLEY IN ARDEN 1914-1919

Douglas Bridgewater

MA (Oxon), MA, PhD (Birm)

Honorary Research Fellow, Centre for War Studies,
University of Birmingham

best wishes

Douglas Bridgewater

August 2014

BREWIN BOOKS

BREWIN BOOKS
56 Alcester Road,
Studley,
Warwickshire,
B80 7LG
www.brewinbooks.com

Published by Brewin Books 2014

ISBN: 978-1-85858-528-4

Printed and bound in Great Britain
by Biddles Ltd.

Contents

In honour
of the men and women of
Beaudesert and Henley in Arden
who during the years 1914 to 1919
dedicated their lives to the service
of their country and in many
cases died for it.

Introduction

IN February 1915 the Henley correspondent of the *Stratford upon Avon Herald and South Warwickshire Advertiser* (hereinafter referred to as the *Herald*) wrote, "The local roll of honour is one to be proud of, and it is to be hoped that a complete and permanent record will be kept of the men concerned, their deeds, and so forth, by the local powers that be.....No trouble should be considered too great in adequately compiling the records of every parish".[1] It is to be regretted that the task was not undertaken when it could best have been done.

This book is an attempt to produce the record called for by the *Herald's* Henley correspondent. It must be recognized that after an interval of a century, full justice cannot be done to all those men who fought and died, to those who fought and survived or to those of both sexes who made their contribution to the war effort by their service on the home front. However, it represents the best acknowledgment I can make to them and I trust it will help others to recognize the sacrifices they made and that more fortunate generations have been spared.

Many sources have been consulted to make this a comprehensive account of the years 1914 to 1919 in the parishes of Beaudesert and Henley. As well as the books listed in the Bibliography, the contemporary issues of the *Herald* have yielded much interesting information: their Henley correspondent was a regular contributor. The increasing availability on line of many of the archives of the Public Record Office, notably the census records of 1901 and 1911 has saved much time and travel. The minutes of the Parish Council of Wootton Wawen, of which Henley was a ward, were remarkable principally for failing to mention that there was a war on at all. Those of the Beaudesert Parish Meeting were a little more fruitful in this regard. Warwickshire County Record Office contains a log book of the Henley Council Schools and the Parish Registers of both Beaudesert and Henley.

Some of the present residents of the town have provided much useful information and interesting photographs. The Henley Heritage Centre is now recognized as the appropriate depository for documents and photographs relating to the history of the town and all those relevant have been examined. The most interesting of its records in this context is the Peace Celebrations booklet printed in July 1919. I was fortunate to have extended conversations in 2004 with Florence Beard (then aged 100) and Norman Welch (85), who were old enough to have memories of the war, and with Walter Haytree and Arthur O'Donnell, who had recollections of some of those who served in the war.

It may be that the publication of this book will bring more information to light and I shall be pleased to hear from anyone who can add to the account which follows.

---

1   *Herald,* 19 February 1915

1. Henley in Arden before 1914

IN 1914 Henley in Arden was a small "market town, head of a petty Sessional division, township and ecclesiastical parish, in the civil parish of Wootton Wawen."[2] It was "in the South-Western Division of the county, the union and county court district of Stratford upon Avon".[3] It consisted almost entirely of a single street, the High Street and in such a one-street town, street names were unnecessary and addresses simply given as, for example, 56 Henley in Arden. Henley was conjoined with the older parish of Beaudesert and by 1914 the name "Henley" was generally understood to include Beaudesert.

At the census of 1901 the population of Beaudesert was 158 and that of Henley 1,014 giving a combined population of 1,172: of these 512 were males (including 20 boys under 14 boarding at Arden House School) and 560 were females (including 19 "lunatics" resident at Glendossil). There were 301 houses, of which 22 were uninhabited. The 1911 census recorded 364 houses (31 uninhabited) and an increase in the total population to 1,249 (Beaudesert 187 and Henley 1,062). The population increase was largely accounted for by an increase in the number of boys

Beaudesert and Henley from the Mount c 1912

2   Kelly 1908, p 133
3   Kelly, p 133

boarding at the town's three private schools from 20 to 51 and an increase in the number of "lunatics" resident at Glendossil and Hurst House from 19 to 35. The number of people who could be said to be actually living in the town showed an increase of only 30 over the ten year period, less than 3%.

Although Henley had the larger population, Beaudesert was almost four times larger in area, with 1,315 acres to Henley's 340. The principal landowners in Beaudesert were C P Wykeham-Martin JP, Frederick Ernest Muntz DL, JP and Charles Couchman JP.

The two parishes had complementary economies. Beaudesert was almost entirely given over to agriculture, with 14 farms held largely by tenant farmers. It had only one tradesman, (a chimney sweep), and one public house, (the Bird in Hand). Henley acted as a service centre for the surrounding area, with a wide variety of shops and tradesmen. The High Street included five stationers, five boot and shoemakers, four butchers, four grocers (plus two green grocers), three bakers and three drapers, as well as plumbers, confectioners and hairdressers, a miller, a watch and clock maker, a wheelwright, a saddler, a fishmonger, a cycle maker, a chemist, a basket maker, an artificial teeth maker and sundry others, including John George Johnson, grocer and carrier, whose family are still in business in the town as Johnsons Coaches. There were nine public houses – the Bear, the Bell, the Black Swan, the Golden Cross, the Nag's Head, the Old Red Lion, the Three Tuns, the White Horse and the White Swan. Private schools and asylums were important employers, as was the Great Western Railway.

The High Street before 1910 (the pinnacles had not yet been removed from St John's).
Note the White Horse

Markets and fairs played a significant part in the life of the town. Henley Auction Sales held a produce market every Wednesday and a stock sale every other Monday. Fairs were held annually on 25 March and 29 October: the Henley Mop, originally a hiring fair, but now a festive occasion, was held on 11 October each year.

Henley Mop 1912

An innovation in 1912 was the Henley Horse and Cattle Show, one of its founder members being Harry Hawkes. It became one of the finest one-day shows in the Midlands.

In the years before the war young men in particular left the town for employment elsewhere. Some moved to Birmingham and other manufacturing towns in Warwickshire and some joined the regular armed services: a significant number emigrated, of whom at least five returned to England with the Canadian Overseas Expeditionary Force during the war.

Henley was a ward within the civil parish of Wootton Wawen. The first Wootton Wawen Parish Council meeting was held on 4 January 1895 in the County Council Schools in Henley and its first chairman was Charles Couchman of Henley, who continued in that capacity until he left the Council in 1910. The members of the Council at the end of 1913 were J Hawkes (Chairman), J H Harris (Vice-Chairman), A C Coldicott, F T Cooper, T Dunstan, H Hawkes, A R Hawkes, F W Harris and R Herring. The Clerk to the Council was C J Atkins.

Beaudesert was represented by a Parish Meeting, first held on 4 December 1894. In May 1914 its Chairman was Revd J Smith Turner and F C Parkes was Assistant Overseer at an annual salary of £8.10s.0d. It was rare for more than four members to attend a meeting. A member occasionally attended meetings of the Wootton Wawen Parish Council.

An interesting anachronism in the town was the Court Leet of the Manor of Henley in Arden. The Lord of the Manor in 1913 was Edward Galton Wheler of Claverdon Leys, Claverdon. The Court Leet was one of the few surviving in the country and rarely met. Its last meeting before the war was on 21 November 1910 at the Council Schools, when Dr Ernest Nelson was elected High Bailiff in place of Charles Couchman, who had resigned the office to which he had been elected at the Court Leet's previous meeting on 28 April 1893. The High Bailiff acted as the ceremonial head of the town. The meeting in 1910 also elected nine other officers: William Coppage, Low Bailiff; Thomas King and F T Cooper, Affearors; A R Hawkes, Ale Connor; R Herring, Butter Weigher; C B Hallett and F W Harris, Brook Lookers; Samuel Harris, Mace Bearer and A E Stokes, Constable. This was its last meeting until 1917.

Virtually all children in the town attended the Council Schools in the High Street. These served Wootton Wawen as well as Beaudesert and Henley and, when opened on 28 April 1884, had been known as the Wootton Wawen and Beaudesert School. They had a capacity of 283 children, with an average attendance in 1908 of 194.

The Council Schools (1955)

The school could boast an open air swimming pool. In 1905 a group of parents, pupils and teachers dredged part of the River Alne near the mill at the north end of the town. It was known as Fletcher's 'Ole and Thomas Franklin remembered using it as a boy.[4] It was also used by the boys from other local schools.

---

4   *Welham,* p 66

A working party at the swimming pool

Children attended the school up to the age of 14. The Register for the Junior School for the years 1864 to 1891 is deposited at the County Record Office and has proved a useful source of information. The Register for the following years to 1901 is missing and this is unfortunate as it would have provided information on more of the Henley men who served during the war. In 1914 Mr Lot Robinson was master of the junior school and Mrs Argyle was head of the infant department.

Henley had three private schools at this time, all of which were preparatory boarding schools. The largest and the oldest was Arden House School, which had its roots in a preparatory school founded in Feckenham in 1869 by the Revd William Nelson. He moved his family and his school to Arden House in 1876. William died before 1881 as in that year his widow Mary married Walter Lionel Bicknell, who was or then became head of the school. Walter Bicknell died in 1896 at the age of 42 and Mary in 1898 at the age of 52. Her sons, Dr William Ernest Nelson and Oswald Thomas Pemberton Nelson, presumably took over the running of the school in 1896 and its ownership in 1898. Oswald was the Schoolmaster in 1901 and the only teacher resident on the premises. He had been a Scholar at Clifton College from 1887 to 1892, going from there to Keble College, Oxford where he took a 2nd Class degree in Classics. The 1911 census shows that the school had 29 boarders, all boys between the ages of 9 and 14: three of them had been born in India of British parents; the others came from all over the country, though predominantly from Midlands counties. The school's records for the period covered by this book have not survived. Its prospectus issued in about 1920 shows that it had "separate grounds for cricket and football, a rifle range, tennis courts and golf links (in the Spring)." Fees were then 160 guineas a year.

Arden House School

Beaudesert Park was the home of H R Heatley at the end of the 19th century. "Mr Heatley coached boys who wanted special teaching, often for army examinations and they came as boarders to Beaudesert, complete with horses, and added considerably to the social life at Henley."[5] When Mr Heatley retired, the house became the home of Beaudesert Park School, founded in 1908 by Arthur Harry Richardson and his wife Margaret as a preparatory boarding school for boys. Harry Richardson was a Classics graduate from Queens' College, Cambridge and

Beaudesert Park School 1913

5   Wagner, p 25

an inspirational teacher. By 1911 Beaudesert Park had 13 boarders, aged between 7 and 13: six of them had been born in India of British parents.

The school also had in residence two governesses, six domestic staff and a nurse. By 1913 the school's numbers had increased to 24 boys, paying 100 guineas a year each.

Beaudesert Park boys swimming in the pool near the Henley Mill

The facilities available to them in the grounds included an outdoor playground, a croquet lawn, a tennis court, a cricket pitch and a 9-hole golf course. Cricket and football matches were enjoyed against Arden House, other local preparatory schools and the Henley and Wootton Scout Troop. The boys also had the benefit of the surrounding countryside: the first fine Sunday of the summer term was the occasion for an expedition to Bushwood for a picnic and bluebell picking, while there were also bird-nesting forays and other excursions by pony and trap, by bicycle and on foot.

The smallest of Henley's private schools was Burman House in the High Street, which had 9 boarders in 1911 (of whom 7 were from Birmingham). The school was run by Francis Morton, who was resident on the premises with his wife Annie Lilian: they had then been married for 14 years and had no children. Burman House had 17 rooms.

There were two lunatic asylums in the town, Glendossil for both sexes and Hurst House for females only. In 1911 both were owned by Dr Samuel Hollingsworth Agar JP, who was resident at Glendossil, together with a Matron and 14 staff. It had 34 patients, 15 men and 19 women whose ages ranged from 16 to 80. They came from as far afield as London and Edinburgh, but were predominantly from the Midlands. Hurst House was run by Mary Agar, Samuel's daughter, though it only had one female patient at that time. While the census recorded the full names of the staff, the inmates of the asylums were identified only by their initials.

Both Beaudesert and Henley had come under the authority of the minster church of Wootton Wawen in Saxon and Norman times. However, while Beaudesert secured its independence from Wootton Wawen in the 12th century due to the power of the de Montfort family, Henley was unable to do so until 1914 even though it had had its own substantial church since 1367. Both parishes were in the rural deanery of Warwick and the archdeaconry and diocese of Worcester.

There were four principal churches in the town, the parish churches of St Nicholas in Beaudesert (12th century, with 189 sittings) and of St John the Baptist in Henley (14th century, with 300 sittings), the Baptist Church (founded in 1688 and rebuilt in 1867 with seating for 200) and the Wesleyan Methodist Chapel (built in 1894 and seating 170): all were in the High Street, with the exception of St Nicholas' which was in Beaudesert Lane. At the end of 1913 the clergy were Revd James Smith Turner, Rector of Beaudesert (since 1901), Revd George Edward Bell, Vicar of Henley (since 1876), Revd James Henry Kelly, Minister of the Baptist Church and Mr T R Perkins, Minister of the Wesleyan Chapel. Roman Catholics were served by their church in Wootton Wawen.

The Choir of St John's Church, c 1906
Sydney Huggard (verger), F Hemming, W Edkins, B Hemming, F Harris, B Findon, C Hemming
L Baker, G Hemming, M Findon, W Washburn, Revd G E Bell, T Herring, R Bell, Mrs F Harris.
Three Robbins brothers, E Hodges, C Huggard, ?

Henley was the focal point of the Henley Petty Sessional Division. In addition to Henley itself, this included Aspley, Bearley, Beaudesert, Bushwood, Claverdon, Kingswood, Langley, Lapworth, Nuthurst, Oldberrow, Packwood, Pinley, Preston Bagot, Rowington, Tanworth, Wootton Wawen and Ullenhall. The new Court House was built at the rear of the Police Station in 1903, prior to which the magistrates sat at the White Swan. In 1908 the magistrates were Sir William Jaffray of Skilts, Studley; Dr Samuel Hollingsworth Agar of Hurst House; James Booth of Claverdon; John Gerald Bradshaw of Hockley Heath; Charles Couchman of Henley; Frederick Ernest Muntz of Umberslade, Hockley Heath; John William Ryland of Rowington and Edward Galton Wheler of Claverdon. The clerk to the magistrates was Theodore Christophers (who was also Coroner to the Southern Division of the county), who was living at Hill Field in Beaudesert in 1911. The Court sat on the second and last Wednesdays of every month. Henley had its own Police Station, built in 1858 and manned in 1908 by Sergeant John Miles Walker and a constable.

Although it was the birthplace of William James, one of the early railway pioneers, the railway did not come to Henley until the last decade of the 19th century. A private company began a railway to link Henley with the main Great Western Railway at Rowington in 1860, but ran out of money. After a number of other failed attempts, it was completed by the GWR over thirty years later and was opened on 6 June 1894, with its station at the north end of the town. For a short period Henley had two railway stations, as the GWR also opened a station on the North Warwickshire line from Birmingham to Stratford upon Avon in 1908 on the newly-built Station Road. The first of these railways had its rails taken up during the war and was abandoned.

Henley Railway Station c 1910

Many businesses in the town used their own horse and cart, or often a hand-drawn cart. Johnsons began a public carrier service in 1909, initially horse-drawn but later motorised. Public motor transport arrived in Henley with the Midland Red service just before the war.

A Midland Red bus and a horse-drawn cart outside the Bear c 1913

The more affluent in the town had their own motor car or horse, but for many others the bicycle provided a reliable and inexpensive form of transport and recreation. Fifteen members of the Harris family appear in the photograph below, all but grandfather having their own bicycle.

The town's water supply came from a reservoir at Ford Hall, Tanworth in Arden, which had been built in 1894, with a capacity of 12,000 gallons. This proved to be inadequate and in 1915 a reservoir with a capacity of 75,000 gallons was built at Liveridge Hill. Sewerage in the town also dated from 1894 with works at the rear of Blackford Mill Farm. These also proved to be inadequate and new works were built at Pennyford Farm, Wootton Wawen in 1912. Henley Gas Works in Beaudesert dated from 1864 and provided lighting to the town, as well as domestic supplies.

Henley's Fire Engine was horse drawn and manned by volunteers. George Rowney was paid an annual retaining fee of £5.0s.0d for horses for the Engine, Mrs Smith £2.0s.0d for the annual rent of the Fire Engine Station and G Hemming £1.5s.0d annually for cleaning the Fire Engine. In 1913 Stratford Rural District Council proposed that the parishes in the Union join with them in the purchase and upkeep of a Motor Fire Engine, for use in any of the parishes in the Rural District. At the Parish Council meeting on 15 May 1913 the Chairman of the District Council (Charles Couchman of Henley) presented this proposal to the Parish Council: it was given short shrift. J H Harris of the Parish Council proposed that "this Council take no further steps in the matter" and this was carried unanimously. A remnant of the old Fire Engine, the jet of the hose, is kept in the Guild Hall.

The major public building in the town was the Public Hall, which was officially opened on 31 December 1908. Henley in Arden Public Hall & Institute Limited had been formed earlier that year, its directors being Charles Couchman (Chairman), Dr W E Nelson (Managing Director), Sir William Jaffray Bart (of Skilts, Redditch), Frederick Huggins (of Hill House, Lapworth), Hugh G Newton (of Barrells, Ullenhall) and G F Lodder (Secretary). The objectives were to "build premises adapted for the purposes of a Working Man's Club, with Reading Rooms, also a Rifle Range, and a Large Room which may be used for Concerts, Theatricals, Dances, Meetings, and Social Gatherings generally".[6] The site on which it was built in the newly created Station Road had been owned by the Loyal Arden Lodge of Oddfellows, which sold it to the company for £50. The Great Western Railway, which owned Station Road, gave a grant of access on payment of £1 annually. The architects were Osborn, Pemberton & White of 40 Bennett's Hill, Birmingham: the estimated cost of the building, including furnishings and architects' fees, was £1,225. The work was carried out by C and G Huins & Sons of Redditch. The *Herald* of 1 January 1909 gave a substantial account of the Public Hall and of its opening ceremony. "The concert hall is a spacious room, capable of seating 430 and is well lighted. The walls are coloured in a pleasing tone with dado, and the ceiling is match-boarded, which, of course, improves the acoustic properties. The stage, 69 ft by 28 ft, is constructed on modern principles with inclined floor… The electric system of incandescent lighting, known as Telphos, has been adopted

---

6   Company Prospectus, 24 April 1908

and can be controlled from the stage by a neat device. There is also a substantial gallery, a commodious reading room, 28 ft by 17 ft, a billiard room of the same size above, while the rifle range, 92 ft by 8 ft wide, runs along one side and this has been furnished in an up-to-date style at the expense of Mr Oswald Nelson."

Despite the presence of a number of notables, including the Lord-Lieutenant of Warwickshire (the Marquis of Hertford), the opening ceremony was performed by Lieutenant-General Sir Frederick Lance, to whom further reference is made later in this chapter. Having declared the public hall and range open, the Lieutenant-General "fired the first shot at the range, and quite in keeping with his high reputation registered a bull's eye".[7]

While "any person in the neighbourhood could join the institute", it would seem that the founding fathers had designed it primarily with men in mind, as Charles Couchman in his opening remarks commented that "the building was there, and now it only remained for the men, and especially the young men of Henley and neighbourhood, to take advantage of it".[8] Membership was two shillings quarterly. The Reading Room and Billiard Room were open every evening from 6.30 to 10.30, excluding Sundays: the Rifle Range was open on Mondays, Wednesdays and Saturdays from 6.45 to 10.00 pm.

The completion of the building was marked by a number of dramatic performances in the first week of January 1909. The first performance on the new stage was by a group of Henley amateurs, who performed Gilbert and Sullivan's *Trial by Jury* on the afternoon of Monday, 4 January. This was followed by a scene from *The Taming of the Shrew*, with Oscar Asche as Petruchio and his wife Lily Brayton as Katherine: they were the Richard Burton and Elizabeth Taylor of their day and had performed the play at the Adelphi Theatre in London the previous year.

Oscar Asche as Petruchio   *Lily Brayton as Katherine*

---

7   *Herald*, 1 January 1901
8   *Herald*, 1 January 1901

The appearance of Oscar Asche and Lily Brayton was a personal triumph for Dr Nelson. In a brief post performance speech, Asche said that "he was glad to come to Henley at the invitation of his friend, Dr Nelson". Asche was not only a famous actor, but went on to write the book and lyrics for *Chu Chin Chow*, in which he and his wife starred and which ran at His Majesty's Theatre from 31 August 1916 to 22 July 1921, breaking all records.

The last item in the programme was *Compromising Martha*. This was a one-act play which had been performed almost 250 times at the Haymarket Theatre. It

Keble Howard

was written by Keble Howard, the pen name of John Keble Bell, one of the four sons of the Revd George Edward Bell, then Vicar of Henley.

The programme was repeated on Tuesday and Wednesday of that week, with the exception that the scene from Shakespeare was replaced by a one-act comedy, *The Ninth Waltz*. One of the principals in this was Barry Jackson, later Sir Barry Jackson and a towering figure in the theatre in the Midlands. It is evident that the Public Hall was given a magnificent launch, the entertainment provided being of a standard which can never have been excelled there in the hundred years since.

The North Warwickshire Hunt held regular meets in and around the town, originally at the White Swan but later, as the High Street became busier, at the Bird in Hand.

The North Warwickshire Hunt meeting at the White Swan

Clubs & societies catered for a variety of interests. The Loyal Arden Lodge of Oddfellows was well established, as were the Foresters' Friendly Society and the Freemasons.

Henley had a number of sporting clubs, prominent among them being the Forest of Arden Football Club and Henley Cricket Club. The Forest of Arden was a thriving Bowling Club. An interesting minority sport was Quoits.

Henley Quoits Club 1905
H Sims, H Hodges, A Stokes, F Harris, Jabbett (landlord of the Bear)
A Lowe, G Coppage, Hodges

Preparations for war

General

National movements to put the country on something approaching a war footing were actively followed up in Henley. At the opening ceremony for the Public Hall in December 1908 Lord Hertford summarized the immediate response: "They heard a great deal of the territorial force, and he was glad to say that in Warwickshire the numbers were very satisfactory indeed. The force was not up to its strength, but very near it: he forgot the exact percentage, but it was very large. It was pleasing to know that Henley in Arden and the neighbourhood had not been backward at all. They had a great many yeomen from that district and a good number of the new horse artillery battery had been recruited in and around Henley....Henley had done well in recruiting men for the Yeomanry and Artillery and he trusted they would not stop there. A large number of men had come forward and joined the territorial force, and perhaps Henley might form a complete company of infantry there."[9]

It is probable that, when Dr Nelson organized the building of the Public Hall, he did so with the idea that it could serve as a temporary hospital. A hall with a seating capacity of 430 was surely not otherwise necessary in a town with a population of 1,100. It was in itself a preparation for war.

Royal Warwickshire Regiment

Haldane's Territorial and Reserve Forces Act of 1907 brought about a significant change in Warwickshire's volunteer forces. The county's long-established 1st Volunteer Battalion contributed eight companies to each of the newly formed 5th and 6th Territorial Force Battalions of the Royal Warwickshire Regiment. The 2nd Volunteer Battalion contributed ten companies to the 7th Territorial Force Battalion and two companies became the nucleus of the 8th Battalion, which was based at Aston. The four new Territorial Force battalions were intended only for the defence of the United Kingdom, with the regular battalions forming an expeditionary force to fight overseas.

Recruits to the Territorial Force signed on for four years and had to be between 17 and 35 years old. They were required to attend for drill (40 times in their first year and 20 times in subsequent years). They were also required to attend a camp in August each year for two weeks, for which they were paid on the same basis as the regular army. Their uniforms, weapons and regimental colours were similar to those of the regulars.

The 5th, 6th, 7th and 8th Territorial Force battalions formed the Warwickshire Infantry Brigade, based at The Old Barracks in Warwick and one of three which made up the South Midland Division. In the years 1909-13 the Brigade attended the following annual camps:

1909   Brockenhurst in the New Forest (a Divisional camp);
1910   Perham Down on Salisbury Plain (a Divisional camp);
1911   Towyn, Wales;
1912   West Down on Salisbury Plain (a Divisional camp);
1913   Beaulieu, Hampshire (when the Brigade was inspected by General Sir Horace Smith-Dorrien).

---

9   *Herald,* 1 Jan 1909

Warwickshire Yeomanry

The Warwickshire Yeomanry had its origins during the Napoleonic Wars. An advertisement in the *Birmingham Gazette* of 2 July 1794 invited "all high-spirited young men" to join the Warwickshire Regiment of Cavalry. It was promised that all would be "mounted on fine hunters, superior to most Regiments of Light Dragoons". The Warwickshire Regiment of Fencible Light Dragoons was formed in 1797 and was one of the senior regiments of Yeomanry in the country, second only to the Royal Wiltshire Yeomanry. The Warwickshire Yeomanry had a strength of several hundred throughout the nineteenth century and was called out on a number of occasions to assist in maintaining civil order. In 1900, a squadron numbering 5 officers and 116 men joined the Imperial Yeomanry on active service in South Africa. In the course of that war, two of its officers and five of its men were killed.

The Territorial and Reserve Forces Act of 1907 recognized the Warwickshire Yeomanry as the cavalry unit of the County Territorial Force. They joined with the Royal Gloucestershire Hussars, the Queen's Own Worcestershire Hussars and the Warwickshire Battery of the Royal Horse Artillery to form the 1st South Midland Mounted Brigade. Members were expected to meet for training on one day each week and to attend a camp of two weeks, held in May each year. The regiment had four squadrons, 'A' based in Birmingham, 'B' in Kineton, 'C' in Leamington and 'D' in Snitterfield (which subsequently moved to Stratford). The Henley troop formed part of 'D' Squadron and, as the name suggests, contained a number of men from the town, including four members of the Harris family.

SSM F W Harris (on the right) with his sons
(left to right) Harold, William and Leonard

'D' Squadron being inspected by the Lord-Lieutenant (the Marquis of Hertford), at Stratford

The Warwickshire Yeomanry held its annual camps at a number of locations prior to the war, often as part of 1st South Midland Mounted Brigade:

1909   Pelham Down, Salisbury Plain;
1910   Windmill Camp, Salisbury Plain (where it was inspected by Major-General E H H Allenby);
1911   Warwick Park;
1912   Combe Park (where the Warwickshire Yeomanry had a complement of 21 officers and 399 NCOs and men);
1913   Salisbury Plain (where it was inspected on separate occasions by General Sir Horace Smith-Dorrien and Major-General Allenby).

Warwickshire Battery, Royal Horse Artillery

Under Haldane's army reforms, the Yeomanry regiments were to be supported by batteries of Royal Horse Artillery which were to be raised in twelve counties, of which Warwickshire was one.

In May 1908 a meeting was called by Charles Couchman (the High Bailiff) at the White Swan, to encourage men to join the 1/1st Battery of the Warwickshire Royal Horse Artillery. The meeting was addressed by the Earl of Warwick and by his son Major Lord Brooke, who had been appointed to command the Battery. A total of 7 officers and 214 men were required of whom 154 were to serve the guns and 60 to provide the Ammunition Column. Enlistment would be for four years: if the men provided their own horse they would receive an annual grant of £5 and an equitation grant of £1; during the annual camp of 16 days each man would receive 4s.0d. per day.[10] Training took place on five nights each week, plus Saturday afternoons, with the object of giving men the opportunity to train at least one day a week. As training was held in the Warwick and Leamington Spa areas, it cannot have been easy for men from Henley to attend.

The number of volunteers had reached 183 by early 1910, 83 coming from the Warwick area, 43 from Coventry, 26 from Stratford, 26 from Henley and 5 from Coleshill. Four sub-sections (a full gun detachment and its wagons) were set up: 'A' and 'B' sub-sections from Warwick and Leamington Spa, 'C' from Coventry and Coleshill and 'D' from Stratford and Henley. The last-named provided most of the men for the Ammunition Column as well as a gun detachment.[11] It also established The Stratford on Avon and Henley Royal Horse Artillery Rifle Club.[12]

The Battery was inspected by General Sir John French in April 1910 prior to going on its first annual camp to Salisbury Plain the following month.

Despite the significant number of volunteers from the Henley area in 1910, only Sgt Frank Moore (*qv*) has been identified as having served with the Warwickshire Battery during the war years. J W Webster (*qv*) served with the Battery from 1908 to 1910, but joined the Royal Field Artillery in 1914.

The Rifle Range

When the Henley Public Hall and Institute was officially opened on 31 December 1908, it was very evident that great importance was attached to its indoor rifle range. Three of the visiting speakers emphasized its significance. The first to do so was Lord Hertford. "It must be of the very greatest possible advantage ….. to have a building … in which they could meet for entertainments, social intercourse, and where the young men could practise using a rifle on the miniature range. He hoped that the young men would take advantage of the rifle range."[13] On closing his address, Lord Hertford asked Lieutenant-General Sir Frederick Lance to declare the building open.

Sir Frederick Lance had been invited to open the building, not because of any association he had with the town or the county, but because he was a representative of the Society of Miniature Rifle Clubs. "The Society had come into existence because of the deficiencies in rifle shooting which became apparent during the Boer War. When in the Boer War they saw so many gallant young Englishmen come forward to fight the battles of their country in South Africa some of them who understood the question could not but feel very grieved that these men, full of zeal and courage, of high physique, and generally fine horsemen should go into battle without any knowledge of the practice and handling of rifles.

---

10 Spinks, p5
11 Spinks, pp 10-11
12 Spinks, p 14
13 *Herald*, 1 January 1909

Although such a range as they now had was extremely useful for winter practice, he hoped the time was not far distant when they would have an open-air range in Henley for a longer distance. The regular forces had benefited by the introduction of these ranges, which were now common in many battalions of the British army. Every man who fired at these ranges was doing a very valuable work in making himself an efficient rifleman. He was very pleased to learn that they had a school in Henley where the boys were taught rifle shooting, and he should like to see it extended to the club, so that boys might have an opportunity of using the range." The school in question was Arden House and their instructor was Benjamin Rhodes (*qv*), formerly of the King's Royal Rifle Corps.

Sir Henry Fairfax-Lucy of Charlecote Park was called upon to propose a vote of thanks to Lord Hertford and Sir Frederick Lance. In doing so, he said that although the territorial force could do very little for miniature rifle clubs, the latter could do a great deal for the territorial force by acting as an incentive for the recruiting of the youth of the district.[14]

The rifle range proved to be popular. "The active career of the Institute and Rifle Club had a very promising opening last Saturday evening. The membership then enrolled numbered sixty and the secretarial department was kept busy. The rifle range was in constant requisition throughout the evening and the reading and billiard rooms proved attractive, the arrangements generally giving satisfaction. It has been decided to open the range on three evenings each week, but the other rooms will be available every night, Sunday, of course, being excepted."[15]

Voluntary Aid Detachments

In 1909 the War Office issued a Scheme for the Organisation of Voluntary Aid, based on the British Red Cross Society and the Order of St John of Jerusalem in England. "Voluntary Aid Detachments were…formed with a view to serving Territorial formations fighting in this country…the general basis of organisation had to be shifted…but that part of it which had reference to the provision of temporary hospitals …was largely available for use as soon as wounded men began to arrive from abroad."[16] Branches of the Red Cross were established on a county basis with units known as Voluntary Aid Detachments (VADs). The members of these units were also known as VADs and were trained in first aid and nursing: they numbered over 6,000 within a year.

Two such units were established in Henley in 1909, one for men (designated Warwick Number 11) and one for women (Warwick Number 32). Members were instructed by Dr Nelson and as well as attending lectures they carried out Red Cross work in the area. Members were examined regularly and Dr Earnshaw Hewer of Stratford upon Avon conducted examinations in December 1913 and

14   *Herald,* 7 January 1909
15   *Herald,* 15 January 1909
16   *Joint War Committee,* p 211

April 1914. The names of the successful candidates were published in the *Herald* of 29 May 1914:

Warwick Number 11 VAD

W Dawes, W Hadley, G Coppage, H Payne, J V Watkins, H Hodges, F Harrison, H H Munro, E Hopkins, E B Berry, P Enstone, E Holtom and R Fisk.

Warwick Number 11 VAD Ambulancet

Warwick Number 32 VAD

Miss Bagshaw, Mrs D Adams, Mrs Cox, Miss M Guinness, Miss Herring, Miss Hardy, Miss M Hemming, Miss F Kirby, the Hon Gladys Moncrieff, Miss B Steele and Miss Wakefield.

Warwick Number 32 VAD

The units also had to raise most of the money required for their work. By May 1914 they were finding this onerous and seeking to raise the £20 they estimated they needed for their annual running costs by attracting a number of vice-presidents and other supporters.

The buildings which were put forward nationally as possible temporary hospitals "were considered from the point of view of Equipment, Doctors, Nursing Staff, and the extent to which the cost of maintenance could be born locally."[17] When the necessary conditions were met, "little difficulty was experienced in respect of funds, local subscriptions and collections of various kinds sufficing to meet the current expenses."[18]

---

17 *Joint War Committee*, p 211
18 *Joint War Committee*, p 212

2. Henley in 1914

The National Situation

On 28 June the Archduke Franz Ferdinand, heir presumptive to the throne of Austro-Hungary, was assassinated at Sarajevo, triggering a series of events which led inexorably to the First World War. Austro-Hungary declared war on Serbia on 28 July and when Russia began general mobilisation Germany declared war on Russia on 1 August. Germany and France mobilised on that day and the British navy mobilised on 2 August. On 3 August Germany declared war on France and invaded Belgium, resulting in a British ultimatum to Germany which was timed to expire at 11.00 pm on 4 August (midnight in Germany). No reply was received and Britain was at war with Germany from that hour.

The following day Field Marshal Lord Kitchener became Minister for War and immediately issued orders for the expansion of the army. He did not believe that the war would be over by Christmas as the popular press supposed, but that it would be long and costly. The highly-trained regular army had 244,000 troops at the outbreak of war and the part-time Territorial Force a similar number.[19] Kitchener had opposed the creation of the Territorial Force in 1908 and now decided to expand the regular army by raising a new army made up of wartime volunteers. Each man would enlist for three years or the duration of the war (whichever was the longer) and would agree to serve anywhere that was necessary. On 6 August Parliament agreed to an increase of 500,000 men of all ranks. Kitchener's "Your King and Country need you: a call to arms" was published on 11 August and asked for 100,000 men to enlist. This was very successful as 300,000 men had enlisted by the end of August and a further 700,000 by the end of the year.[20]

The first British troops arrived in France on 7 August and Germany invaded France on 23 August. The British retreat following the Battle of Mons on that day was halted at the Battle of Le Cateau on 25 to 27 August. After the German capture of Antwerp on 9 October, trench warfare on the Western Front began on 29 October. On the same day Turkey entered the war on the side of Germany. Britain declared war on Turkey on 6 November.

At sea, a British squadron was defeated by a numerically superior German squadron at the Battle of Coronel off the coast of Chile on 1 November. This defeat was avenged on 8 December, when a larger British squadron under Admiral Sturdee defeated von Spee's squadron at the Battle of the Falkland Islands, sinking his principal ships the *Gneisenau* and the *Scharnhorst*.

The war reached the British mainland when the German fleet shelled Scarborough and Hartlepool on 16 December.

---

19   Winter, p 29
20   Winter, p 30

The Royal Warwickshire Regiment

The Royal Warwickshire Regiment had many battalions during the war: the 1st and 2nd Battalions were part of the regular army; the 3rd, 4th, 12th, 13th and 17th were reserve battalions and remained within the UK; the 5th, 6th, 7th and 8th were Territorial battalions and the 9th, 10th, 11th, 14th, 15th and 16th were Service battalions, part of Kitchener's New Army. The last three of these were also known as the 1st, 2nd and 3rd Birmingham Battalions – the "Birmingham Pals". They were recruited following an advertisement which appeared in the *Birmingham Daily Post* on 1 September, calling for "non-manual workers aged 19 to 35 to join". Within a week the list had closed at just under 4,500 "young men of the middle class". None of the Henley men enlisted in these battalions at that time, but a number joined them or were transferred into them from other battalions later in the war.

It is impractical to follow the fortunes of all of these battalions, so only the history of the four Territorial Battalions, the 5th, 6th, 7th and 8th which made up the Warwickshire Brigade, will be detailed further.

On Saturday, 1 August the Warwickshire Brigade entrained for Rhyl in North Wales for their annual camp. The following day the War Office cancelled all Territorial Force annual camps and the Brigade immediately returned home to await further instructions. The order for the Territorials to mobilise was given on the afternoon of 4 August. Parading at 6 am on the morning of 5 August, the Warwickshire Brigade marched to New Street Station in Birmingham and entrained for Weymouth. They did not remain there long, but moved by train to Swindon and thence to Leighton Buzzard. From Leighton Buzzard they marched to Chelmsford, averaging 16 miles each day, by way of Tring, Waltham Cross and Chipping Ongar. They were met at every village by crowds offering hospitality. At Chelmsford each member of the Brigade was asked individually if he wished to volunteer for service overseas: almost all agreed to do so.

The Brigade spent the rest of the year billeted in private houses in Essex, despite having been told on 9 September that they would be sent out to France in six weeks.

The Warwickshire Yeomanry

The year began as it normally did for the Warwickshire Yeomanry, which assembled for its annual fortnight's training in early summer. On Saturday, 23 May 1914 the Henley troop of 'D' Squadron paraded at the White Swan in Henley to march to Warwick Park via Claverdon. The troop consisted of RQMS Tippett, SQMS F T Cooper, Sergeants F C Parkes and H G Morris, Lance-Corporals F T Cox, I B Whitehouse, W Whitehouse, H Digwood, H P Hawkes and E J Cox, Saddler Lance-Corporal W Dyer, Staff Sergeant R Haycock and Privates E B Berry, T Cooke, D J Faithfull, A Hanson, F T Hobbs, H Johnson, W E Lyde, C H Lyde, T Meredith, W Price, R Russell, A Steele, J Spencer, W Stiles, H Willis, P Yeomans, A Cumbley and G Finch. The troop left Henley under Sergeant Parkes at 9.30 am and met up with the other troops of 'D' Squadron (those of Stratford upon Avon, Weston-sub-

Edge and Salford Priors) at Longbridge Manor near Warwick at 11.30 am, before moving to join the rest of the regiment in Warwick Park at 1.00 pm. "Year by year the selected exercises and tests are calculated to promote more and more the thorough efficiency of this important branch of the country's service. In addition to grants and allowances, prizes of £5 and £2 will be given to the best horses in each squadron and £10 for the best horse in the regiment".[21] The *Herald* reported that during the camp the Henley troop (not all of whom were resident in Henley) "well sustained the good reputation of the locality for smartness and efficiency": the jumping prize was awarded to Corporal Percy Hawkes and his section. On 6 June the men then dispersed to their normal occupations, but not for long.

Anticipating Germany's negative response to the British ultimatum, the order to mobilise the Warwickshire Yeomanry was given during the afternoon of 4 August. 'A' Squadron assembled at Birmingham on 5 August, but was immediately broken up, as only three squadrons were called for in the war-time establishment of a cavalry regiment. One-third of its men were transferred to each of the other three squadrons. On the same day, 'B' Squadron assembled at Warwick, 'C' Squadron at Coventry and 'D' Squadron at Stratford.

D Squadron leaving Stratford for Warwick and the war, 10 August 1914

The squadrons marched to Warwick on Monday, 10 August where they and the Headquarters staff paraded on Warwick Common. The Regiment assembled at Shire Hall on 12 August where it was addressed by its commanding officer

---

21   *Herald*, 22 May 1914

Lieutenant-Colonel F Dugdale and by Brigadier-General E A Wiggin, commanding 1st South Midland Mounted Brigade. The men's conditions of service did not oblige them to do so, but the very large majority of them volunteered for service overseas.

The following day the regiment entrained at Milverton Station for Bury St Edmunds, arriving there on 14 August and being joined by the Royal Gloucestershire Hussars and the Queen's Own Worcestershire Hussars, the other regiments in the 1st South Midland Mounted Brigade. On 31 August the brigade entrained for Newbury where they camped on the Race Course until they returned to Norfolk on 16 November, remaining in Norfolk for the rest of the year.

Henley

There was an initial enthusiastic response in the town to the call to arms. The first to leave from Henley were the local members of the Warwickshire Yeomanry, who left for the headquarters of D Squadron at Stratford upon Avon on Wednesday, 5 August. "The township has always provided one of the best and strongest troops in the Warwickshire Yeomanry."[22] On 10 August the regiment concentrated at Warwick, the men of D Squadron marching there from Stratford. The Headquarters Staff of the regiment included RQMS George Tippett of Henley.

Another nine men left Henley on Monday 24 August for more varied locations. These men and their destinations were:

Ernest Jones	ASC, Woolwich
Raymond Bayliss	ASC, Aldershot
Fisher Webster	Royal Artillery, Portsmouth
James Webster	Royal Artillery, Portsmouth
James Harris	Royal Artillery, Portsmouth
George Holt	King's Royal Rifle Corps
J Holt	King's Royal Rifle Corps
William Daniel White	King's Royal Rifle Corps
Arthur Ford	Hussars, Colchester

They left in some style, being photographed as they left for Birmingham in three cars.[23] Those joining the KRRC had clearly been influenced by Benjamin Rhodes, the instructor at the Miniature Rifle Range in the Public Hall, whose original regiment it had been. All of them had enlisted in Birmingham, but early in the war a recruiting station was established in Stratford upon Avon at 4 Sheep Street, where men could be medically examined and attested if found suitable.[24]

---

22 *Herald*, 7 August 14
23 *Herald*, 28 August 1914
24 *Herald*, 4 September 1914

At least one local employer actively encouraged his men to enlist. Mr F E Muntz of Umberslade Hall was one of the principal landowners in both Beaudesert and Henley. He gave a donation of £2 to any of the men on his estate that enlisted and guaranteed that their places would be kept open for them until their return. Any married man living on the estate would retain his house and his dependants would be allowed to live rent free until his return.[25]

Joseph Hawkes had succeeded Charles Couchman as Chairman of the Parish Council in 1910. He was re-elected Chairman at the Council meeting on 17 April 1914. At this meeting it was proposed and carried unanimously that the Clerk be instructed to write and convey to Cllr T Dunstan "their deep sympathy for him in his recent bereavement." Two councillors and the Parish Clerk each lost a son in the course of the war and it seems strange that no such proposal was made following those sad events. The first Parish Council meeting to be held during the war years took place on 28 September 1914, chaired by Joseph Hawkes. Other members were J H Harris (Vice-Chairman), A C Coldicott, F T Cooper, H Hawkes, R Herring, T Dunstan and A R Hawkes. W T Taylor in his capacity as Rural District Councillor was also present at that meeting. The Parish Council had a number of Committees: the Henley, Wootton Wawen and Ullenhall Footpath Committees reported their footpaths to be fair, satisfactory and good respectively; the Fire Engine Committee stated that the Fire Engine was in good condition and had been re-painted and the Council instructed the Clerk (C J Atkins) to send to the Local Government Board their resolution, "That the Wootton Wawen Parish Council request the Local Government Board to regulate the speed limit of Motors through Henley in Arden". The war and its local consequences did not appear on the agenda and they did not do so at any Parish Council meeting during the war years.

The Parish Meeting of Beaudesert on 8 September 1914 noted that Mr F C Parkes had resigned his position as Assistant Overseer of the parish "on being called up with the Warwickshire Yeomanry for war service". Mr Herbert George Parkes was appointed in his place at the same annual salary of £8.8s.0d.

There was some excitement on Wednesday, 16 September 1914 when Inspector Wright of Henley arrested Charles Gotz as a prisoner of war. Gotz was working in the nurseries of Mr Woolley in Lapworth, was living in lodgings at Canal Cottages in Lapworth and was said to be a German reservist. The following day he was sent with an escort to the camp for aliens in Newbury.[26]

Refugees from the war did not take long to arrive in Henley. A family of three Belgian refugees was staying at Mrs Argyle's bungalow in the town by early September.[27]

All the churches supported the war. The Revd J Smith Turner, Rector of Beaudesert, was appointed as the representative in the immediate locality for the

25   *Herald*, 11 September 1914
26   *Herald*, 4 September 1914
27   *Herald*, 11 September 1914

Inns of Court Officer Training Corps, for those who wished to obtain a commission in the cavalry or infantry. "Men of the University and Public School class, and particularly those of sporting or out of door experience, or used to handling men, are the most suitable."[28] Since there were few such men in the area, his role was a light one. The Revd Leonard D Schofield was appointed minister of the Baptist Church on 7 June 1914. He later gave a series of sermons on the subject of the war, concluding on 4 October with a rousing address entitled, "Will You Join the Army?"[29] In December there was a crowded audience at a patriotic concert in the Wesleyan schoolroom.[30]

The local schools continued to operate as normally as possible. Beaudesert Park School played three football matches during the year against the Henley and Wootton Boy Scouts, all of which they won convincingly. They played eight games of cricket, five of them against the local schools of King Edward's, West House and Packwood Haugh.

The first contingent of wounded arrived at Henley's VAD Hospital on 28 November, being brought by motor ambulance from Birmingham. The nine wounded included men from the Black Watch, the Cameron Highlanders and the Royal Irish Rifles. Although there were several serious cases, it was reported that none had lost limbs.[31]

The newly opened Hospital
Quartermaster William Dodds is standing on the left

28   *Herald,* 4 June 1915
29   *Herald,* 9 October 1914
30   *Herald,* 10 December 1914
31   *Herald,* 4 December 1914

In the early months of the war, the children made 100 sandbags for a scheme organized by Miss Guinness of Wootton Wawen Hall. [32]

Hunting continued during the war, but not on its pre-war scale. This was inevitable, since by the end of September 1914 some 300 horses had gone from the North Warwickshire Hunt for war purposes and 65 members of the Hunt had joined the army. [33]

Many clubs and societies were formed in connection with the war. The Snapshots from Home League sent photos of relatives and of local scenes to members of the forces. [34] The Helping Hand League was established to send comforts to the troops. [35]

William John Fieldhouse bought the title of Lord of the Manor of Henley in Arden in 1914 from Edward Galton Wheler. He took his newly acquired duties very seriously and immediately set about restoring several of the older buildings in the town and reviving the Court Leet.

32   *Herald*, 10 December 1914

33   *Herald*, 2 October 1914

34   *Herald*, 26 November 1914

35   *Herald*, 10 December 1914

3. Henley in 1915

The National Situation

The first Zeppelin raid on Britain took place on 19 January and Germany extended the war against merchant ships by authorising their attack by U-boats. The *Lusitania* was sunk on 7 May, resulting in an international outcry. As a consequence of this Germany ended its unlimited submarine warfare on 1 September.

On the Western Front there were notable battles at Neuve Chapelle in March, at Ypres in April and May, at Artois in May and June and at Loos, where battle commenced on 25 September and resulted in the heaviest British casualties to date. On 17 December Haig replaced French as the British Commander-in-Chief in France, largely as a result of French's failure to follow up the early British advantage at Loos.

Britain bombarded Turkish forts in the Dardanelles as a preliminary to the landing on Gallipoli on 25 April. The campaign proved unsuccessful, heavy casualties were incurred and on 23 October the decision was taken to evacuate the peninsula, though this did not take place until the end of the year.

In Mesopotamia, Allied troops entered Kut el Amara on 28 September and their siege by the Turks began on 7 December.

The Warwickshire Brigade

The Warwickshire Brigade remained in Essex in the early part of 1915, each of its battalions being quartered in a different village. At this time each battalion's eight companies were reorganized into four companies. The Brigade numbered 176 officers and 4,053 other ranks: it formed part of the South Midland Division and went overseas from Southampton on 23 March 1915, landing in Le Havre.

Moving by train to Cassel, they marched about 12 miles to Bailleul on 28 March and some 8 miles to Armentieres on 1 April. There they were trained in the arts of trench warfare before taking over a section of the front line south of Ypres and northeast of Ploegsteert.

The 5th and 7th battalions were the first to serve in the front line, with the 6th and 8th going into reserve. After four days they exchanged duties and continued to do so as a matter of routine.

The front line trenches were not yet continuous and during April the Brigade's essential task was to link up the existing trenches and to put in place a second line of trenches and a system of communication trenches at right angles to these. This work was carried out at night to minimise casualties.

On 13 May 1915, the 1st South Midland Division became the 48th (South Midland) Division and the Warwickshire Brigade was renamed the 143rd (Warwickshire) Infantry Brigade.

After two months at the front, 143rd Brigade had a brief four days respite as the divisional reserve before moving back into the line. At the end of June the Brigade made a four day march south to Lozinghem, where it again spent some time training. In July the Brigade moved to the front line north and east of Hebuterne in the Somme sector, then one of the quietest sectors of the line. On 7 August it moved a little further south to Collincamps and the men spent much of their time in maintaining the trench system which had been damaged by heavy rain.

Its next move came in September, when it took over part of the line at Fonquevillers, to the north of Hebuterne. There it experienced a number of casualties as a result of its trenches being shelled by German Minnenwerfers (10 inch mortars). Bad weather again made life difficult. The Brigade was now experienced and efficient in trench warfare and spent some time passing on its experience to battalions of Kitchener's New Army. In the last quarter of the year the Brigade's losses were comparatively light, 77 men being killed or wounded.

The Warwickshire Yeomanry

The Warwickshire Yeomanry spent the first quarter of the year in Norfolk, but in April they were ordered overseas. On 10 April the first party of the Yeomanry left Avonmouth for Alexandria on the *Wayfarer*, together with the regiment's horses.

HMT Wayfarer *at Avonmouth*

The greater part of the regiment sailed the following day on the *Saturnia*, which reached Alexandria on 24 April. The *Wayfarer* was torpedoed some 60 miles northwest of the Scillies on 11 April with the loss of four men. The rest of the men got away safely in their lifeboats and were picked up by the *Framfield*, which had been sailing close behind the *Wayfarer*, but the horses were left on the *Wayfarer*. However, the *Wayfarer* did not sink and a party of the Yeomanry under Major Richardson returned to the ship to look after the horses, while the *Framfield* towed the *Wayfarer* into Queenstown, which was reached on 13 April. Only three of the 760 horses on board were lost. The Yeomanry who had been on the *Wayfarer* eventually reached Alexandria on 14 May.

The Regiment was in Chatby Camp, just outside Alexandria, and was part of the 1st Mounted Brigade, 2nd Cavalry Division. On 14 August most of the Regiment left on the *Ascania* for Gallipoli where it was to serve as infantry: about one-third of the regiment stayed behind to look after the horses. It landed at Suvla Bay, disembarking under enemy fire.

Warwickshire Yeomanry on the beach at Gallipoli

The Regiment left the peninsula for Mudros on 31 October and returned to Alexandria on 28 November on the *Themistocles*. During its time in Gallipoli the Regiment lost 11 men killed, four died of wounds and four died of disease: in addition 2 officers and 92 men were wounded. Some of those left at Chatby served with the Western Frontier Force, which was assembled to fight the Senussi in the Western Desert: of these, three were killed in an action on 11 December.

Henley

On 16 March 1915 the *London Gazette* announced that by an Order in Council dated 11 March the benefices of the Rectory of Beaudesert and the Perpetual

Curacy of Henley in Arden, being contiguous to each other and having a combined population not exceeding 1,500 were to be combined into a single benefice of Beaudesert-cum-Henley in Arden. The union had been agreed by the Bishop of Worcester, who held the right to nominate to the Rectory of Beaudesert, and by the High Bailiff of Henley, who held the right to nominate to the Perpetual Curacy of Henley. The right to nominate to the combined benefice was to be vested in the High Bailiff on the first occasion and on the second occasion in the Bishop of Worcester; they were to nominate alternately thereafter. Added to the new parish were Whitley from Wootton Wawen and Impsley and James' farms from Ullenhall. The Rectory of Beaudesert was to be the house of residence of the united benefice. For six weeks previously notices had been fixed on the principal door of each church, inviting anyone who objected to the proposed union to write with their objections to the Archbishop of Canterbury. No such objections having been received, the union came into effect on 20 March. The right of nomination to the combined benefice was formalized on 2 June and appeared in the *London Gazette* of 11 June 1915. One advantage for the people of Henley was that they now had the privilege of burial in Beaudesert rather than being buried in Wootton Wawen.

On 18 June the Revd J Smith Turner left Beaudesert to take up the living of Shelsley Beauchamp in Worcestershire following the amalgamation of the parishes of Beaudesert and Henley. The Revd Francis Dalrymple Lane took over the joint benefice.

On the academic front, Alice Tippett, the younger daughter of RQMS Tippett and his wife of Henley won an entrance scholarship to King Edward's School at Stratford from the Henley Council Schools, as her elder sister Mary and her brother Edward George had done before her.

The children of the Henley Council Schools again made 100 sandbags for a scheme organized by Miss Guinness.

In January it was announced that Henley Cricket Club was to be discontinued in the coming season.[36]

Some entertainment was continued however. The choir of St Nicholas' Church enjoyed their annual outing in Evesham, while Henley and Alcester had a bowls match.[37] The *Herald* of the following week noted the forthcoming Horse Show and Sale at Henley.

A meeting of the Bird in Hand Pig Club was held in 1915 and it was reported that the Wesleyan Church ladies were working on comforts for the troops.

In November the North Warwickshire Hunt was again hunting in the area. The Forest of Arden Bowling Club was ticking over and the White Swan Bowling Club had recently been formed.

The North Warwickshire Hunt met again in December and there were a number of Christmas festivities.

---

36   *Herald,* 22 January 1915
37   *Herald,* 10 September 1915

White Swan Bowling Club 1915

The Bear was refused a license, on the grounds that it was one of 10 fully licensed houses in Henley, the population of 1,023 had been practically stationary for years and agriculture was the only industry. These reasons were equally applicable to the other licensed houses in the town, so it is not clear why the Bear was singled out in this way.

The Bear

Dr Samuel Agar advertised in the *British Medical Journal* of 26 June 1915 that considerable improvements had recently been made in both Glendossil and Hurst House. He claimed that they were "in every way adapted for the care and treatment of the mentally afflicted of the upper and middle classes".

There was a crowded audience at a patriotic concert in the Henley Wesleyan School Room early in December.

Early in 1915, "few young, and above all, robust men are now to be seen in the immediate locality".[38]

A presentation was made to Private William Bonehill, who had been called up on 5 August 1914 and wounded on 9 November. He was given a subscription of £2.10s.0d. Sergeant Cyril Huggard was badly wounded and lost an arm.[39]

In March 1915 a company of the 1st Birmingham Battalion of the RWR (also known as the 14th Battalion RWR) under Captain Cooke was billeted in the town for manoeuvres. "People were asked to accommodate the troops. Where people agreed the soldiers number was chalked on the front door. On some houses there were two or three numbers showing".[40] "Skirmishes and night attacks under war conditions have formed a prominent part of the exercises." They arrived in the town on Friday, 19 March and left the following Friday to return to Sutton Coldfield.[41]

An unidentified company of the 14th Battalion RWR parade in the Market Square

---

38   *Herald,* 5 February 1915
39   *Herald,* 22 January 1915
40   Mary Howard, quoted in Welham, p 126
41   *The Picture World,* 26 March 1915

Cyrenius Herring and RQMS Tippett were reported safe following the *Wayfarer* incident[42]. Both of them had in fact sailed on the *Saturnia*.

Frank Stokes and William Findon, formerly of Henley, who had emigrated to Canada before the war, were back in the country with the Canadian Expeditionary Force.[43]

A recruitment meeting was held at the Market Cross on 23 June, preceded by a parade through the town by the band of the 8th Battalion RWR. The meeting was chaired by the High Bailiff. The Henley correspondent of the *Herald* was doubtful whether it would meet with any great success. "In conversation with a leading resident of the neighbourhood it was pointed out that the supposed available recruits resident in Henley could probably be numbered on the fingers of one hand, whilst very few remained in the hamlets around. The fact was also emphasised that Henley and the district had already responded splendidly to every patriotic call, and that not a few lives had been laid down from the immediate neighbourhood in the present struggle."[44]

The *Herald* reported on a number of cases where a family had several sons in the forces. Mr & Mrs Holt's five sons were all in or had volunteered for the army: Richard had joined the 3rd Battalion of the RWR and after training on the Isle of Wight was now in the trenches; Owen had been with the RFA on Salisbury Plain; Harry, a married man with a child was also with the RFA; an elder married son William had volunteered for service, while George had joined the KRRC but had since been invalided home and was now working in a gun factory in Birmingham. Of the four sons of Mr & Mrs Thomas Robbins, two were in the army and two were employed by the GWR: Thomas Robbins had himself served in the Royal Warwicks. Private Leslie Huggard of the Coldstream Guards, who was previously wounded in the hip at the Battle of Mons, had now been shot through the jaw. His brother, Sergeant Huggard of the East Yorkshire Regiment, who had also been seriously wounded in the early weeks of the war, was now much improved in health after a long and tedious convalescence. A younger brother (Gordon Cuthbert) had now been commissioned. Their widowed mother was entitled to take pride in her patriotic sons.

Private H R Arnold of the Coldstream Guards was killed on 6 July 1915. He was the eldest son of Mr & Mrs Harvey Arnold, who had a boot and shoe establishment at 281 High Street.

Harry Arnold had assisted in his father's business before enlisting and had been an active member of the Baptist Church. A memorial service was held for him in the Baptist Church on the evening of Sunday, 18 July, conducted by the Revd Leonard Schofield. Harry had been a member of the Fire Brigade, which was in attendance under its Captain, Godfrey Hemming. The local British Red

---

42 *Herald,* 16 April 1915
43 *Herald,* 23 April 1915
44 *Herald,* 25 June 1915

Cross Society also attended in uniform, under its Quartermaster William Dawes, as did the local scout troop.[45]

William Bonehill was wounded again, this time in the thigh, and was in hospital in Dublin. On a happier note, Sergeant Cyril Godfrey Huggard was married in Southam to Gladys Mary Plummer, also lately of Henley: the wedding had been postponed because of the war, as the banns had first been read in Henley in July 1914. Mr J G Hotchin was now at the front with the Warwickshire Battery of the Royal Horse Artillery.[46] His connection with the town was that he had formerly worked for Mr T R Perkins of the Henley Pharmacy.

RQMS Tippett was serving in Alexandria with the Warwickshire Yeomanry. Two former members of the clerical staff at Henley Station had enlisted: Mr R Roy was with the RAMC in the Dardanelles and Mr C B Finney, who had subsequently moved to Lapworth Station, was also in the forces. It was noted that work on the railway was now recognized as national service.[47]

The Henley men in the Yeomanry survived their experiences in Gallipoli. Private Edward Hopkins of the 9th Battalion RWR was not so fortunate and died of wounds on 8 October, aged 21. On the evening of Sunday, 24 October a Memorial Service was held in St John's Church for him. He had sung with the church choir for some years and at the service a wreath was hung in his former place in the choir stalls. The service was attended by the High Bailiff (Dr Nelson), members of the Henley VAD and members of the Foresters Society, of which he had been a member. Several soldiers from the hospital also attended.

Rifleman William Robbins of the 1st Battalion KRRC was now in Henley. He had been on active service in France since May and was wounded in the stomach on 27 September during the battle of Loos. This was a very narrow escape from death as the bullet had ripped through a tobacco tin and pierced a half-franc piece. He was transferred to a hospital in Leicester at the beginning of October and discharged on 30 October. He was said to be at home on leave until 8 November.[48]

The Henley correspondent of the *Herald* reported on 19 November that "the patriotism of this part of the country has been most gratifying. Few remain of military age without a good reason, a number of men having been rejected through no fault of their own and others placed in their proper class of the reserves. Patriotic funds and movements have also been well supported in the district".

---

45 *Herald*, 16 July 1915

46 John George Hotchin was born in Sutton, Lincolnshire and mobilized with the Warwickshire Battery as a Driver on 5 August 1914. He was subsequently promoted to Corporal and died in Flanders on 25 July 1917, aged 27

47 *Herald*, 3 September 1915

48 *Herald*, 5 November 1915

4. Henley in 1916

The National Scene

Conscription was introduced on 27 January 1916, when the Military Service Act came into operation. All unmarried men between the ages of 18 and 41 were required to enlist, with the exception of those who were unfit, were in exempt occupations or had a conscientious objection to war service. Many men claimed to be in one or other of these categories when they received their papers. Local tribunals were set up to hear these cases. In May compulsory service was extended to married men when the desired increase in the number of recruits failed to materialize.

Compulsory military service was not extended to Ireland, where the Easter Rising against the British in Ireland took place on 23 April.

The nation was shocked by the death of Lord Kitchener, drowned when the cruiser *Hampshire* was sunk by a mine off the Orkneys on 5 June when taking him to Russia.

On the western front much the biggest engagements of the year were the Battle of Verdun, primarily involving the French, from 21 February and the first Battle of the Somme, primarily involving the British, between 1 July and 18 November. The first day of the Somme on 1 July saw the largest loss ever suffered by the British army in a day: a total of 58,000 casualties were sustained of which 19,000 were killed. By the end of the battle British casualties totaled almost 419,000 men.

In the Middle East, the withdrawal from Gallipoli at the end of 1915 enabled British forces to push forward from the Suez Canal into Sinai and Palestine. April proved to be a bad month with the defeat of the 5th Mounted Brigade (formerly the 1st South Midland Mounted Brigade) in Sinai on 23 April by a German led Turkish force and the surrender of the British garrison of Kut el Amara in Mesopotamia to the Turks on 29 April. The British setback in Sinai was temporary and they advanced into Palestine, winning an important battle at Romani on 3 August. On 13 December they went onto the offensive again in Mesopotamia.

The Battle of Jutland on 31 May and 1 June was the only full-scale battle between the British and German navies during the war. Although the result was inconclusive, the Germans never sought battle again. The U-Boat campaign was renewed on 15 October, having been cut back on 10 May.

David Lloyd George became Prime Minister on 7 December.

The Warwickshire Brigade

Some specialization took place within the Brigade, with the establishment of a Brigade Machine Gun Company in January and the Light Trench Mortar Unit attached to the Brigade being renamed the 143rd Trench Mortar Battery in March.

A demonstration by the latter in front of the whole Brigade in May unfortunately resulted in 14 of its members being killed or wounded. In the same month the Brigade took over a section of the line at Hebuterne, one of the quietest sections of the front, opposite the German position at Gommecourt. The Brigade's first task was to dig a new trench 800 yards long and 200 yards in front of the existing one. Digging took place at night and was resisted by the Germans. During the first night of digging 29 men were casualties. In June the Brigade incurred 183 casualties, mostly during digging, rather more than it had incurred in the whole of the preceding eight months.

This rate of casualties increased dramatically with the onset of the Battle of the Somme on 1 July. The Brigade's battalions were divided into two, with 5th and 7th being attached to 48th Division and forming part of the reserve, while 6th and 8th were attached to 11th Brigade of 4th Division which went into the attack. The 5th and 7th battalions lost 52 men killed or wounded on 1 July: the 6th and 8th battalions lost 472 and 584 men respectively – horrendous casualty rates of 60% and 55%.

The 5th and 7th Battalions went into the front line later in the battle. A private in the 5th battalion who had cracked and left the line was court-martialed on 10 July and sentenced to death. Although the panel recommended leniency, General Rawlinson decided to make an example of him, this being the first case on the Somme, and Private Earp was shot at dawn on 22 July. The 5th Battalion was part of a force involved in heavy fighting near Ovillers from 15 to 17 July, cutting off the German garrison there, capturing many prisoners and incurring 121 casualties.

Men of the Warwickshire Brigade resting during the Battle of the Somme

The Brigade was re-united in August and spent some time in training out of the line. On 2 September Lieutenant-Colonel Sladen, commanding 5th Battalion, was promoted to Brigadier-General and took over command of the Brigade. It continued to spend much time in training, absorbing the drafts of men to replace the casualties of the Somme. It left the Somme in mid-December and moved to Albert.

Lieutenant Carrington, the battalion's historian, kept a comprehensive record of his time with the 5th Battalion in 1916. He spent 101 days in the front line under fire, 120 in reserve, 73 at rest and 72 days in courses, leave, travelling and in hospital. He had packed up and moved 80 times.

The Warwickshire Yeomanry

Following the defeat in Gallipoli, action in the Middle East moved to Sinai and Palestine as British troops left the comparative safety of the Suez Canal and sought to advance against the Turks in this area. The campaign began badly. The 2nd South Midland, now renamed the 5th Mounted Brigade, found itself in Sinai in advance of the main British force, defending a number of oases at Oghratina, Katia, Hamisah and Romani. Commanded by Brigadier-General Wiggin, the Brigade was spread thinly among the oases and was surprised by an attack from a considerable Turkish force. It suffered a heavy defeat on 23 April, a day still commemorated as Katia Day by the three Yeomanry regiments concerned. The Worcestershire and Gloucestershire Yeomanry suffered most, the Warwickshire Yeomanry losing only one man killed and seven men wounded.

Later in the year, the advance in Sinai resumed and the Yeomanry took part in the Battle of Romani, in which they lost three officers killed and two wounded, together with five other ranks killed, 22 wounded and two taken prisoner. By the end of the year the advance had reached El Arish.

Henley

The annual meeting of the Farmers' Union in January emphasised the importance of farming, claiming that "many could render more useful service to their country in their everyday occupation than as active members of the forces".[49] As a result of the shortage of men, farmers' wives were doing men's work: this was not enough and it was hoped that "in the spring and summer we shall not only see farmers' wives but every woman who is able doing something towards relieving the present shortage of labour".[50]

The shortage of labour was re-emphasised in the following month, when it was claimed that "Henley and many parishes round have almost been denuded of young men by the national claims. Even rejected men have offered themselves more than once in a number of cases. It is evident, however, that some are offering

---

49   *Herald*, 14 January 1916
50   *Herald*, 28 January 1916

useful service at home, and where necessary the cases are coming before the district tribunals, which have been kept pretty busy since the closing of the original Derby scheme".[51] There were now considerable additions to the number of men enlisting as a result of conscription. "It is the dread of being forced to undertake duties for which they are entirely unsuited and not any lack of patriotism which has kept many back in Warwickshire as in other parts of the country." The unfairness of the system was bemoaned: "while many unfit have been taken, thousands of the more robust have been left untouched".[52]

The first recorded meeting of the Stratford Rural District Tribunal was on 28 February. It was chaired by Charles Couchman of Henley and had seven other members. Mr R C Cox appeared for the Recruiting Officer of Stratford, Major Bairnsfather (father of the war's most famous cartoonist), to put forward the army's case in each instance. The chairman was reported as strongly deprecating the practice of certain people in canvassing members of the Tribunal. No men from Henley appeared before the Tribunal on this occasion.

A number of men served as Special Constables, those named in early 1916 being F T Cooper, W T Taylor, Harry Hawkes, Francis Morton, H F Hands and Robert Newcombe. Henley had its own Magistrates' Court and its own bench. Offences against society were generally minor. The principal offences at one session in October were failing to display rear lights on a cycle, driving a motorcycle with an ineffective silencer, too brilliant a light shining from the Ullenhall vicarage and the theft of three guinea fowl. At a sitting later in the month, William Jamieson of the White Swan applied for the transfer of the licence to his wife Florence Emma

The North Warwickshire Hunt entertaining the troops

---

51 *Herald*, 4 February 1916
52 *Herald*, 3 March 1916

Jamieson, as he had been called up for active service. Sarah Argyle, newsagent of 102 High Street, was fined 10s.0d for showing a light after dark. No doubt to his personal embarrassment in view of his position as a Special Constable, Harry Hawkes was summoned for failing to produce a driving licence: the case was dismissed on payment of 4s.0d costs. In December the Bench heard cases involving the showing of lights after dark in the Three Tuns, riding a cycle without lights and failing to produce a driving licence.

The North Warwickshire Hunt met at the Bird in Hand in February and twice in March, with its next recorded meeting being at 10.00 am on 18 November.

On 29 March 1916 the Beaudesert Parish Meeting recorded its thanks to Mr S K Cattell "for his generous gift of land for the extension of the church yard". It was pleased "that the privilege of burial has been offered to the parishioners of Henley in Arden". Prior to this time the parishioners of Henley were buried in Wootton Wawen. There were only four members at the meeting (the number never exceeded six during the war years).

The Bear Hotel closed in April. It was in a run-down condition and at the hearing for the renewal of its license it was argued that there were more than enough premises in the town without it. Its case cannot have been helped by the absence of so many men in the armed forces. It was sold at auction in May for £260.

Henley Auction Sales Limited held its annual meeting in April. The Henley Horses and Foals Sale and Show was held on Wednesday, 27 September with numerous entries. Although very successful, there were fewer entries than last year, which was "not surprising in view of the numbers commandeered by the Government".[53] The Christmas Fat Stock Show was held in December.

The Baptist Guild of Help held a rummage sale on 2 October 1916 and raised £12 to be used to acquire materials to make up into useful gifts for soldiers and sailors.

The annual treat for the children of the Henley Council Mixed and Infants' Schools was given by Mrs Richardson of Beaudesert Park: 180 children attended, 60 from the infants and 120 from the mixed. Mrs Argyle was Head of Infants and Mr Lot Robinson Head of Mixed.

The *Herald* reported regularly on news of Henley men in the forces. In January Mrs Sladen of Hillfield (at the top of Liveridge Hill) was collecting socks, "which are urgently needed for the 1/5th Royal Warwickshire Regiment". Mrs Sladen was well informed on this shortage, as her husband Lieutenant-Colonel Gerald Sladen (*qv*) was commanding the regiment at the time: he was mentioned in dispatches soon afterwards and awarded the DSO in the same month. This was not the end of his exploits during the year: in September he took over command of the Warwickshire Brigade with the rank of Brigadier-General and was awarded a Bar to his DSO in November.

---

53 *Herald*, 29 September 1916

RQMS Tippett (*qv*) of the Warwickshire Yeomanry was home on leave in March. "His long experience of military matters and his enthusiasm have proved of much service in the present campaign … The RQMS who responded at the outset of the war as an old campaigner is certainly now entitled to a share of less exciting duties." George Tippett was fortunate to get leave from Egypt and his age is likely to have been a factor (he was then 53).

The experiences of Warrant Officer Peter Newcombe (*qv*) were reported upon in February and March. He had served in the Royal Navy before the war and had just retired when war broke out. He immediately re-enlisted and served in HMS *Kent*, which took part in the Battle of the Falkland Islands on 8 December 1914. Peter Newcombe came home on leave in March, having left the *Kent* and been transferred to another ship. He was the elder brother of Robert Newcombe, who ran the Henley Garage.

The part being played by the Holt and Robbins families of Henley was highlighted in March. Richard and Ellen Jane Holt of the Tanyard had four sons in the forces and a fifth on munitions work (who had previously enlisted but had been discharged from the army on health grounds). Both Owen and Harry Holt (*qv*) were with the RFA in France; Richard Holt (*qv*) was with the 7th Battalion of the Warwicks, had been wounded twice and was also in France, while William Holt was with the RAMC. George Holt (*qv*) was an ammunition worker, while a brother-in-law, Francis Thomas Maine, was with the Worcesters.[54] Thomas and Ellen Robbins, of 82 High Street, also had four sons serving or about to serve with the forces. Their eldest son William (*qv*), who had been wounded at Loos in September 1915, had been much troubled by his wound and was in hospital in Brighton: Arthur Robbins (*qv*) had been in France but was sent to Salonika in January, while Harry Robbins (*qv*) was in the Royal Naval Reserve; their fourth son Frank had also volunteered. Their father Thomas was a former member of the forces.

The role of the sons of Mr Edmund Shilton, a dentist in Henley, was next to feature in the *Herald*. Corporal Roy Shilton (*qv*), a graduate of Birmingham University, had enlisted in the Coldstream Guards and was wounded in France in March 1915. On his return to active service he was transferred to the Royal Engineers because of his knowledge of chemistry and was commissioned as a 2nd Lieutenant. His two brothers, both Birmingham University students, were also in the forces, one being a Lieutenant in the RAMC, the other in the Inns of Court Officer Training Corps.[55]

In April there was news of Leslie Duggan (*qv*), the only son of Mrs Duggan of Glendossil. He was educated at Solihull School and while there had four years in the Officer Training Corps, becoming a sergeant in charge of the armoury. He left the school in August 1915 and joined the 13th Battalion of the Warwicks. He

---

54 Francis Thomas Maine was the younger brother of Frederick George Maine (*qv*)
55 Frederick Walton Shilton (*qv*) and Arthur Shilton respectively

was promoted to Lance Corporal immediately afterwards and was now a Corporal, aged 17 and stationed at Blandford, Dorsetshire.

2nd Lieutenant K Westmacott Lane (*qv*), the only son of the Revd F D Lane, Rector of the joint parish, was dangerously wounded in France while serving with the 1st Worcestershire Battery of the Royal Field Artillery. The Rector was able to visit his son twice in May and 2nd Lieutenant Lane was later reported to be out of danger and making good progress.

Other Henley men reported on in May were Percy Hawkes (*qv*), "now on leave, looking well and hearty after his exciting yeomanry experiences" and 1st Class Air Mechanic W Franklin (*qv*) of the Royal Flying Corps, who "has been looking up his Henley friends. He has already seen some interesting service at the front".

In June the *Herald* reported on several former members of the town and district who had emigrated to Canada before the war. They were now serving with the forces either at home or in France, while some had recently been able to pay a short visit to their former home. Those named were W Findon (*qv*) and F Stokes (*qv*) (serving in France), P Hemmings (*qv*) of the Canadian ASC, T Beck (*qv*) of Strathcona's Horse, A R Hodgkins (*qv*) and A E Atkins (*qv*) (who was expected on leave shortly).

The *Herald* of 14 July gave a belated account of the defeat at Katia on 23 April and of the death at that time of Lieutenant Sir J H Jaffray of Skilts, Studley a former pupil of Arden House School. Two weeks later it carried an account of the marriage of his sister, Mabel Violet Mary Jaffray to Major C R H Wiggin of the Staffordshire Yeomanry.

In August the *Herald* reported on two sons of James Hodges, a baker in Henley. Private W J Hodges (*qv*) was serving with the 1st Birmingham Battalion of the Warwicks (the 14th Battalion) and had been wounded in the neck and arm by shrapnel on 30 July. He was progressing well in the Wellington Road Hospital, Liverpool. Private D T Hodges (*qv*) was serving with the South Staffordshire Regiment and was in Dublin, where he had seen active service "during the late rebellion".

The *Herald* of 22 September carried a letter from Michael Bell (*qv*), a chaplain in the forces, who had sailed over 50,000 miles during the war in Australian Hospital ships. He was a son of the former Vicar of Henley, the Reverend G E Bell, and requested the addresses of those from the town and district who were serving in the forces, "many of whom I have known personally for some years". He stated that he might be able to visit some, but would in any event write to them from time to time. He was then billeted at the Hotel Victoria in Aldershot.

Sapper F C Atkins (*qv*) was one of those who wrote to Michael Bell (then at Newark) informing him that his brother, Sergeant A E Atkins (*qv*), had come over with the Canadian contingent, been wounded in the leg and was in hospital in Woolwich. Sapper Atkins had himself been wounded and sent to a hospital in the north of England: he was expecting to go back to France.

Another who wrote to him was Corporal Raymond Bayliss (*qv*), "one of the four soldier sons of Mr & Mrs Bayliss", who had been wounded by shrapnel on 22 August: he found that he had 53 marks, "but only 15 were very bad". Corporal Bayliss was now back on duty. Another of Michael Bell's correspondents was Private J H Beard (*qv*), who was "about 20 miles from the firing line, so having a good rest". Jack Beard had gone to a large church service the previous Sunday night in the open air, where the divisional band played the music. "It was the largest service I have seen."

5. Henley in 1917

The National Scene

The year was notable for significant changes in alignment among the principal protagonists. The Russian Revolution led to the abdication of Tsar Nicholas II on 15 March. The Bolsheviks seized power on 7 November and signed an armistice with Germany on 15 December. The withdrawal of Russia from the Allied cause was more than compensated by the USA declaring war on Germany on 6 April, its first troops landing in France on 25 June. The fighting capability of the French was damaged by mutinies in their army from 29 April to 20 May: Marshall Petain took over as the French Commander-in-Chief on 15 May, while Clemenceau became their Premier on 19 November.

Trench warfare continued on the Western Front. The Germans withdrew to the Hindenburg line between 23 February and 5 April. The British went on the offensive at Arras in April and captured the Messines Ridge in June. The third battle of Ypres began on 31 July and ended on 10 November. British forces arrived in Italy on 4 November.

In Palestine the arrival of Allenby saw a major improvement in the British campaign. At the conclusion of the third Battle of Gaza, the town was seized by the British on 7 November. They went on to capture Jerusalem on 9 December.

Germany resumed its unrestricted U-Boat campaign on 31 January and losses in its shipping led to Britain belatedly introducing the convoy system on 10 May.

The Warwickshire Brigade

The Brigade spent the first six months of the year in France. Conditions were difficult, as heavy snow and severe frosts prevailed until mid-April. During a temporary thaw in mid-February most trenches were up to the knee in water and in some instances it was up to four feet deep. In March the Germans went onto the defensive, withdrawing to prepared positions on the Hindenburg Line. The Brigade crossed the Somme by pontoon, all the bridges having been destroyed. The advance was hampered by booby traps and the scorched-earth policy the Germans had adopted. The Brigade was relieved on 20 April and employed in training and in repairing roads around Peronne in the Somme. On 13 May they moved up east of Bapaume, facing the Hindenburg Line. The enemy was a mile away and the front was very quiet.

On 5 July the Brigade began to prepare for operations in the Ypres Salient and moved there by train on 20 July. The 3rd Battle of Ypres, or Passchendaele, had begun on 7 June in an attempt to clear the Germans from the Salient. The Warwickshire Brigade went into the front line on 17 August. The ground had been so fiercely fought over for so long that the trenches had disappeared, leaving a waste of mud and water with countless shell holes and dead bodies, both British and German. All of the battalions were heavily involved in an attack on a German strongpoint at Springfield Farm, which they finally took and held. In August 1917, the wettest in Flanders for 30 years, the Brigade suffered over 1,000 casualties. It spent the month of September resting and training and moved back into the Salient on 30 September, where it was involved in very heavy fighting in the first week of October. In that time each of its four battalions lost on average about 10 officers and 250 other ranks.

Very few of the men who had landed in France with the Brigade in March 1915 now remained. On 9 October it moved back to Poperinghe and reinforcements began to arrive, including about 100 from the newly dismounted Warwickshire Yeomanry who had been sent back from Palestine. Passchendaele was captured by the Canadians on 7 November and the 3rd Battle of Ypres came to an end on 12 November: in its course the BEF incurred about 240,000 casualties and the Germans some 260,000.

On 20 November the Brigade had a complete change of scene when it entrained for Italy, part of the British and French support for the Italian army which had been badly beaten by German and Austro-Hungarian troops. The Italians were holding a line along the Piave River in Venetia with the British and French providing a strategic reserve to the west in case the Italian line was broken again. The Brigade were billeted in the area and remained there until 26 January 1918.

The Warwickshire Yeomanry

During the year the advance into Palestine continued, the 5th Mounted Brigade being part of the Desert Mounted Column which also included the Anzac Mounted Division and the Camel Corps. At the Battle of Rafa in January the Warwickshire Yeomanry lost five men killed and two officers and 42 other ranks wounded. The border into Palestine was crossed on 21 March. In an interval in the fighting the first Grand Palestine Race Meeting took place, in which the premier event, the Sinai Grand National was won by Captain Gooch of the Warwickshire Yeomanry on his horse *Clautoi*. This horse had been on board the *Wayfarer* when it was torpedoed and was wounded in battle no fewer than three times. It became the best known horse in Palestine, subsequently winning three more races.

The first Battle of Gaza took place on 25 March, but the attack failed as did another on 17 April. The actions in the first six months of 1917 resulted in the regiment losing one officer killed and five wounded, together with 16 other ranks being killed and 46 wounded. The failure to capture Gaza led to General Sir Edmund Allenby replacing General Murray as Commander in Chief of the Egyptian Expeditionary Force. The Force was revitalized and after a period of consolidation Beersheba was captured on 31 October, finally being taken by a brilliant charge by the 4th Australian Light Horse. Gaza was taken on 7 November. On the following day, the Warwickshire and Worcestershire Yeomanry shared the honours of a famous charge against the Turkish guns at Huj, in which they routed a force more than ten times their number. 'B' and 'C' Squadrons of the Warwickshire Yeomanry took part and in the course of the charge lost three officers wounded (Captain R Valintine of Snitterfield later dying), 13 other ranks killed and 20 wounded (two of whom subsequently died) and 45 horses killed. The advance continued into the Judean Hills through very difficult conditions and adverse weather. Jerusalem surrendered on 9 December. The 5th Mounted Brigade ended the year at El Birj, many suffering from sickness.

Henley

The *Herald* began the year with 8 pages and sold for 1d. By 23 March it had halved in size, as a result of the shortage of newsprint. Attendances at church services were considered to be generally good. For Easter 1917 there were 184 communicants at St Nicholas' and St John's. Attendance at Easter was significantly better than at Christmas when there had been 121 communicants at the two churches.

The annual meeting of the White Swan Bowling Club was held on Friday, 5 May. Play commenced on the following Sunday, "when the green was found to be in very good condition". The patients of the VAD Hospital, which adjoined the club, were allowed free use of the green on all but three evenings a week, reserved for members.

William John Fieldhouse had bought the title of Lord of the Manor of Henley in Arden in 1914 from Edward Galton Wheler. He took his newly acquired duties seriously and set about restoring several of the older buildings in the town and reviving the Court Leet. The *Herald* of 6 July reported that "the town has been wonderfully improved by the splendid work carried out by Mr W J Fieldhouse. The restoration of the Guild Hall from its previous very dilapidated condition is a thing of architectural beauty and Henley possesses in it a historic building of which it may be justly proud." On 7 July the Red Cross Gift House was formally opened at the Corner Shop (in the same block as the Guild Hall and now occupied by Lloyds TSB Bank). Mr Fieldhouse had placed the building at the disposal of the Red Cross "free of rates, taxes and other expenses". It was "devoted to the sale of rummage" with all proceeds going to the Henley Red Cross Hospital. It was opened by the High Bailiff, who welcomed all donations to the Hospital: though the war had now lasted almost 3 years and the prices of everything had more than doubled, the grant which the government allowed to the Hospital had not been increased. The shop took over £50 in its first week and was closed on Wednesday, 26 September having raised £264.9s.1d in eleven weeks.

Dr Nelson, High Bailiff, Commandant of the Hospital and local medical practitioner, was presented with the OBE by King George V personally at Buckingham Palace on Thursday, 27 September.

A meeting of the Court Leet was held on 14 November 1917. The proceedings, presided over by the Lord of the Manor, were attended by a large number of

The Corner Shop and the Market Cross

"Henley's prominent citizens". The Town Crier, Mr F W Harris, the fourth generation of his family to hold the office, opened the court. The High Bailiff was at one end of the table, the Lord of the Manor at the other. The Steward of the Manor, Mr G F Lodder, empanelled a large jury and Dr Agar was chosen as its foreman. Dr Nelson was re-elected as High Bailiff and other officers elected were William Coppage, Low Bailiff; George Busby, Constable; Algernon Hawkes, Ale Taster; Robert Herring, Butter Weigher; Howard Sinclair-Brown and F W Harris, Brook Lookers and Harry Hawkes, Mace Bearer. Dr Agar said that it was the unanimous wish of the jury that the court should meet each year and this was agreed to by the Lord of the Manor: the Steward thought that the second Wednesday in November would be a suitable day. This "interesting revival" was fully reported in the *Herald* of 16 November.

A Court Leet service was held in St John's at 3 pm on Sunday, 2 December 1917. This was the first such service to have been held for over 40 years, the last occasion being during Dr Diamond's period of office (1850-1855). In the course of the service the Rector appealed for a generous offering in aid of a fund to be raised for a permanent war memorial to the men on the Roll of Honour of the parish: the collection amounted to £4.5s.9d.

Sunday School treats exercised the minds of teachers and others "since the food problem became of such absorbing interest". The Baptist Sunday School decided that for the next treat each child would be rationed and parents would be asked to bring their own food.

The *Herald* commented in August that facilities for young people were generally very poor in the town. There was not even a recreation ground, so the children had to play in the street and were "in frequent danger from the numerous motors". However, the Scouts were keeping together well under the leadership of their Scoutmaster, the Revd L G Schofield, despite the difficult conditions under which they operated. They pitched their tents for their summer camp at Bickerscourt Farm, Danzey Green on 4 August and came home on 9 August, having had a very happy time despite the miserable weather. In November scouting activities were suspended for the winter.

On Thursday, 2 August the staff of the Hospital were entertained at Crocketts by Mr & Mrs Clifton Mitchell.

During the war years Henley was a source of recreation for many of its neighbouring towns and cities. In August it was reported that "the holiday week in Henley has been one of the busiest in recollection". All available accommodation in the town was taken and many could not be accommodated due to lack of rooms. Fishing was a popular pastime for male visitors. Many visitors came to see their friends and relatives in hospital. "It was pleasant to note that the soldiers from the Hospital took full advantage of the presence of their friends in the town and these in turn were delighted to find their men folk in such comfortable and well-situated quarters."

The Henley Bench heard several cases involving the use of motor spirit to drive a car or motorcycle, following the Motor Spirit Restriction Order of 1917.[56]

Another symptom of the food shortages was that the Stratford Food Control Committee met in early October under the chairmanship of Charles Couchman. Under the Milk (Prices) Order the maximum price for the retail sale of milk in the Stratford District was 2s.0d per gallon during October and would then be raised to 2s.4d per gallon until the end of March 1918. Couchman commented that the price did not seem too high considering the scarcity of labour and other winter difficulties. Under the Potatoes Order, after 30 September no person, other than a grower selling his own potatoes, could offer them wholesale or retail unless he was registered to do so. It was pointed out that a retailer must display, in his shop or on his barrow, the price at which he was selling his potatoes. Under the Meat (Maximum Prices) Order butchers in the Borough of Stratford were being asked to send in returns for a period to show what their profit had been. Couchman thought it would be a good idea if they invited the butchers in the Rural District to come and talk the matter over with the Committee. This was agreed: it was also agreed that the butchers ought to display the price of meat on their carts when they went round the villages. W T Taylor said that he had been asked to mention the matter of proprietary bread. Some bakers were making it and charging what they liked. Couchman observed that proprietary bread could be sold by a dealer

---

56   *Herald*, 30 November 1917

with a reasonable addition to the fixed price of 9d for a 4lb loaf, but he must still be willing to sell the customary bread for 9d. Couchman said that it was absolutely necessary to engage an officer to see that these regulations were carried out. He proposed that the matter be brought before the District Council: this was seconded by W T Taylor and carried.[57]

Air Raid precautions also created some interest. Instructions were received by the local police authorities to take the necessary steps against air raids. Special constables were dispatched all over the district. It is apparent that they were not always well received, as the comment was made that "it would greatly facilitate the work of the authorities if householders would attend promptly to the order for lowering lights, instead of manifesting an inclination to prolonged argument."[58]

The Food Control Committee met again in December, a month which also saw a meeting of the Rural District Coal Committee. At the latter, Mr Truelove spoke of the problem of displaying the price of coal: coal dealers were allowed to put 1d per mile on the price, which would therefore have to be altered every mile.

News of Servicemen

A Memorial Service was held on the evening of Sunday, 4 February for F C Atkins and F H Woodward. Both men had attended St Nicholas' and St John's during their last leave and Woodward had been a chorister at both. Eighteen wounded soldiers from the hospital also attended, by special permission (under Army Regulations soldiers in hospital were not normally allowed out after 4.00 pm in the winter time).

Sergeant H D Cooke (qv), son of Mr & Mrs Cooke of The Gables, was wounded on 25 February. He was "an old Henley boy" and had served in Gallipoli. He was sent home for treatment and ultimately arrived at the Henley Hospital, where he made a good recovery. Sergeant Cooke is the only Henley soldier known to have been treated in its hospital. Harold Beard was reported to be in hospital in France, while L (sic) Beard was in Bristol suffering from rheumatism.

On 26 March the Beaudesert Parish Meeting resolved to write a letter congratulating F Hodgkins of the Canadian Force (Alfred R Hodgkins qv) on his award of the Military Medal.

Private Maurice Horsnett (qv) of the 13th Battalion RWR was buried in St Nicholas' churchyard on Sunday, 15 April with full military honours. A full choral service was held in the church. Maurice had died on 8 April at Salisbury Plain, where he had been training: his body had been sent home at the request of his relatives.

A crowded Memorial Service was held in St John's Church on Sunday, 20 May for Private George William Andrews (qv) of 11th Battalion RWR, who was killed in action in France on 25 April. He was 20 years old and prior to enlisting had lived

---

57   *Herald*, 12 October 1917
58   *Herald*, 26 October 1917

at 54 High Street. He had been employed by the Great Western Railway at Danzey Green Station. The service was attended by some of his former colleagues and by representatives of the Foresters' Friendly Society, of which he had been a member.

Private William Sutton Findon (*qv*) of Henley, who had emigrated to Canada in about 1913 and had volunteered in 1915 died of wounds on 3 July. He had been warmly welcomed to Henley on his visits while he was training in England. His widow, who was still living in Canada, was the granddaughter of James Argyle of Henley. It was said that much sympathy was felt for those bereaved. Concern was expressed for his sister, Miss E S Findon, who was seriously ill. She had been thrown out of a trap while making a bread round for Mr Welch, a duty she was undertaking because of the shortage of men.

Corporal John George Hotchin of the Warwickshire Royal Horse Artillery was killed in action on 25 July. He had been assistant to Mr T R Perkins of the Henley Pharmacy for three years from 1908 to 1911.

The death of Mr Thomas Robbins after a long illness was reported. He had been employed by the Great Western Railway for about 20 years as a ganger on the line to Lapworth. He left a widow and several children, some of whom were serving in the forces.[59]

The *Herald* of 21 September contained information on several Henley servicemen. News had been received by Mrs Holt of the death of her husband, Driver Harry Hugh Holt of the Royal Field Artillery, in letters from his commanding officer, his Chaplain and a comrade. All testified to the high esteem in which he had been held. He had been about to return from taking ammunition to the trenches on 10 September when he and his two horses were killed instantly by a shell. He had been expected home on leave in the same week in which the news of his death was received.

Mrs Robbins of Henley had been notified by the Record Office in Winchester that her husband Rifleman William Thomas Robbins of the 12th Battalion King's Royal Rifle Corps had been posted missing since 12 August. Fortunately on the morning of 20 September she received a postcard from him stating that he was wounded and a Prisoner of War in Germany: he was going on very well.

Mrs Margaret Maud Hodges had been informed by the Admiralty of the feared loss of the merchant boat on which her son Able Seaman Lawrence Hodges was serving. Nothing definite was yet known of the fate of the ship. In fact Lawrence Hodges died on 21 August 1917, while serving on HMS *Vala*. She was a ship of 1,016 tons, built in 1894. *Vala* had been a collier, but was taken over by the navy in 1915 as one of its Special Service Ships, commonly known as Q Ships. Posing as a merchant ship, the *Vala* was armed and manned by a naval crew. After losing many U Boats to Q Ships, the German navy had become suspicious of merchant ships sailing unescorted. *Vala* was torpedoed and sunk with the loss of all hands

---

59   *Herald*, 31 August 1917

by the German submarine UB 54 on 21 August, some 120 miles south west of the Scilly Isles on a voyage from France to Queenstown in Ireland.

Private Jack Beard was welcomed home on leave in September and was spending 10 days with his parents. He was an old boy of the Baptist Sunday School and originally a member of the VAD. He had seen 2 years and 8 months active service, mostly in Belgium. Three of his brothers were also serving in the army. One of them, Private Harold Beard, who had also been home on leave recently, was wounded for the second time and in a London hospital where he was progressing favourably. Private Harry Lowe, a well known local footballer, had also been wounded in France where he was in hospital, later being moved to a hospital in Stafford.

In December Brigadier-General G C Sladen DSO, MC was mentioned in Sir Douglas Haig's dispatches for distinguished and gallant service and devotion to duty. He was then serving in Italy.

6. Henley in 1918

The National Scene

Butter, margarine, lard, jam, sugar and meat were all subject to rationing in April 1918, with the weekly ration being set at 4 ounces of fats, 8 ounces of sugar, 15 ounces of beef, mutton or lamb and 5 ounces of bacon.

March marked the beginning of the German Spring Offensive, a desperate attempt to secure victory before the Americans could make a major impact. On 21 March they broke through on the Somme and on 9 April began their Lys offensive in Flanders. They went onto the offensive on the Aisne on 27 May, but their retreat began at the second Battle of the Marne from 15 to 18 July. The Allied offensive continued and 8 August became known as "the black day of the German army". The final offensive on the Western Front began on 26 September and British troops broke through the Hindenburg Line on 5 October, with Germany requesting an armistice on the following day. The war finally ended on 11 November when Germany signed the armistice.

The war in the Middle East in 1918 was one of continued success for Allenby and his Egyptian Expeditionary Force. The Turks were defeated at Megiddo (Armageddon) in September and on 1 October British forces entered Damascus. Turkey made peace on 30 October.

At sea the British were steadily winning the war against the U-Boats and Germany abandoned submarine warfare on 20 October. The German High Seas Fleet mutinied on 29 October. Following the Armistice, the German High Seas Fleet surrendered to Britain on 21 November.

In November the Ministry of Labour stated that "When general demobilization begins, priority of release will be given to officers and men who have definite employment awaiting them".[60]

The war had claimed an estimated 16 million lives, but this number was dwarfed by the estimated 50 million people which were killed throughout the world by the influenza pandemic of 1918. This was a more deadly disease than any other in recorded history, attacking one in five of the world's population. Frequently known as "Spanish flu", the disease appeared first in the late spring of 1918, when few deaths were reported and most victims recovered after a few days. When the disease surfaced again later in the year, it was far more severe. Some victims died within hours of their first symptoms, while others succumbed after a few days. It was a true pandemic, finding its victims in every continent and every age group, in the trenches and among civilians in urban and rural areas.

---

60 *Herald,* 29 November 1918

The Warwickshire Brigade

In late January the Brigade moved west of Treviso with the rest of 48th Division to act as a reserve behind the front line along the Piave. In early March they took over a stretch of the line on the Piave and in mid-March moved to the front line on the Asiago Plateau. This was some 50 miles west of Venice and was cold, being over 3,000 feet above sea level. The Plateau was also short of water – a serious disadvantage in the heat of an Italian summer. In early May the Brigade was hit by the influenza epidemic, which was beginning to sweep across Europe. Many men went to hospital. While the average battalion strength at the end of April had been 702, this had reduced to 411 by 15 June.

On 15 June the Austrian army began a heavy offensive, their artillery firing gas shells as well as high explosives and shrapnel. The 5th Battalion, which was the forward battalion in the line, found itself outnumbered by eight to one and suffered heavily. The 6th, 7th and 8th Battalions moved forward to reinforce the position and the ground lost was re-captured the following day. This was the Brigade's first defensive battle during the war and it suffered 201 casualties (12 officers and 189 other ranks). On 26 June the Brigade went into reserve on the Lombardy Plain with the rest of 48th Division.

They returned to the Asiago Plateau on 17 July, taking over a position on the front line on 30 July. On 8 August the 7th and 5th Battalions made a successful raid against the Austrians, capturing one officer, 115 other ranks and 2 machine guns at little loss to themselves. A much less successful attack was made by 5th Battalion on 9 September, in which 8 of its officers and 87 of its other ranks were casualties. When gallantry medals were presented to the Brigade on 17 September, the officers and men of the 5th Battalion, which had borne the brunt of the fighting, were awarded one DSO, 4 MCs, 3 DCMs, 17 MMs and a bar to an existing MM.

In the summer the army's brigades were reorganized, their four battalions being reduced to three. As a consequence of this, the 8th Battalion returned to France, where Corporal William Amey won the VC on 4 November during an attack on Landrecies. His story is worth giving in some detail: "On his own initiative he led his section against a machine gun nest, under heavy fire, drove the garrison into a neighbouring farm and finally captured about 50 prisoners and several machine guns. Later, single-handed, and under heavy fire, he attacked a machine gun post in a farmhouse, killed two of the garrison and drove the remainder into a cellar until assistance arrived. Subsequently, single-handed, he rushed a strongly-held post, capturing 20 prisoners. He displayed throughout the day the highest degree of valour and determination."[61]

The three battalions of the reconstructed 143rd Brigade continued to serve in Italy and went into the front line again on 18 September. The 6th Battalion mounted a successful attack on the Austrian lines on 4 October. The Brigade was

---

61   *London Gazette*, 31 January 1919

in reserve when British and Italian troops defeated the Austrians at the Battle of Vittorio Veneto on 29 and 30 October. On 1 November the 6th Battalion captured Asiago and was joined in its advance by 5th and 7th Battalions. They had advanced 35 miles in 3½ days when the armistice with the Austrians came into force, 6 days before the armistice with Germany. On Sunday, 17 November all 95 officers and 2,410 men of the Brigade attended a church parade and thanksgiving service at Valdagno.

The Warwickshire Yeomanry

The regiment began the year at Belah, resting after the strenuous autumn campaign of 1917. A Divisional Sports Day was held on 9 March, in which a troop of D Squadron won the competition for the best troop of the Division. Two race meetings were held in which Captain Gooch, who had just been awarded the Military Cross, further distinguished himself by winning the Palestine Grand National on his horse *Clautoi* at the 22nd Mounted Brigade races on 6 March and the Grand Military Steeplechase at the 7th Mounted Brigade races on 16 March.

Selected for dismounted service in France with the Machine Gun Corps (MGC), the Yeomanry and the South Nottinghamshire Hussars formed what subsequently became the 100th Warwick and South Nottinghamshire Battalion of the MGC with Lieutenant-Colonel H Gray-Cheape of the Warwicks in command. They left Alexandria on 23 May on HMT *Leasowe Castle*, which was also carrying another battalion of the MGC. Just after midnight on 27 May the ship was struck by a torpedo. Most of the troops were able to escape, as the water was calm and warm and the moon clear and bright. However, when the ship went down at 2.00 am 108 men were lost, including Lieutenant-Colonel Gray-Cheape together with one other officer and 8 other ranks of the Warwickshire Yeomanry.

Leasowe Castle

The battalion returned to Alexandria and embarked again on HMT *Caledonia* on 17 June. They reached Taranto on the south coast of Italy on 21 June and left the following day by train. A long, slow journey brought them to the depot at Etaples on 29 June. Many men were then able to go on leave to the UK. After intensive training in their new role, the battalion began their active service on the western front on 4 September, joining 58th Division. They were heavily involved until the Armistice on 11 November. During their time in France 3 officers and 24 ORs were killed and 1 officer and 51 ORs wounded or gassed.

Henley

Considerable difficulties were experienced with the meat supply on Saturday, 5 January 1918, the local butchers being unable to meet the demand. One way around problems caused by food shortages was the use of allotments. On 8 March 1918 the *Herald* reported that the Allotment Holders Association was now fully organized and fresh land had been obtained, which would result in a considerable increase in food production in the locality. Following the Henley Sale on Monday of that week the farmers met at the Golden Cross to form a Selection Committee under the Meat Distribution Order. A Pig Assurance Association was formed, with Dr Agar as President. An advertisement in the *Herald* on 5 April 1918 urged people to plant more potatoes.

The Golden Cross

Owing to floods in the middle of January, the mail van was unable to get along the Birmingham Road and was delayed for several hours, though the North Warwickshire Hunt was still able to hunt in the area at the end of the month. There was some unseasonal weather in June, when the town was subjected to a violent hailstorm with the hail settling to a depth of several inches.

The Baptist Church held its annual social in March and in August the Baptist Sunday School held their annual treat at Buckley Green Farm, by courtesy of Mr and Mrs F C Parkes.

Henley Auction Sales reported a record year in April and many horses of quality were entered in the Henley Horse Show and Sale on 25 September 1918. W J Fieldhouse, the Lord of the Manor who had been awarded the CBE in January, gave a cup at the Show.

Henley was well patronised by visitors during the Whitsun weekend in May 1918 and many of the men in hospital were visited by their friends.

On 28 June the *Herald* was still running at only four pages, but the price had increased to 1½d. The *Herald* of 12 July contained an advertisement urging people to apply for their new ration books.

On 27 July a score of German POWs arrived in Henley from Stratford and were "accommodated near the railway station", but due to "the lack of various facilities" they had to return the following afternoon. Farmers in the locality were keen to make use of them on the land, but during the night of Wednesday, 25 September four German POWs escaped from Henley, where they were doing farm work: they were still at large the following afternoon.[62]

In July 1918 a few cases of Spanish flu were reported in Henley, but none were regarded as really serious. It was not the only disease to trouble the town, as in September the Deputy Medical Officer of Health for Stratford Rural District reported that there had been 26 cases of measles since the last meeting, of which 25 were from Henley. He recommended closing Henley Schools from 27 August to 30 September 1918.

A day of national prayer and thanksgiving was held on 4 August. At the close of the usual evening services, all the churches united in an open-air service in the market place. There was a large and representative gathering: the lesson was read by Mr A C Coldicott (Rector's Warden).

The scarcity of manpower created a problem in the farms. Gangs were established for threshing, each having its own machine. In the Stratford area the workers included a few men, some of whom were POWs, but the great majority of the workers were women. By August there were fifty gangs of women in the county, each made up of 6 women and a forewoman.

On Monday, 19 August 1918 the Girl Guides and Brownies from Henley went by train to Wootton Wawen to be inspected by Lady Baden-Powell. Following the inspection the girls and their officers were given refreshments and then marched home to Henley.

---

62 *Herald,* 27 September 1918

Henley Brownies 1919
Mildred Hodges, Doris Mole, ?, Hannah Forest, Alice Watkins, Ella Carrington
(Leader)   (Brown Owl)
Muriel Bonehill, H Hawley, Lucy Harris, Florrie Bonehill, O Hawley, Amy Fewtrell, Ruth Rhodes

There was a Wolf Cub pack in Henley and in September there was a merger of the Henley and Wootton Wawen Scout troops.

Beaudesert School outgrew its premises when its numbers increased to 30 and moved to Minchinhampton in Gloucestershire in 1918. It continues there to this day and has retained the name of Beaudesert Park School.

The boys of Beaudesert Park School 1918

The school had a fine academic record during its ten years in Henley, with 11 boys gaining scholarships to major public schools and eight others winning cadetships to the Royal Naval College at Osborne. One member of its staff, Mr Nathan, had enlisted in 1915 and was seriously wounded but returned to the school. Another member of staff, Mortimer Southern, applied to the Tribunal for exemption from military service but was probably called up at the end of 1916. Twenty of its old boys served in the Great War, five of whom were killed (see Roll of Honour).

A considerable number of Henley people were now commuting to Birmingham and Stratford by rail. On Tuesday, 24 September they were astonished to find that no trains were running due to a strike. Munitions workers in particular were greatly inconvenienced, though they were able to get to work the following day. Public sympathy was against the strikers, as their action was unofficial and their occupation protected them from military service.[63]

Dr Nelson chaired a meeting held in the Church of England School rooms to organize a scheme to offer hospitality to American soldiers in the Henley area.

In October influenza returned to the town, this time in a more virulent form. Attendance in the Junior Department of the Council School on Wednesday, 29 October was only 74 out of 120. The outbreak was still going on in November, so that no indoor service of thanksgiving took place on 11 November, the High Bailiff advising that it would be unwise. A number of deaths occurred as a result of the outbreak, including those of Miss Lizzie Saddler, Mrs Finch, Mr Price (manager of Lloyds Bank) and Mr Theo Bioletti "a young man prominent in the Scouts, known and loved by all".[64] Lizzie Saddler was one of the six daughters of William and Alice Saddler, whose only son Tom had died of wounds on 4 April.

News of the Armistice reached Henley on the morning of Monday, 11 November. It is thought that the first person in the town to know the war was over was Florence Watkins, housekeeper to Dr Nelson at his house and surgery at Greengates in the High Street. Telephones in Henley were few and when she made a call to a pharmaceutical company in Birmingham she was greeted with the news that church bells were ringing all over Birmingham and that the war was over at last. Her response was to arm her children with bells, tin trays and saucepan lids and send them out into the street to make as much noise as possible and to cry, "The War is over!"[65] In a very short time the householders were displaying flags and joyous peals were rung on the church bells. Celebrations went on throughout the day and well into the night. The many public houses in the town were full to overflowing with members of both sexes, some of whom were uncontrollable.

It was hoped to have an indoor service of thanksgiving, but owing the prevailing sickness Dr Nelson advised against it. A short meeting was held on Tuesday, 12

---

63   *Herald,* 27 September 1918
64   *Herald,* 15 November 1918
65   Rita Redfern (Florence Watkins' granddaughter)

The Market Place, 12 November 1918

November in the market place, those on the platform being Dr W E Nelson, Revd L G Schofield, Mr T R Perkins and Revd F D Lane (who conducted the service).

On Saturday, 16 November there was a bonfire and a firework display on the top of Swan's Croft. A torchlight procession formed at the Hospital and in the centre of the procession was an effigy of the Kaiser, subsequently burned on the bonfire. It had been made by wounded soldiers from the Hospital. Dr Nelson was in charge of the fireworks, the cost of which was met by public subscription. On 17 November a special thanksgiving service was held in St John's, combined with the annual Court Leet Service.

The Court Leet met on 13 November and noted that "The end of hostilities had now been brought about and an Armistice had been arranged with the enemy".[66]

There were meetings of the Warwickshire and North Warwickshire Hunts in November and December.

On Monday, 16 December two German guns captured by the RWR were displayed at the Market Cross for a short time.[67]

The *Herald* of 27 December referred to complaints about indecent language from the youth of the town of both sexes.

News of Servicemen

The *Herald* gave news of Henley men in the armed forces throughout the year. In January Lance Corporal A Atkins was an anti-gas instructor working among Canadian soldiers in England. Corporal W Richards was serving in France, while

---

66   Court Leet Minutes
67   *Herald,* 20 December 1918

Henley boys on Salisbury Plain

several Henley boys were together on Salisbury Plain, including Privates W Beard, Harry Edgington and G Horsley.

The Revd Michael Bell was now vicar of Over Kellet and Capernwray in Lancashire and the Australian Government had awarded him the medal issued to those formerly on active service. Private Fred Stinson was in hospital: he had met another old Henley boy, Private Frank Davis, who had been with the GWR. Private W E Beard reported himself well, while good news had also been received from Jack Beard, who had seen a very long period of active service. Private Sammons was home on leave.

In February it was reported that Mr A W Farr, who had been at the local branch of the London City & Midland Bank, had recently visited Henley after being discharged from the army. He had been severely wounded in the left arm some 18 months earlier and unfortunately his wound had only healed slowly: he was resting prior to taking up another clerical appointment. Private Harold Beard expected to receive his discharge after having been wounded some months previously. A E Atkins, who was an old Henley boy serving in the Canadian army, had been promoted Corporal and was an instructor, having passed his examination in anti-gas precautions. Sergeant Frank Parkes, son of Mr George Parkes, was expected in Henley for a day or two, while Privates H Smallwood and G Coppage had recently been home on leave.

Reports on several Henley soldiers were given in the *Herald* in April. Private A Harris had been wounded and Howard Wright, the son of Police Inspector George Wright of Henley, reported himself well after a trying period in the trenches. A E Atkins serving in the Canadian Army, had been promoted Sergeant.

A service was held in the Baptist Church on Monday, 8 April for W E Hayward of the Royal Navy Volunteer Reserve, who had many friends in Henley and had died in London on 3 April. The mourners included his widow, his parents and his brother Lance Corporal B Hayward. On Sunday 21 April "a very quiet and impressive service" was held in the Baptist Church for Private Tom Saddler of the Royal Warwicks, an old scholar of the Baptist Sunday School: although in an exempt category, he had volunteered and had been in France for two years. His parents had been informed by telegram on 9 April that he had died in a base hospital on 4 April, two days after being wounded.

The German Spring Offensive caused heavy casualties and the men of Henley were not spared. Private George Spears of the Dorset Regiment was killed in action on 12 April. The son of Mr & Mrs Spears of the High Street, Henley he was only 19 and had been in France for barely three weeks. He was killed instantly by a shell. An officer of his battalion wrote that "he was buried at a small village behind the line and I have had a white wooden cross put up, with his name, regiment and date on it".

A Memorial Service for Driver Owen Holt and Private Sidney Bickley was held in St John's Church on Sunday, 28 April when there was a large congregation present. Drive Holt had joined up soon after the outbreak of war at the age of 17, was sent to France after six months and had seen continued active service. The first news received by his parents was in a letter from his Battery Major, stating that their son had been seriously wounded by several pieces of shell, mostly in the chest. His death from his wounds on 11 April was announced in a later letter. This was the second son that Richard and Ellen Jane Holt had lost in the war: two others were still in the army, one in England and one in France. The latter, Corporal Dick Holt of the Royal Warwicks, had been awarded the Military Medal for gallantry in the field. Private Sidney Bickley, a son of Mrs Bickley of Henley, had been in France for about nine months and had been killed in action on 23 March. He was 22 and had worked for Mr Burman of Earlswood. Sidney's brother Peter was serving in Egypt.

On a more positive note, there had been much concern on behalf of Harry Lowe, who had been through the recent heavy fighting and posted missing. News had now been received that he was safe and well after several perilous experiences and had rejoined his unit. Staff Sergeant James Perks of the Army Service Corps had been awarded the Distinguished Conduct Medal. His citation read, "On several occasions he displayed great courage while in charge of convoys under heavy fire and his personal example and untiring energy largely assisted in preventing casualties".

On 31 May the *Herald* gave an account of three Henley soldiers who were missing. Private Thomas Wall of the 1st Royal Marine Battalion had not been heard of for two months, but his wife had never given up hope. Her hopes were fulfilled when she received a letter from him on 25 May which had been posted in early April: in it he reported that he was a POW in Limburg, having been captured on 26 March. Private Albert Sammons, a young soldier who went out to France in Easter Week, had been missing since 25 April. Private Howard Hobbins had been officially reported wounded between 20 and 27 April and was missing. Any hopes regarding the last two were in vain. Albert Sammons was subsequently discovered to have been killed on 25 April and Howard Hobbins had died of wounds on 27 April, though his parents were not informed of this until July. Howard had been within a few days of his 19th birthday.

In July the Wesleyan congregation was pleased to see Sergeant J H Steele of Mays Hill, who was enjoying a well-earned leave after serving with the Warwickshire Yeomanry for about 3½ years.

Captain A C Coldicott MC of the RWR, the elder son of Mr & Mrs A C Coldicott, was reported as having been wounded for the third time on 25 June: on 11 July the original report was corrected to "wounded and missing". He had been 21 in February, was a Foundation Scholar of King Edward's School Birmingham and had seen much service in France and Italy. The *Herald* of 28 July reported that Captain Coldicott's parents had now heard that he was a POW in Germany. There was good news of another missing soldier, as "The friends of Mr Harrison of Mays Hill will be pleased to hear that, although reported missing some time ago, his wife has now heard that he is a POW in Germany."

Private William Bonehill of the 15th Battalion RWR was awarded the Military Medal for gallantry and devotion to duty. When on a bombing raid on 19 July he killed nine of the enemy and captured a machine gun. He lived in Beaudesert and before the war he had worked for the GWR in Henley in the delivery of parcels.

In August Private Geoffrey Horsley, a well-known Henley lad, was seriously wounded, but was progressing as well as could be expected. His father Walter had been on active service almost from the start of the war.[68]

Private Edward Harrison of 16th Battalion Royal Warwickshire Regiment had been wounded in the shoulder and was in Fushill War Hospital, Carlisle in September. He had been on active service since early November 1917. He had also been wounded in April last, but did not then get back to Blighty.

2nd Lieutenant Jack Hawkes died on 12 September of wounds received the previous day. Formerly of the Warwickshire Yeomanry, he had been commissioned into the Leicestershire Regiment and had only gone to France with the 7th Battalion in June. After a short but eventful period he was killed leading his men.

Private Harry Lowe was reported to have taken advantage of a period of rest to play various games. He had captained a hockey team, the other members being American, and had won a cup. Private Geoffrey Horsley, who had been very severely wounded was progressing favourably but would be bed-ridden for some considerable time.

---

68   *Herald,* 30 August 1918

Corporal (Aerial Gunlayer) Leonard Allen of Henley was awarded the Distinguished Flying Medal. "He has frequently been in action with enemy aeroplanes and has flown for 100 hours on photographic and reconnaissance flights."[69]

On 22 September a Memorial Service was held at St John's for 2nd Lieutenant Jack Hawkes, conducted by the Revd F D Lane. The service was exceedingly impressive and very well attended. The congregation included wounded soldiers and nurses from the Hospital.

Corporal Howard Wright of the King's Own Liverpool Regiment, the son of Inspector and Mrs Wright of Henley, was wounded while serving in France and was now in hospital in Lincoln. Only 19, he had enlisted about 2½ years ago and had recently seen about 7 months of hard fighting.

2nd Lieutenant F C Mannox, Royal Munster Fusiliers, the only son of Mr F H Mannox of Whitley House, Henley was wounded on 7 October and was in hospital. He had been commissioned last April and had been in France since July. Captain A C Coldicott, the elder son of Mr and Mrs A C Coldicott of Church House, Henley who had been a prisoner since June had died in Dortmund of wounds received on active service. Although his death was not reported until October, he had died two months earlier on 14 August.

Private Donovan Hodges, son of Mr and Mrs J E Hodges, had been missing since 3 October. He was serving with 1/5th Battalion of the South Staffordshire Regiment and was one of the first from Henley to enlist, having done so in September 1914 at the age of 16½.

The last of Henley's men to die on active service was Private Stephen Hastings, who died in hospital in Le Havre on 8 November from bronchial pneumonia. He was a baker in the Royal Army Service Corps and had been employed in that capacity by Mr James Welch of Henley. He left a widow and four children and a Memorial Service was held for him in the Baptist Church on Sunday, 1 December.

Corporal Richards, a much-travelled soldier, arrived home for Christmas leave from France on 10 December. On 12 December has was taken to 1st Southern General Hospital and operated on immediately for appendicitis. The following day another operation for a separate condition was required and his parents were sent for. Shortly afterwards Corporal Richards was said to be slightly better.[70]

69   *Herald,* 27 September 1918
70   *Herald,* 20 December 1918

7. Henley in 1919

The National Scene

On 4 January the Peace Conference was convened in Paris. The German Fleet was scuttled at Scapa Flow on 21 June. The Treaty of Versailles, setting out the terms of the peace treaty, was drawn up on 28 June, ratified by Germany on 9 July and by Britain on 21 July. Peace celebrations were held on 19 July.

The Warwickshire Brigade

The troops of the Brigade now spent their time in training, sports and educational classes. By mid-January 500 men had been demobilized. In February they were joined by another 1,000 but the 7th Battalion was selected to join a mixed brigade of four battalions to oversee the transition to peace. It was made up to strength by volunteers and recent drafts from the rest of 48th Division and moved to Egypt in May, not returning home until January 1920. The remainder of 143rd Brigade was disbanded on 26 March 1919. Not all were happy to go: Lieutenant Carrington of 5th Battalion wrote, "The end of the war has no attraction for me. It will be the severance of ties and friendship…and the loss of a well-paid job."

The Warwickshire Yeomanry

Five officers and 165 other ranks of the 100th Warwickshire and Nottinghamshire Battalion of the Machine Gun Corps were demobilised in January. By 6 February the Battalion was down to two companies, that representing the Warwickshire Yeomanry being under the command of Captain Motion. They were based at Haversin in the Belgian province of Namur. In March they moved back to Ciney, ten miles to the North West, where they had spent some time in December. On 1 May the last remaining elements of the Yeomanry moved to Antwerp and embarked for Tilbury on 9 May. From there they moved by train to Barrow in Furness and then marched to their final camp. They were finally dispersed on 17 May.

Henley

News was gradually received of the Henley men who had survived the war. On 10 January the *Herald* reported that Sergeant Howard Cooke, son of Mr & Mrs Cooke of The Gables, had been mentioned in dispatches by Sir Douglas Haig. He had been in the regular army for many years and had seen active service since 1914 on various fronts.

Corporal William Richards was making satisfactory progress. Sergeant Arthur Atkins was in the town on leave and hoped to be discharged soon, though he might have to return to Canada. Corporal Howard Wright was at home, having received his discharge; his wounds were quite serious, though he was able to get about. Cadet Wallace Steele was at home on leave, having done much flying in the last two months.

In the following week, Mr and Mrs Hodges of South End, Henley received very welcome news. They had not heard of their son Donovan since the end of September. An official communication had stated that he was wounded and missing and they had almost abandoned hope. They now heard that he had been wounded in the leg and had been a prisoner in Germany. Several letters he had sent home had not arrived. He was now in France and hoping to be home soon. The *Herald* of 24 January gave news of several men who had been discharged or demobilised. Donovan Hodges was now home with many interesting tales to tell of his experiences as a POW in Germany. Other returning prisoners were Private Thomas Wall and Rifleman William Robbins.

In March it was reported that the young men of the Wesleyan congregation who joined the army had all come safely through and had been demobilised. Sufficient men had now returned for there to be a football match between the demobilised of Henley and of Stratford. This was held on 15 March, Stratford winning by 3 goals to 2. There were no further reports until May, when it was announced that Mr Frederick Stinson had been demobilised and had re-opened his premises at Mile Stone Works (183 High Street). This was the last Henley demobilisation to be reported by the *Herald*.

Life in the town gradually returned to normal. The North Warwickshire Hunt met on 3 January 1919 and later in the month a Social Club and YMCA were formed, which it was thought would meet a very real need. The annual meeting of the Henley Garden Allotment Association was held at the White Swan in February. Mr A E Berry was elected Secretary: he was welcomed after much service on mine-sweepers in the North Sea. The Council Schools closed for over a week in March because of an outbreak of measles and opened again on Wednesday, 19 March.[71] On 24 March the Beaudesert Parish Meeting had some discussion "with regard to the erection of houses in the Parish and it was considered at least 6 should be built for the benefit of workers on the land". The VAD Hospital closed on 5 April.

Members of the County Education Committee met in the Council Schools on Thursday, 1 May to hold an inquiry into the conviction of Lot Robinson by the magistrates earlier in the year. The case of Rhodes v Robinson had filled Henley's new Court Room to overflowing on Wednesday, 29 January. Lot Robinson, the head of the Council Schools, came before the magistrates charged with a common assault on one of his pupils, Norah Rhodes aged 11, in his classroom.[72] He was remembered as being very strict. Annie Elvins, one of his pupils, spoke of how "he would walk around the class with one hand behind his back holding a cane which would be hidden up the back of his jacket"; another, Mary Howard, remembered

---

71 *Herald*, 21 March 1919

72 Norah Rhodes was a daughter of Benjamin and Jane Rhodes of Beaudesert. Her father was serving in the Army at the time (see his entry in the Roll of Honour)

an occasion on which "Nutty Beard was caned, he was often in trouble but was never upset at being punished"; on this occasion he had pleaded his innocence, which was later established and Robinson apologised.[73] The magistrates found Robinson guilty and fined him 5s.0d. The Education Committee confirmed the decision of the magistrates.[74]

The War Pensions Committee met at the Court House the following week.

The Committee for Entertaining American & Colonial Soldiers, chaired by Dr Nelson, held its final meeting in May. The organizer, Mr H V Potter, reported that the scheme had been quite successful. Nearly 40 "Americans and Colonials" had been given hospitality in the district although sufficient homes had not been found for all who might have been placed. In every case the cordial welcome and treatment by their hosts and hostesses had been highly appreciated by the soldiers. The secretary to the Committee was Mrs Potter. The accounts showed a balance of £1.12s.6d and it was decided to hand this over to the local Peace Celebration Committee for entertaining local men who joined the army during the war.[75]

On 16 June the Beaudesert Parish Meeting (with no fewer than 10 attendees) agreed that its Chairman, the Revd Lane, should meet the Henley Parish Council "to lay before them the resolution of the meeting that the 4 houses to be built in Beaudesert Parish should be built in a field on the right of Liveridge Hill (towards Birmingham)".

A crowded meeting of the Discharged Soldiers and Sailors Federation was held in the Golden Cross on 5 July, made up of its members and members of the public. The High Bailiff took the chair and the meeting was addressed by Mr Albert Yarwood, the secretary of the Federation, who encouraged former servicemen to join. This was one of four National Organisations of ex-Service men which combined to form the Royal British Legion on 15 May 1921.

Peace Sunday was celebrated on 6 July, with services being held in St John's, St Nicholas' and the Baptist and Wesleyan churches.

Peace celebrations had first been considered at a town meeting held in the Guild Hall on Thursday, 13 February 1919. A committee was formed comprising:

Dr W E Nelson OBE (Chairman)
Revd L G Schofield (Hon Secretary)
W Taylor (Hon Treasurer)
F Bayliss
H Sinclair Brown
G Busby
F W Harris
J Harris

---

73   Welham, pp 116 & 125
74   *Herald,* 2 May 1919
75   *Herald,* 23 May 1919

T Hazelwood
Revd F D Lane
G F Lodder
F Maine
C Mitchell
F Morton
H H Munro
R L Newcombe
T R Perkins
E J Stephens

The day of national celebration was to be Saturday, 19 July. By the beginning of July considerable progress had been made for the arrangements on the day. The programme for Henley's celebrations was set out in a commemorative booklet prepared by the High Bailiff, which was produced as a souvenir of the occasion and distributed to every household in the town. The booklet contained 20 pages and included a very detailed programme of the day's events; a list of those who had died; a list of those who had served in the armed forces and a list of those who served in the Voluntary Aid Detachments. Everyone was invited to join in the procession, the order of which was as follows:

Inspector of Police
The Constable
The Mace Bearer
The High Bailiff
The Low Bailiff
Officers of the Court Leet
The Navy
The Army
The Royal Air Force
Members of the Women's Auxiliary Forces
VADs
Boy Scouts
Girl Guides
Council School Children and Teachers
School Managers
Members of Friendly Societies
Fire Brigade
Members of Public Bodies
Private Schools
General Public

Henley Fire Brigade, 19 July 1919
Five of the men are wearing their newly issued medals

All those entitled to do so were requested to wear their uniforms, decorations and badges of office.

The procession formed at the Market Cross at 10.30 am and at 10.50 am marched to St Nicholas' Churchyard, where they were met at the Lych-gate by the choirs, church wardens and chapel officials and the officiating clergy and ministers (Revd F D Lane, Revd L G Schofield and Mr T R Perkins). The procession formed into a hollow square in a prescribed order and a service began at 11.00 am.

The *Herald* of 25 July 1919 reported that the celebrations were adversely affected by rain, but that the procession contained almost everyone in the town who could walk. The weather meant that the High Bailiff did not speak in the churchyard as planned. "At 1.00 pm about 70 discharged and serving members of the army and navy were entertained to a superb lunch at the Golden Cross. Captain Elkington DSO and Corporal Rhodes voiced the thanks of the men, who honoured the High Bailiff by singing 'For He's a Jolly Good Fellow'.[76] Pipes, cigarette cases, tobacco and cigarettes were distributed." A local group of juvenile entertainers put on a concert in the afternoon, followed by tea and the presentation of medals by Mrs Nelson. In the evening a company of *pierrots* played to a packed house in the Public Hall and dancing took place in a pavilion. The planned fireworks display was postponed until Monday, when the whole neighbourhood was brilliantly

---

76   Christopher Garrett Elkington DSO, 13th Battalion Gloucestershire Regiment. His DSO was awarded "For conspicuous gallantry in action. With six men he attacked and silenced an enemy machine gun. Later, he displayed great courage and ability in organizing the defence of the position. He was twice wounded, but remained at duty directing operations until he was again severely wounded." (*LG* 28 January 1917)

illuminated. Donations amounted to over £80. Following the Peace Celebrations the Committee had a balance in hand of £2.14s.0d.[77]

On Monday, 11 August a meeting of the Forest of Arden Football Club was held. A unanimous vote of thanks was given to the President, Charles Couchman, who had now left the district; Mr W J Fieldhouse was elected in his place. Mr Harry Lowe was elected Captain and Mr Henry Hughes Vice-Captain. Mr F W Harris was Secretary of the White Swan Bowling Club.

A freehold shop and dwelling house at 251 High Street sold for £420.[78] This belonged to Harvey Arnold, one of the town's boot and shoe makers. His eldest son Harry had joined him in the business in 1908, but enlisted in the Coldstream Guards on 6 October 1914 and was killed on 6 July 1915.

A two-minute silence was held in the town at 11.00 am on Tuesday, 11 November establishing a tradition which continues to this day. A wreath was placed on the market cross by several discharged men in memory of their fallen comrades.[79]

The Court Leet Service was held in St John's on Sunday, 16 November.

The Rural District Council election was held on Monday, 8 December when Mr W C Jamieson was elected to represent Henley, the losing candidate being Mr H Sinclair Brown.

77   *Herald,* 5 September 1919

78   *Herald,* 31 October 1919

79   *Herald,* 14 November 1919

8. The Triumvirate

THERE were three men who were of particular influence in Henley during the war years, one by virtue of his wealth and philanthropy and the other two by virtue of the offices they held.

Charles Couchman JP (1858-1932)

He was born at The Yew Trees, Henley in Arden on 21 September 1858, the eldest son of Thomas Barnes Couchman of Beaudesert Park and his wife Sarah Whitby (*nee* Smith). He was baptised at St John's Church on 18 October 1858. He was educated at Rugby School. Thomas Couchman was one of the partners in the firm of Henley Solicitors and when Charles left Rugby he was articled to his father. On 29 May 1884 he married Florence Catherine, the eldest daughter of Revd Richard Thursfield, Rector of St Michael in Bedwardine, Worcestershire and a former vicar of Ullenhall. He was a solicitor and member of the firm of Lea and Couchman, solicitors, Henley in Arden. He succeeded his father in the practice in 1889 and some two years later took Theodore Christophers into partnership. Shortly after this he retired from active participation in the practice and entered into public life.

He was a magistrate for the Henley Petty Sessional Division from 1897 to 1919; a member of the Stratford upon Avon Board of Guardians for 25 years, of which he was vice-chairman for six and chairman for sixteen. He represented Henley on Stratford Rural District Council, of which he was chairman for many years. He was chairman of the War Tribunal throughout its duration from 1916 to 1918 and was High Bailiff of Henley from 1893 to 1910. "To these offices… he brought exceptional ability and energy and was a wise and firm manager of public affairs who won the respect of all." Couchman was elected Henley's first Honorary Burgess in 1919.

On retirement from his legal practice he moved to Ireland's Farm. He later returned to Henley, where he lived at The Elms, before building a house called Whitley in Preston Bagot in 1910: he was living there in 1911 with his wife and two female servants.

Charles Couchman left the area in 1919 and moved to Jesmond, Bristol Road, Weston-super-Mare where he died without issue on 18 July 1932. He was buried in St Nicholas' churchyard, Beaudesert on 21 July 1932. On 28 September of that year probate was granted to Henry Boteler Couchman, estate agent, Arthur Whitby Couchman, chartered accountant, and John Horace Thursfield, solicitor: his effects were valued at £4,340.

William John Fieldhouse CBE, FSA, JP (1857-1928)

He was a native of Newport, Shropshire where his birth was registered in the first quarter of 1858 and where he was baptised on 23 January of that year. His parents, Thomas Fieldhouse and his wife Ann (*nee* Hall) had been married in Newport on 10 January 1850. In 1861 he was living in the High Street, Newport with his parents Thomas (46) and Ann (34), his sister Matilda (9) and his elder brother Thomas (6). His father was a Master Maltster and his mother a Milliner. Also living with them was an apprentice milliner and a house servant. The family were still living in the High Street in 1871 though his elder brother Thomas seems to have died by this date: Thomas Fieldhouse was now described as a retired Auctioneer: the millinery business of his wife Ann was thriving, as also living in the house were five assistant milliners and dressmakers. William moved out of the family home some time before 1881 when he was living as a boarder at 197 Lozells Road, Handsworth with a Commercial Traveller and his wife, William and Annie Addis, their two young children and a 14-year-old servant. William Fieldhouse was only three years younger than his landlord and was working as an Iron Merchant's Salesman. By 1891 he had married and was living at 198 Hamstead Road, Handsworth with his wife Lucie (6 years younger than himself), his two sons Seymour (5) and Ernest (4) (both of whom had been born in Handsworth) and a female servant: he was described as an Ironfounder. He was still living at the same address in 1901 with his wife, his daughter Nancy (8), his niece Sarah Wood and two servants: his sons are likely to have been away at school. In 1911 the family was living at The Priory in Wootton Wawen: the household then comprised William (now described as an Ironfounder and Wheel Maker), his wife Lucie, his daughter Nancy, his niece Sarah (described as a Companion) and one servant.

His principal commercial activities were with the St Stephen's Wheel Works and the Griffin Foundry in Birmingham.

His elder son Seymour was killed by a boar while on a pig-sticking expedition in Ceylon (now Sri Lanka) at some time before the Great War. The incident is commemorated by plaster plaques William placed on several buildings in Henley and Wootton which he renovated or built.

Plaque on the north east corner of The Corner Shop (now Lloyds Bank)

Towards the end of the war he was awarded the CBE (Supplement to the *London Gazette* 7 January 1918).

He restored and furnished the Guild Hall in Henley and revived the Court Leet. He took a great interest in the parish church of Wootton Wawen and contributed greatly to its restoration. He also helped generously with the excavation of Anglo-Saxon work at Bidford and the restoration of examples of mediaeval art discovered in the Beauchamp Chapel at Warwick.

Fieldhouse was associated with Sir John Furley in arranging for and supervising the construction of the first hospital train used in the Boer War. In August 1914 the two men undertook the provision for the Red Cross Society of portable hospitals and later improvised an ambulance train from French rolling stock.

He was a generous donor to the Stratford upon Avon General Hospital. He financed the excavations on the Stratford upon Avon Golf Links from 1925 to 1927 when important Roman pottery and metal ornaments were found. He had a remarkable collection of leather jacks and bottles and other antiques including carved coffers and dower chests. He financed the printing in 1921 of *Black Jacks and Leather Bottells* by Oliver Baker of Stratford upon Avon. He was a liberal supporter of the Birmingham Archaeological Society and was clearly a noted industrialist and philanthropist.

He established the Lucy Fieldhouse Charity in 1921 with the sum of £200, the interest on which was to be distributed amongst poor children attending schools within the parish of Wootton Wawen. In 1923 he gave land and five houses at Wootton Wawen, with £6,000 in consoles as an endowment, to establish the Seymour Fieldhouse Homes (commemorating his elder son) for use as alms houses. In 1926 he gave £6,240 in consoles to establish the William John Fieldhouse Charity in memory of his wife Lucie, the interest to be paid annually as pensions to poor men and women of good character living in Wootton Wawen.

Bronze head of W J Fieldhouse

His bust was formerly in the Guild Hall, but was unfortunately stolen. It was the work of Reginald R. Goulden.[80]

William Fieldhouse died at Austy Manor on 28 October 1928 at the age of 71. His funeral was held at Wootton Wawen on 31 October with no fewer than four officiating clergy: Canon Eagles (Coughton), Canon Cartwright (Henley in Arden), Revd F H Hodgson (Clopton) and the Revd E C Hanson (Shipton Olliffe and Shipton Sollars). The principal family mourners were his son Mr Ernest Fieldhouse and his wife, and his daughter Mrs Nancy Barnard and her husband Captain Cyril W Barnard MC. The officers of Henley Court Leet attended along with representatives from many public bodies, including six justices of the peace. There were five representatives of the Birmingham Archaeological Society, led by its president Mr John Humphreys. Over 50 other people were named, including Dr Ernest Nelson, five representatives from St Stephens Wheel Works and one from each of Ariel Wheel Works, Griffin Foundry and Guest, Keen & Nettlefold.

He left £291,321 gross at his death. Among the bequests set out in his will were £500 to each of the Children's Hospital, Birmingham; Stratford upon Avon General Hospital; the Vicars and Churchwardens in each of the parishes of Wootton Wawen and Henley in Arden for bread and meat for the poor on Christmas Eve and to his general managers H J Johnson and J A Hollings. He gave the large book containing copies of the Court Rolls and other ancient documents to the High Bailiff and burgesses of the borough of Henley in Arden to be displayed in the Guild Hall. William Fieldhouse left the title to the manor of Henley in Arden jointly to his son Ernest Fieldhouse and his daughter Mrs Nancy Barnard. The balance of his estate after his death he left in trust for his son and daughter, encouraging them to be always charitably disposed.

Birmingham Mail 29 October 1928, *Birmingham Post* 1 November 1928, *Evesham Journal* 3 November 1928, *Birmingham Post* 28 February 1929.

---

80 Born in Dover in 1877. Educated at Dover College, he went on to the Dover School of Art, where he won a scholarship to the Royal College of Art in London. He served in the front line in France in 1915 and 1916 and was mentioned in dispatches. He specialised in statues, memorial fountains, busts and panels, and after the war designed and executed many war memorials all over the country

Dr William Ernest Nelson OBE, MA (Cantab), JP, MRCS, LRCP (1871-1933)

He was the elder son of the Revd William and Mrs Mary Nelson and was born in 1871 at the Manor House, Feckenham, where his father had a preparatory school. The school moved to Arden House in Henley in 1876. Ernest was a pupil at Arden House in 1881 and was later educated at Bilton Grange preparatory school, Haileybury (1885-1888) and Clare College, Cambridge (matriculated 1890, Rugby blue 1892, BA 1893, MA 1898). He went on to study medicine at St Thomas' Hospital, London and qualified MRCS and LRCP in 1900. Ernest married Rosa Gertrude, daughter of A J Tompkins of Park Terrace, Cambridge in 1899. They had a son John Pemberton (baptised in St John's on 28 June 1904) and a daughter Irene Mary (baptised on 23 January 1907). He bought Dr James Arthur's medical practice at Greengates in the High Street and also went into a partnership of Arden House School with his

brother Oswald, who acted as Headmaster. Ernest was the driving force behind the construction of the Public Hall in Henley in 1908. He was High Bailiff from 1910 to 1922 and was made an Honorary Burgess in 1923. He hunted regularly with the North Warwickshire and served as Medical Officer of Health for the Wootton Wawen District of the Stratford upon Avon Union. From 1914 to 1919 he was Commandant of the Hospital in Henley, for which service he was awarded the OBE in 1917. He retired from general practice in 1930, but retained his interest in the school. John Pemberton Nelson succeeded his uncle Oswald as Headmaster in 1937.

Ernest Nelson was the author of *Canal Barges Adapted for the Transport of Wounded (RAMC Journal, 1912)* and *Open-Air Treatment for Wounds: A Simple and Inexpensive Form of Open-Air Ward, as Used in the VAD Hospital, Henley in Arden (British Medical Journal*, 28 August 1915).

He died on 8 October 1933 and is buried in St Nicholas' churchyard with his wife, who died on 2 January 1949 at the age of 82.

Haileybury Register 1862-1946 (Col N C King (ed)); J E Venn (compiler), *Alumni Cantabrigiensis*, Part II, Vol IV, pp 524-525; Medical Directory, 1920; Obituary *Times*, 11 October 1933.

9. Henley in Arden Red Cross Voluntary Aid Detachment Auxiliary Hospital

IN 1909 the War Office issued a Scheme for the Organisation of Voluntary Aid, based on the British Red Cross Society and the Order of St John of Jerusalem in England. "Voluntary Aid Detachments were…formed with a view to serving Territorial formations fighting in this country…the general basis of organisation had to be shifted…but that part of it which had reference to the provision of temporary hospitals …was largely available for use as soon as wounded men began to arrive from abroad."[81] It was designed to aid the Territorial Forces Medical Service in the event of war. Branches of the Red Cross were organized on a county basis, units being known as Voluntary Aid Detachments (VADs). The members of these units were also known as VADs and were trained in first aid and nursing: there were over 6,000 members within a year. In 1914 the Red Cross and the Order of St John combined to form the Joint War Committee to enable them to carry out their work more efficiently and economically, their units operating under the protection of the Red Cross name.

They organized and administered auxiliary hospitals and convalescent homes in which qualified nurses were also employed. The buildings which were put forward as possible temporary hospitals "were considered from the point of view of Equipment, Doctors, Nursing Staff, and the extent to which the cost of maintenance could be born locally."[82] When the necessary conditions were met, "little difficulty was experienced in respect of funds, local subscriptions and collections of various kinds sufficing to meet the current expenses."[83]

Two VADs were formed in Henley in 1909, one for men (designated Warwick Number 11) and the other for women (Warwick Number 32). Members were instructed by Dr Nelson. As well as attending lectures and carrying out Red Cross work in the area they also had to raise most of the money required for the work. By May 1914 they were finding this onerous and were seeking to raise the £20 they

---

81   *Joint War Committee,* p 211
82   *Joint War Committee,* p 211
83   *Joint War Committee,* p 212

estimated they needed for their annual running costs by attracting a number of vice-presidents and other supporters.

Members were examined regularly and Dr Earnshaw Hewer of Stratford upon Avon conducted examinations in December 1913 and April 1914. The names of the successful candidates were published in the *Herald* of 29 May 1914:

Warwick Number 11 VAD	W Dawes, W Hadley, G Coppage, H Payne, J V Watkins, H Hodges, F Harrison, H H Munro, E Hopkins, E B Berry, P Enstone, E Holtom and R Fisk:
Warwick Number 32 VAD	Miss Bagshaw, Mrs D Adams, Mrs Cox, Miss M Guinness, Miss Herring, Miss Hardy, Miss M Hemming, Miss F Kirby, the Hon Gladys Moncrieff, Miss B Steele and Miss Wakefield.

An annual inspection and field display of the VADs was held in Henley just after the outbreak of war, on Thursday, 6 August 1914. The *Herald* reported that the detachments had "long enjoyed a high reputation in official circles for smartness and practical efficiency".[84] Those mustering on the occasion were as follows:

Warwick Number 11 VAD	Dr W E Nelson (Commandant and acting Medical Officer), Quartermaster William Dawes, Sergeant-Instructor Jenner, Section Leaders H H Munro, F Stinson and O James; W Hadley, A J Dalby, G Coppage, H Payne, J V Watkins, H J Hodges, E Hopkins, W Eccles, T Coysh, F Watkins, P J Woodfield, L L Stanton, R Turner, W Sly, T O'Donnell, J Beard, A J Heraper, R J G Fisk, F G Holtom, H Elvins, E T Everix and H Beard.
Warwick Number 32 VAD	Mrs Nelson (Commandant), Mrs Lodder (Lady Superintendent), Miss Joyce Agar (Quartermaster), Mrs Harry Hawkes and Miss Herring (cooks), Miss Moore (Ward Clerk), Miss Steele (pack store clerk), Miss Bagshaw, Miss Wakefield, Miss Grace Richards, Miss F Kirby, Miss Munro, Mrs Leonard Cox, Miss Hardy, Miss Guinness, Mrs Blackwell, Mrs Adams, the Hon Gladys Moncrieff and Miss Moore.

---

84   *Herald,* 14 August 1914

Mrs Phoebe Lodder & Mrs Rosa Nelson

The chief inspecting officer for the day was Lieutenant-Colonel Barling.[85] Those displaying their interest by attending included the Countess of Craven (President of the County Association), Mrs Guinness, Brigadier-General Morcy Quayle-Jones CB (of Claverdon Hall, County Director), Mrs Onslow and Mrs Ryland (Preston Bagot), Mrs Charles Couchman (Whitley Hill) and Mrs and Miss Strang (Yew Trees).

The day's scheme was intended to show how the two detachments could provide accommodation for one hundred sick and wounded in temporary hospitals at 24 hours notice. The roll call for the men's detachment was taken at Green Gates and for the women's at the Council Schools: exercises by the members of the men's detachment involving company drill, stretcher drill and the collecting of wounded took place in Dr Nelson's field at Green Gates. The "wounded" were played by local Boy Scouts and were conveyed on stretchers by improvised transport to the temporary hospital at the Council Schools. Four wards were provided in the schools, one acting as the operating theatre complete with every modern appliance. The hospital kitchen was located in the infant department, as were the quartermaster's stores.

Brigadier-General Quayle-Jones warmly complimented the local detachments on their display and equipment. Lieutenant-Colonel Barling said he understood that the schools would be one of the temporary hospitals in case of grave necessity and thought that, as arranged on the day, they would make an excellent institution of that kind. He considered both detachments to be most efficient and congratulated the officers, non-commissioned officers and members upon a very praiseworthy display.

Further examinations in Hygiene and Sanitation were held in the autumn. The examinations were again conducted by Dr Hewer. The preliminary course of lectures had been attended by 25 men, of whom 19 presented themselves for examination and of whom 16 exceeded the pass mark of 50%. Those who passed were A R Jenner, H H Munro, W Sly (90); H Hodges, E Hopkins (80); T Coysh, H

---

85   Lt-Col Harry Gilbert Barling (1855-1940) then Consulting Surgeon to Southern Command. By1919 he was Colonel Sir H G Barling CB, CBE

Payne (75); F W Hemming, O James, F Stinson, J V Watkins (70); G Coppage, W Dawes (65); T O'Donnell (60); A J Dalby and F K Watkins (55). It was announced that a series of six classes on First Aid would be held on Wednesday evenings from 4 November. A plea was issued for volunteers to fill the 12 vacancies in the men's VAD caused by members having enlisted in the forces: married men up to the age of 50 were particularly asked to join.[86] It has not been possible to identify 12 men who had enlisted by October 1914; those identified as having enlisted then or later are Harry Arnold, Frederick Charles Atkins, Harold Beard, Jack Beard, Eric Berry, George Coppage, Arthur Ford, Jack Hawkes, Albert Heraper, Edward Hopkins, Oliver James, Tom O'Donnell, Leonard Stanton, Fred Stinson, Frank Watkins and John Watkins.

This plea for volunteers was repeated in the *Herald* of 6 November 1914, when it was confidently stated that the Public Hall had been ready for some time to receive wounded and that everything would be ready on 24 hours notice. It is likely that the Public Hall had been regarded as a potential hospital by Dr Nelson even before it was built in 1908. The miniature rifle range attached to it had a clear military purpose as has been shown and the size and layout of the Public Hall were well suited to its conversion to a hospital. The initial drawings given to the architects had been sketched out by Dr Nelson and the Hall's ability to seat 450 when the population of the town was only 1,100 indicates a purpose other than simply providing the townspeople with a venue for entertainment. Nelson was a man with many contacts and an early interest in the Red Cross movement: he was the Medical Director of the Warwickshire Branch of the British Red Cross Society and immediately took on the role of Commandant of the Hospital when it was opened.

Dr W E Nelson, Commandant

It was a hospital for Other Ranks only. The first wounded arrived by motor ambulance from Birmingham on 24 November 1914. There were several serious cases, but none had lost limbs: they were from a variety of regiments, including the Black Watch, the Cameron Highlanders, the Royal Irish Rifles and the Royal Artillery. The Hospital was attached to 1st

Southern General Hospital, located on the Edgbaston campus of the University of Birmingham, and was open for a longer period than any other unit attached to that Hospital. Although manned largely by local volunteers, it was under military control and inspected from time to time by Lieutenant-Colonel F Marsh RAMC, or one of his officers from 1st Southern General.

VAD Hospital c 1915 (J V Watkins standing on the left)

It had 22 beds when it opened, but by August 1915 it could accommodate 32 patients and in July 1916 the number went up to 40. The Hospital did not have an operating theatre until early 1916, operations previously being carried out in the bathroom or in the wards: the theatre was created from part of the rifle range.[87] Its eventual capacity was 82 beds, 52 being in Henley in Arden and 30 in an extension opened at Wootton Hall, Wootton Wawen in June 1917. Nationally the average number of patients per hospital was 48.7 so that Henley was one of the country's larger hospitals. The average stay of a patient nationally was 37.4 days, but no information is available on the average stay of patients in Henley.

Wootton Hall was the home of Mr and Mrs Robert Darley Guinness, who had bought the property in 1912. Robert Guinness was a practising barrister, educated at Harrow and Trinity College Dublin. He had married Lydia Lucy Lyster Smyth in 1887. They had two children, Richard Smyth Guinness (1888-1979) and Elizabeth Muriel Smyth Guinness (1892-1974). Richard served during the war as a Lieutenant in the RNVR: his sister Muriel was a member of Warwick Number 34 VAD throughout the war and was awarded the ARRC. Mrs Lydia Guinness was Honorary Assistant Commandant at the Wootton Hall Extension.

---

87   *Herald,* 7 April 1916

The Henley Hospital never closed, although in July 1915 no fresh cases were admitted while it was thoroughly cleaned and redecorated.[88] By July 1915 almost 150 soldiers had been treated, with very satisfactory results.[89] The number treated had gone up to about 230 by November of that year.[90] In all a total of 1,576 servicemen were treated in the Hospital, only two of whom died while a patient there. Soldiers appreciated the benefit of staying in such hospitals rather than military hospitals, because of "their milder discipline, more generous conditions and homelier surroundings".[91]

On 30 July the *Herald* announced the imminent departure of Private Crowley from the Henley Hospital. He was its longest serving patient, having been there "since its earliest days towards the end of November". He was born in Nechells, Birmingham: in 1901 he had been eleven years old and living in an orphanage in Marston Green with his elder brother and over 400 other boys. Private 8855 Thomas Crowley of the Coldstream Guards had gone over to France on 12 August 1914, one of the "Old Contemptibles". His wounds had clearly been severe and he was discharged from the army shortly after his release from hospital. In September another of the Hospital's patients was in the news, this time Lance Corporal H J Quinault of the 2nd Royal Munster Fusiliers. He had been in the Hospital from 20 August to 10 September, having been wounded in the back at the Dardanelles, and recommended for a VC.[92] The *London Gazette* of 16 September 1916 subsequently reported that he had been awarded the Military Medal for bravery in the field. CSM Field, 3rd Battalion Worcestershire Regiment was the highest-ranking of the Hospital's patients recorded.[93] The only local soldier named as having been treated in the Hospital was Sergeant Howard Cooke, whose parents lived at The Gables in the High Street.

The Open Air Ward, showing its location on the west side of the Hospital

88 *Herald,* 30 July 1915
89 *Herald,* 23 July 1915
90 *Herald,* 12 November 1915
91 *Joint War Committee,* p 214
92 *Herald,* 24 September 1915
93 *Herald,* 7 August 1915

The Hospital's Open Air Ward was the first of its kind in the country. An article by Dr Nelson entitled *Open-Air Treatment for Wounds: A Simple and Inexpensive Form of Open-Air Ward, as Used in the VAD Hospital, Henley in Arden* was published in the *British Medical Journal* of 28 August 1915, setting out its benefits.

The ward was open on both sides, only the ends being closed in, and had accommodation for 8, although the design could accommodate any number from 2 to 30 patients. The architects were Messrs Osborne, Pemberton & White of Birmingham. Dr Nelson claimed six advantages for this particular form of building:

- The ward was open on both sides, but having four feet high screens at the back of the bed heads meant that there was a continual current of fresh air but no draughts.
- Deep sloping eaves meant that rain could not drive in. "The past month of July has had not a single day without rain and we have had some of the most severe thunderstorms I have ever seen, but the interior of the ward has always remained dry."
- If desired one side could be closed in by screens.
- It was easily built, the materials being wood and asbestos sheeting, the latter being cheaper than wood and having the advantage of being fireproof. It stood a foot from the ground on small brick pillars.
- It was quickly and easily erected, being put up complete in four days (ten days from the date of order).
- It was easily connected to the main building by a covered way.

The Henley Open Air Ward

Following its success a larger Open Air Ward with 18 beds was opened early in 1917, the gift of Mr F E Muntz of Umberslade Hall, after whom it was named.

The town took the Hospital to its heart. As well as relatives of the patients, many locals called in to visit them. A list of donors of money and of gifts in kind was published in the *Herald* each week. A typical list appeared in the *Herald* on 11 August 1916:

Cash: Lieutenant R Guinness (Wootton Hall) £7.7s.0d; W C Jamieson (White Swan collecting box) 11s.0d; F W Harris (sale of roses) 7s.0d; A H Richardson (Beaudesert Park) £2.2s.0d.

Gifts in Kind: Infant School children; Mrs Mitchell; Mrs Grierson; Mrs Cranmer (Lapworth); Mrs Webb; Miss Bonberry; Lady Moncrieff; Mrs Keighlty-Peach; Mrs Griffiths; Mrs Ryland; Mrs Grazebrook; Mrs Couchman; Mrs Bell (Lapworth); Mrs King (Shrewley); Miss Pain (Shirley); Mrs Burbidge; Mr Hopkins (Mobbs Farm); Mrs Guinness; Mr Welch; Mr Harry Hawkes.

Mr F E Muntz

From time to time shortages of supplies resulted in specific appeals for donations. On 1 October 1915 an urgent request was issued to the public for dressing gowns, blankets and sheets, the appeal for blankets being repeated the following week. On 22 October, there was a request for slippers, pyjamas, cigarettes, tobacco and armchairs. Bed linen was urgently needed in July 1916, following the increase in the number of beds in the Hospital. A particularly beneficial fund-raising exercise came about as a result of the generosity of Mr W J Fieldhouse: he had restored the Corner Shop (a building now occupied by Lloyds Bank) and placed the building at the disposal of the Red Cross Society, free of rates, taxes and other expenses. It was formally opened by the High Bailiff on Saturday, 7 July 1917 and was devoted to the sale of rummage, all proceeds going to the Hospital. Dr Nelson pointed out the need for more donations, as in the time since the Hospital had opened, prices had almost doubled, while the grant allowed to the Hospital by the government was almost unchanged. The shop's takings in its first week were over £50; the following two weeks brought in a further £50: up to 12 September 1917 a further £100 was received.

Such donations were very necessary. The daily capitation rates per bed per day were 3s.0d in November 1914, 3s.3d in December 1917 and 3s.6d in December 1918. When the highest capitation rates were being paid, the government was obtaining full hospital treatment for each patient, including food and every hospital outgoing, for £1.4s.6d per week![94] In 1917 the question of making some payment to local doctors for their services was raised. The War Office agreed to make a payment of 3d per equipped bed per day, up to a maximum of 12s.6d per day. It was acknowledged that "the public will probably never fully appreciate the amount of unostentatious voluntary work given by the Medical Profession".[95] The roles of Commandant and Quartermaster were honorary positions, as were many others. "In many cases ladies in the neighbourhood gave part-time services…assisting in such ways as laying and preparing tea, washing up etc. It was of course in many cases necessary to supplement voluntary labour by paid labour, as in the case of cooks."[96]

On Christmas morning 1916, 18 of the 49 patients attended the service at St John's Church, followed by a sumptuous lunch. A magnificent Christmas tree, laden with gifts, was presented by Mr Muntz.

Patients were regularly seen throughout the town and were frequently visited by relatives and the local inhabitants. Seats were provided for them in the town, two being given by Mr & Mrs Newcombe and placed outside their garage in the High Street; a further two, including one outside the Police Station, were given by Mrs Sladen (wife of Brigadier-General Sladen) and Mrs Strachey-Clitheroe of Outhill. The patients had some restrictions as Army Regulations did not permit wounded soldiers to be out after 4.00 pm in the winter months.

Recreation and suitable entertainment were not forgotten. Concerts were regularly given to the patients. In such a concert in February 1917 some of the less seriously wounded took part, namely Lance Corporals W Cupit and F Coates and Privates F Harvey and C R Hill.[97] Patients were treated to car rides in the area by Mr F Mahler of Alvechurch and Mr R D Guinness of Wootton Hall, and carriage rides by Mrs Strang of Yew Trees in the High Street.

---

94   *Joint War Committee,* p 219
95   *Joint War Committee,* p 215
96   *Joint War Committee,* p 215
97   *Herald,* 9 February 1917

In June 1916, Harry Payne, Mrs Strang's coachman, reported that driving wounded soldiers out was his principal employment. Mr W T Geary and Mr Percy Fewtrell, hairdressers in the town, treated them to haircuts and shaves.[98] The White Swan Bowling Club had its green next to the Hospital and patients had free use of the green except on three evenings of the week, which were reserved for members.[99]

In June Mr & Mrs Guinness enabled a further 20 beds to be provided by offering the use of Wootton Hall as an extension of the Hospital. This was regarded as an ideal location for the more convalescent cases.[100]

The ward at Wootton Hall

The *Herald* of 20 July 1917 gave a comprehensive report on the hospital and highlighted the role of the Nelsons. "The little town has a splendid worker and organizer in Dr Ernest Nelson, the commandant and medical officer and his services have been freely placed at the disposal of those who conceived and helped forward the undertaking. He has been ably seconded in all his efforts…by Mrs Nelson, the assistant commandant…Although Dr Nelson attends to all the medical officer's work…Dr Agar is always willing to render assistance when anaesthetical or extra medical service is required." The matron Sister Stevenson was also highly praised: "She is a lady brimful of sympathy, sheds brightness wherever she goes and possesses that fine Irish spirit and cheerfulness which contribute so much to raising the spirit of her wounded patients."

98   *Herald,* 19 November 1915
99   *Herald,* 11 May 1917
100 *Herald,* 22 June 1917

A Hospital Christmas

Particular festivities were laid on at Christmas. In 1917 Christmas stockings were filled for all patients and 5 large turkeys and 8 plum puddings were consumed for dinner; games took place in the evening, while a Whist Drive was held on Boxing Day (prize winners being Privates Bates, Ham, Grazaini and Lock, Sapper Sparrow, Gunner Hills and Lance Corporal Tanser). Father Christmas visited on 27 December. Nor were the staff of the hospital forgotten: in October 1918 they were entertained to tea at Crockett's Farm by Mr and Mrs Clifton Mitchell – the third successive year they had done so.[101]

The hospital closed on 5 April 1919. A valedictory article appeared in the *Herald* on 16 May 1919. It held that the hospital had been administered "with a care and efficiency that could certainly not be excelled". The credit for this was largely due to the "energy, skill and unfailing resource" of Dr and Mrs Nelson. To mark the closure of the hospital, the Nelsons invited past and present members of the two detachments to a supper, whist drive and dance in the hall. At the conclusion of the festivities, Dr Nelson presented the matron Miss Stevenson with a gold watch: she had been matron during the whole period the hospital was open and "won for herself, by kindness and devotion to duty, the warm admiration of the wounded, the staff and the visitors". A silver cake dish and a coffee service were presented to Mrs Cox, Quartermaster of Warwick Number 32 Detachment, and a silver inkstand to Mr H H Munro, Quartermaster of Number 11. An address was presented to Dr and Mrs Nelson by Mr Lodder, who gave an eloquent testimony

101 *Herald*, 4 October 1918

to the work which they had performed. In his reply, Dr Nelson thanked all those who had worked with him so loyally and so well: "it was the united efforts of all and not the work of individuals that had contributed to the success the hospital had achieved". Eighteen members of its staff served throughout the period during which the hospital was open.

On the closure of the hospital, the two open air wards, the Henley in Arden Ward and the Muntz Ward were presented to Bramcote, the County Tuberculosis Hospital near Nuneaton, complete with their beds and bedding.

The Peace Celebrations Booklet named the following who served with the Warwick VADs Numbers 11 and 32 during the war.

W Ernest Nelson OBE	Commandant & Medical Officer
Rose G Nelson	Assistant Commandant
Lydia Guinness	Honorary Assistant Commandant, Wootton Hall Extension
N Stevenson ARRC	Matron
Phoebe F Lodder	Lady Superintendent
Amy F Cox	Quartermaster
Joyce Agar	Quartermaster
William Dawes	Quartermaster & Pack Storekeeper
H H Munro	Quartermaster & Pack Storekeeper
T R Perkins	Pharmacist
Kathleen Wilcox	Night Sister
Elizabeth Hawkes	Relief Sister
Lilian Heynes	Masseuse
G F Lodder	Auditor
A L Robbins	Secretary
Revd F D Lane MA	Chaplain

VAD Nurses

Annie Albrighton	Mary Avery	Emily K Bagshaw
Nellie Belcher	Annie Blackwell	Lucy Brettell
V Daly	Ruth Dodd	V Grazebrooke
Muriel Guinness ARRC	Lucy Hands	M Hemming
Madge Jamieson	Flora Kirby	Maud Lively
Hon Gladys Moncrieff	D Moore	Marion Moore
Grace Richards	Catherine M Ryland	Mabel Sladen
Beatrice Steele	E Strang	L Teece
H Wakefield	L Whitehead	W Wright

VAD Cooks

Annie Atkins	Annie Coldicott	Hannah Crookes

Q Davis	Mabel Dixon	Mary Dixon
Elsie Hackwood	C Hartley	Mary J Hawkes
Ina Herring	T Heynes	Edwina Stephens
Margaret Stephens		

VAD Orderlies (Women)

R K Baker	A Bonberry	D Chrisp
Rona Stacey-Clitheroe	Gertrude Collins	Gertrude Cooper
Hylda Edkins	Elizabeth Hawkes	Florence Hazelwood
L Hirons	Ada Hodgkins	Phyllis Kitching
Dorothy des Longrais	Helena Newcombe	S Owens
D Robertson	Dorothy Saunders	Gwendoline Taylor

These lists are not necessarily complete: Florrie Beard recalled that her mother worked at the hospital for two years with Mrs Jackson.

Men's Detachment

Oliver James (Section Leader)
Frank Stinson (Section Leader)
Alfred Jenner (Sergeant)

Frank Bioletti	George Coppage	Arthur Dalby
William Eccles	Walter Hadley	Frederick Hemming
H Hodges	B Sly	William Sly
Leonard Stanton	Reginald Turner	J V Watkins
L Watkins		

Public recognition was given to Dr Nelson in the form of an OBE, awarded to him by King George V at Buckingham Palace on Thursday, 27 September 1917. Miss Stevenson became an Associate of the Royal Red Cross (ARRC) 1st Class; Miss Muriel S Guinness, VAD nurse Wootton Wawen, was awarded the ARRC 2nd Class. Mention was made of the services of Mrs A Cox and Mr H H Munro.[102] Quartermaster William Dawes died in harness in 1917 at the age of 74 and is commemorated on the memorial tablet in the Baptist Church: he was a Pensioned Postal Clerk and lived in Beaudesert with his wife Sarah Ann.

The VADs nationally had played a significant part in treating the wounded throughout the war. By its end Henley was one of 43 Auxiliary Hospitals in Warwickshire and one of over 3,000 in the country, which were manned by over 90,000 VADs.

---

102 *London Gazette* – reported in the *Herald* of 15 August 1919

10. Conscription and the Stratford upon Avon Rural District Tribunal

ABOUT one quarter of the adult male population of the country served in the army during the war. Of these, just under half were volunteers, the rest being conscripted under a number of Military Service Acts. The first of these took effect on 27 January 1916 and provided for the conscription of bachelors and widowers between the ages of 18 and 41 and without children or dependants. The Act did not extend to Ireland or to men in work of national importance: the medically unfit and conscientious objectors were excluded. Insufficient numbers were recruited and just three months later on 25 May 1917 the Act was extended to include married men.

A second Act, introduced in February 1918 raised the age limit to 50 and provided that, if need arose, this could be extended to Ireland and to men up to the age of 56. The schedules of work regarded as being of national importance were revised several times and in July 1918 the minimum age of exemption for such occupations was raised to 23.

Over two and a half million men were conscripted from January 1916. The largest number of them served in the infantry and, whereas those volunteering had normally been recruited into their local regiment, conscripts were allocated to regiments on an "as required" basis. It became common for men to be trained in one regiment and moved into another when they reached the infantry base depots at Etaples.

The infantry normally accounted for half the strength of British fighting units in France and Flanders, the artillery being the next most significant in numerical terms, followed by the Royal Engineers. The Army Service Corps was the most numerous of the non-combatant troops, followed by the Royal Army Medical Corps. However, by the end of the war the Labour Corps, which had been formed in January 1917, contained the largest number of non-combatants and amounted to more than 10% of the army: many of its members had been wounded when serving with other regiments and were no longer fit for service in the front line.

Many of those appearing before the Tribunal pleaded that they were unfit for military service. The principal medical categories into which men were placed were:

A   Able to march, see to shoot, hear well and stand active service conditions
B   Free from serious organic diseases, fit for service in Lines of Communication
     in France or in Garrisons in the tropics
  B1   Able to march 5 miles, see to shoot with glasses and hear well
  B2   Able to walk 5 miles, see and hear sufficiently for ordinary purposes
  B3   Only suitable for sedentary work
C   Free from serious organic diseases, fit for service in Garrisons at home
  C1   Able to march 5 miles, see to shoot with glasses and hear well
  C2   Able to walk 5 miles, see and hear sufficiently for ordinary purposes
  C3   Only suitable for sedentary work
In practice, C3 men were not called up.

Stratford Rural District Tribunal

With the advent of conscription came an appeals procedure, initially through local
Wartime Tribunals. Men who received their calling-up papers had seven days to
appeal against their conscription and to apply for exemption on a permanent or
temporary basis to their local tribunal. Henley was covered for this purpose by the
Stratford upon Avon Rural District Tribunal, the chairman of which was Charles
Couchman. The men from the Henley area who appeared before the Tribunal
claimed exemption on occupational or medical grounds: there are no instances of
conscientious objection. There are no records of men being presented with white
feathers, but applying for exemption was not always without consequences: Mrs
Rowney for example was shunned on visits to Henley after her husband (George
Rowney) applied for and was given exemption.

The first meeting of the Tribunal to be reported in the *Herald* was held in the
morning of Tuesday, 28 February 1916.[103] In addition to the chairman seven other
members were present, together with a military representative Mr R C Cox. The
last named appeared for the Stratford Recruiting Officer, Major Bairnsfather. At
this first meeting, the chairman strongly deprecated the practice of certain people
in canvassing members of the Tribunal. Some of those rejected attempted more
than once to enlist, but some men "are offering useful service at home, and where
necessary the cases are coming before the district tribunals".[104]

When a message was read at the Tribunal on 11 August 1916, urging upon
it the necessity of finding men for the army, Couchman commented, "I feel
that the country districts have been bled pretty freely", contrasting this with the
availability of men in the larger towns such as Wolverhampton.[105] His interventions
were unsympathetic at times, as when considering the case of Oliver James of
Henley, a boot repairer, he remarked that it might be better if people bought

---

103 *Herald,* 3 March 1916
104 *Herald,* 4 February 1916
105 *Herald,* 18 August 1916

new boots rather than had them repaired.[106] It was noted in the *Herald* on 5 May 1916 that many agricultural occupations were now no longer exempted. The Tribunal met, normally at fortnightly intervals, until late in 1918 and had about a dozen members: the meeting on Friday, 22 June 1917 for example comprised C Couchman (Chairman), the Honourable Mabel Verney, W W Hutton, E D Kennard, W Hawkes, G B Sims, R J Day, W T Taylor and W Parrott, with R C Cox, J Fielden and Lieutenant Jackson representing the military and T S Smith watching the agricultural interest. The Tribunal believed it was having its last meeting on 12 April 1918, when a vote of thanks was proposed to its chairman. However, it continued in existence for some months, its final meeting being held on 8 November 1918, when Couchman was again in the chair.

The Tribunal could be very busy, hearing 41 cases on 11 August 1916 and 40 cases at the following Tribunal on 25 August (seven of which were from Henley). In January 1917 the Tribunal met twice within a week, on 12 and 16 January. Appeals against the decision of the Tribunal could be made to the Warwickshire Appeal Court and ultimately, in medical cases, to the Central Medical Board in London.

At their meeting on 12 January 1917 a letter from the Adjutant of the 2nd Battalion of the Warwickshire Volunteer Regiment was received by the Tribunal. He pointed out that many men who had been ordered to join the Volunteer Regiment had not attended the drills regularly and that many men who had obtained temporary exemption had not joined the Volunteers although they had plenty of spare time to do so.[107]

The meeting of the Tribunal on 27 April 1917 had a letter from Brigadier-General Grove, commanding the District, read to them. The country required another 500,000 men by 31 July: "All loopholes, all bolt holes must be stopped. Fraud and influence, social and business, must be rooted out once and for all. Men who are fit to serve must come into the Army".[108]

At their meeting on 27 June 1917, the agricultural representative Mr T S Smith told the Tribunal that the County War Agricultural Committee had received an important telegram from the War Office. As from 14 June 1917 no man certified by the County Executive Agricultural Committee as being engaged whole time on farm work of national importance was to be passed for service with the colours or called up for examination or re-examination. Another 3,000,000 acres were to be put into cultivation, of which Warwickshire's share was 60,000. G B Sims, a member of the Tribunal, said that they ought to be careful to differentiate between men genuinely employed on the land and those who had slipped into agriculture to avoid military service. On the basis of this telegram the cases of Wallace Steele and Clement James Jones (*qv*) were adjourned for a month.[109] At the following

---

106 *Herald,* 2 June 1916
107 *Herald,* 19 January 1917
108 *Herald,* 4 May 1917
109 *Herald,* 29 June 1917

meeting Couchman remarked that they had not had any official information on how they were to deal with the cases of men employed in agriculture. Under the present regulations, an attested man had to apply to the Tribunal within 7 days of receiving his calling-up notice. Couchman thought that the best plan would be to give a fairly long adjournment in the agricultural cases, but it was pointed out that this was just what the military did not want. It was decided that cases would be dealt with on their merits.

At the meeting on 8 February 1918, the military representative said that there was now quite a call for C2 men.[110]

No meetings of the Tribunal were reported by the *Herald* between 14 September and 16 November 1917.

Fifty-seven men from Beaudesert, Henley and the surrounding villages appeared before the Tribunal in the course of its existence. Their names are given in alphabetical order for ease of reference. Unless otherwise stated, they are not mentioned in the records of the Tribunal beyond the date given, nor is there any evidence that they subsequently enlisted though that must be the presumption.

Albert C Atkins (27) was a cowman employed by Mr Chandler of Botley Mill, Henley in Arden. He applied for Atkins' exemption before the Tribunal on 12 May 1916 on the grounds that he was unable to find a replacement. Atkins was given exemption until 12 September.[111]

Arthur Bayliss – see his entry in the Roll of Honour.

John Blackwell, blacksmith of Henley, was given conditional exemption by the Tribunal on 30 November 1917. It is likely that this exemption continued until the end of the war. In 1911 he was 30 and living with his widowed mother Susannah in a three-roomed house at 229 Henley in Arden.

John Blackwell at his smithy in the High Street: the man shoeing the horse is probably T C Burton

T C Burton (22, single) in the employ of the above John Blackwell had passed fit for general service and at the Tribunal on 16 November 1917 the military could not agree to him being given exemption. Blackwell said he did the shoeing for 40 farmers and also repaired agricultural implements. The Tribunal thought Blackwell might get an older man than Burton, who was given exemption for 3 months. T S Smith, representing the agricultural interest, suggested Blackwell should try to get a certificate for Burton from the War Agricultural Committee.[112] It is probable that he did so, as Burton's name does not appear in the further records of the Tribunal.

Arthur Chambers (27, single) was stockman to Clifton Mitchell of Beaudesert Farm, who asked for conditional exemption for Chambers on 9 February 1917. Mitchell stated that he had a farm of over 200 acres and Chambers was the only man he had left. His wagoner, cowman and another employee were already in the army. There was a great scarcity of labour, but "he had just got an alien allotted to him". Chambers was granted exemption until the military found an efficient substitute.[113]

Herbert H Chandler of Whitley House appeared before the Tribunal on 11 August 1916 and stated that he had just taken a farm of 57 acres and also assisted his father. The Chairman said that in training with the Yeomanry, Chandler had been injured with a lance and he believed that Chandler held a certificate of unfitness. Chandler said that he had only been passed for garrison duty. He was given a conditional exemption while in his present occupation.[114]

George Coppage – see his entry in the Roll of Honour.

Wilfred James Dobbs, was one of three employees of Hawkes & Sinclair-Brown, millers of Henley, who appeared before the Tribunal on 20 July 1917, the others being Richard Haines and Thomas Wall (*qv*). Dobbs was a mill engineer and foreman, with the control of three floors of machinery, the suction gas plant and the electric lights. He had been rejected several times, but had now been passed C2. Before the war the mill had employed 9 men. The employers had been trying to get men under the National Service Scheme since February, but had only succeeded in getting one. Dobbs was granted conditional exemption.[115] At the meeting held on 8 November 1918 he was given exemption until 1 April 1919.[116]

Samuel Elvins – see his entry in the Roll of Honour.

Percy Albert Fewtrell (40), hairdresser and umbrella repairer of Henley, had only been passed for home service, as grade C2. He was given exemption by the

---

112 *Herald*, 23 November 1917
113 *Herald*, 16 February 1917
114 *Herald*, 18 August 1916
115 *Herald*, 27 July 1917
116 *Herald*, 15 November 1918

Tribunal on 25 August 1916.[117] His case came again before the District Tribunal on 18 January 1918. Fewtrell did not think he would be doing better for himself in the army: his heart was good, although his legs were bad. The Chairman (W T Taylor) said his breath was also bad! The case was adjourned to the next meeting.[118] At the meeting held on 8 February, Fewtrell gave domestic reasons why he shouldn't join the army (these were not elaborated). The military said there was now quite a call for C2 men. Fewtrell was given a final exemption of one month.[119] However, he took his case to the Warwickshire Appeals Tribunal which gave him a conditional exemption, the condition being that he was to give free attendance to soldiers in three local hospitals and to work on the land for twenty hours each week.[120] He was still a hairdresser at 128 High Street in 1936.

Sidney Fisk (18) was employed as an assistant cowman and ploughman by Mr Heler of Grange Farm, Henley. Heler said he was very short-handed and should like to retain Fisk's services for the summer at least. He had 326 acres (128 arable), 40 cows in milk, 112 head of cattle and 110 sheep. Fisk had an agricultural certificate and the case was adjourned *sine die*.[121] Heler had earlier obtained exemption for another of his employees Sidney Gardner (*qv*).

David Augustus Florence was a farmer working for his father at Kyte Green in Beaudesert. He was given conditional exemption by the Tribunal on 12 January 1917.[122]

Sidney Gardner, employed by Mr Heler (see Sidney Fisk above), had the military representative assent to his conditional exemption at the Tribunal held on 2 March 1917.[123]

Vivian Garratt (28) of the High Street Henley, colonial butcher, claimed his occupation was exempt and was given exemption for six months by the Tribunal on 7 April 1916.[124] He appeared before the Tribunal again on 22 September, when he suggested it was in the national interest that he should remain in his occupation: the money that would buy 3 lbs of English meat would buy 4 lbs of colonial. All his money was invested in the business and he also assisted a farmer for 3 days a week. He was given exemption until 27 November 1916.[125]

117 *Herald,* 1 September 1916
118 *Herald,* 25 January 1918
119 *Herald,* 15 February 1918
120 *Herald,* 8 March 1918
121 *Herald,* 10 May 1918
122 *Herald,* 19 January 1917
123 *Herald,* 9 March 1917
124 *Herald,* 14 April 1916
125 *Herald,* 29 September 1916

Richard Haines (28) was a mill hand and carter, class B2, who appeared before the Tribunal on 20 July 1917 with his fellow workers Dobbs and Wall (*qv*). He was granted conditional exemption but appeared before the Tribunal again on 8 November 1918, when he was given exemption until 1 April 1919.[126]

Edward Richard Harrison – see his entry in the Roll of Honour.

Stephen Hastings – see his entry in the Roll of Honour.

Henry Hawkes, farmer of Henley, was now over military age, but had been called up and it was necessary for him to obtain the leave of the Tribunal to appeal. He was engaged on the land (350 acres) for the whole of his time and his appeal was granted. The Clerk said he had advised Hawkes to apply to the War Agricultural Committee for a certificate.[127]

Frederick William Paley Hemming was employed by Christophers & Lodder in Henley and had been exempt as the Law Society considered that he could not be spared. However, at the meeting of the Tribunal held on 8 November his absolute exemption was withdrawn and he was given exemption until 1 May 1919.[128]

Sidney W Hemming (34), general wheelwright of Henley, claimed to be the only wheelwright in a 4-mile radius. His chief work was the repair of carts and implements for the local farmers. The men who formerly worked for him had enlisted and he was now single-handed, with more that 6 months work in hand. He was given conditional exemption when he came before the Tribunal on 15 December 1916.[129]

Walter Ethelbert Hemming was 44 and had been graded C2 when he appeared before the Tribunal on 23 August 1918. He was a watch and clock maker and repairer and asked for exemption on the ground that this was work of real national importance. He was also not satisfied with his medical examination, but unfortunately the time had expired during which he might appeal. His was a one-man business and the only one of its kind in the district. His case was adjourned for a medical examination.[130] At the meeting of the Tribunal on 13 September 1918 the panel was informed that Hemming was being re-examined on that day and his case was adjourned.[131] Hemming had been re-examined when he again appeared before the Tribunal on 4 October. He was still dissatisfied and had appealed to go before the

126 *Herald,* 15 November 1918
127 *Herald,* 21 September 1917
128 *Herald,* 15 November 1918
129 *Herald,* 22 December 1916
130 *Herald,* 30 August 1918
131 *Herald,* 20 September 1918

special assessors. His case was adjourned.[132] At the final meeting of the Tribunal on 8 November 1918, it was reported that Hemming had been put down to grade 3 on his medical re-examination: he therefore did not require exemption and could wait until he was called up.[133] He was a watchmaker at 131 High Street in 1936.

Willoughby George Hemming, jeweller, appeared before the Tribunal on 2 June 1916 and asked for exemption on the grounds of serious hardship: he did all the outside work in the business while his brother did all the benchwork. He was given exemption for three months (*Herald* 9 June 1916). When he reappeared in September, he had moved to Redditch and was now working in a munitions factory, suggesting that it was in the national interest that he should remain there. The Chairman, in giving him 14 days exemption, said that he appeared to have got into a more remunerative occupation.[134]

William Hewlett (38) was wagoner to Walter Richmond of Liveridge Farm in Beaudesert, which comprised 107 acres, 23 of which were arable. The case was adjourned by the Tribunal on 27 April 1917 to see if the military could find a substitute for him.[135]

Oliver James – see his entry in the Roll of Honour.

William C Jamieson – see his entry in the Roll of Honour.

† *Clement James Jones (1898/9-1918)*
Private 51015, 12th Battalion Somerset Light Infantry (Prince Albert's).

Clement Jones was born in Bromsgrove, the son of Frederick and Sarah D Jones. His father was a market gardener. The family was living in Broad Street, Bromsgrove in 1901, Clement then having a younger brother, Robert F Jones.

Clement was 19 when he came before the Tribunal on 25 May 1917. His father, then a farmer in Preston Bagot, sought exemption for him on the grounds that Clement was a stockman and the only assistant he had on a 63 acre farm. The military representative thought that the young man should join up. Jones said that before the war he had employed two men but now had to rely on his son and a younger boy of 16 (it later emerged that this was his younger son). The case was adjourned for two weeks to enable Clement to be medically examined. At the tribunal on 22 June his case was adjourned for one month to enable instructions from the War Office to be clarified: a telegram had been received stating that from 14 June 1917 no man certified by the County Executive Agricultural Committee to

---

132 *Herald,* 11 October 1918
133 *Herald,* 15 November 1918
134 *Herald,* 29 September 1916
135 *Herald,* 4 May 1917

be engaged whole time on farm work of national importance was to be conscripted. At the Tribunal on 20 July Clement was given exemption until 1 November.

Shortly after this date Clement enlisted at Leamington in the 12th Battalion, Somerset Light Infantry. This was a Territorial Force unit, formed in Egypt on 4 January 1917 from the dismounted West Somerset Yeomanry. The battalion left Alexandria for France with 74th Division on 30 April 1918 and landed at Marseilles on 7 May. Clement joined them after this date: he was wounded in France on 13 October 1918 and brought back to hospital in England, where he died on 31 October, aged 20. He is buried on the south side of Preston Bagot Church where his father was buried alongside him in 1928, aged 66.
1901 census; CWGC; SDGW; James, p 57.

William King (36), a farm worker employed by Mrs Steele of Mays Hill Farm, was given conditional exemption by the Tribunal on 30 November 1917.[136]

British War Medal, Victory Medal.

Frederick George Maine – see his entry in the Roll of Honour.

Robert L Newcombe, cycle and motor dealer of Henley, appeared before the Tribunal on 30 November 1917. The military asked for the withdrawal of the certificate of exemption held by him, arguing that it was in the national interest that he should be employed on military service. Newcombe stated that he had a contract to look after the motor ploughs in the district and at present had five machines to keep in order. When the war broke out, five of his employees had joined up: he acted as a Special Constable and also did Red Cross work. He was given a final conditional exemption until 1 February 1918.[137] Towards the end of March he appeared before the Warwickshire Appeals Tribunal, when he was stated to be a garage proprietor and engineering mechanic, aged 38, married and Class A. The Board of Agriculture Commissioner could not give him a certificate for tractor maintenance, as he was a contractor and not a direct employer. All efforts to find someone to take over the work had been unsuccessful. The case was adjourned so that definite information could be given to the Tribunal of the efforts to find a substitute.[138] He was living at 84 High Street in 1936 and died on 20 May 1947, aged 67. He is buried in St Nicholas' churchyard.

Herbert George Parkes (39), secretary of the Henley in Arden Gas Board, appealed for exemption to the Tribunal on 22 October 1916. The Chairman, Charles Couchman, stated that, being a director of the company, he would not adjudicate in this case; he said that the directors supported the appeal, as gas was a public

---

136 *Herald,* 7 December 1917
137 *Herald,* 7 December 1917
138 *Herald,* 22 March 1918

service and Parkes ran the whole thing under the orders of the directors. Parkes was only passed for garrison duty at home. He was granted exemption until 31 March, with leave to appeal again.[139] A further appeal was heard on 27 April 1917. Charles Couchman said that he and another member of the Tribunal, being directors of the company, would not adjudicate on this case. Parkes had been to Budbrook for his medical and had been classified C1. He was one of only two employees. He was given conditional exemption.[140] He was a stationer at 197 High Street in 1936.

Harry Payne (40) was the coachman for Mrs Strang of the Yew Trees, who asked for a temporary exemption for him at the Tribunal on 16 June 1916, until such time as she had disposed of her horses. Payne said that he was a member of the Red Cross Society (he was an active member of Warwick Number 11 Voluntary Aid Detachment in 1914) and his principal employment now was driving wounded soldiers out. He was given exemption for 2 months and told that if he returned at that time and said he was working in munitions he would be permanently exempt.[141] It is very likely that he did so.

Robert George Pickard (37) worked for his father, a farmer, at Harper's Hill, Henley. The farm comprised 40 acres, with 6 milking cows and 25 stock. Dr Agar attended to testify to the ill-health of Pickard's father and Pickard was given conditional exemption when he appeared before the Tribunal on 25 August 1916.[142] Dr Agar's testament proved to be fully justified on this occasion, as Pickard's father died on 5 September.[143] Pickard was still farming at Harper's Hill in 1936.

Walter Pinfold, cowman, working for Mrs Steele at May's Hill Farm, had his conditional exemption agreed to by the military representative at the District Tribunal held on 11 May 1917.[144]

William Price – see his entry in the Roll of Honour.

Frank Rathbone – see his entry in the Roll of Honour.

William Reynolds (39, single), an agricultural labourer, appealed on the grounds that he was constantly being seen by the doctor. He was classed C3. The military agreed to his exemption when he appeared before the Tribunal on 17 November 1916, until those in grade C3 were called up.[145]

---

139 *Herald*, 27 October 1916
140 *Herald*, 4 May 1917
141 *Herald*, 23 June 1916
142 *Herald*, 1 September 1916
143 *Herald*, 15 September 1916
144 *Herald*, 11 May 1917
145 *Herald*, 24 November 1916

George Rowney (37), hay and straw dealer and farmer of Henley, appeared before the Tribunal on 11 August 1916 and claimed exemption on the grounds that it would mean selling up his home and everything if he enlisted. He didn't think it would be possible to pick up the business again. He was given two months exemption.[146] When he reappeared before the Tribunal on 13 October, he stated that he had for some years provided the horses for the Henley fire engine. If he had to join the army, he would sell his horses and the business would be wound up. He had not been examined at Budbrook. He was given a conditional exemption.[147]

Alfred Sammons (38), greengrocer of Henley in Arden, applied for exemption before the Tribunal on 2 June 1916. The Medical Board had said he was only fit for garrison duty at home. He was given exemption until 30 September. When he appeared again before the Tribunal on 17 August 1917, calling himself a greengrocer and allotment holder, it was stated that he had originally been granted exemption on the condition that he went into munitions work and he had done this while his son worked the allotment. His son had now joined up (see A A Sammons in the Roll of Honour). Under the orders of his doctor Sammons had now left munitions work and wished to keep his business together. He was classified B2. The military suggested his wife could look after the shop but the Tribunal granted him exemption, conditional upon him putting in 2 days each week on farm work.[148]

John H Shepherd (40) was a carter employed by Mr Harry Hawkes of Henley, who claimed before the Tribunal on 12 May 1916 that he was a farmer of 200 acres and would be caused hardship if Shepherd were to be taken. Hawkes had two younger men working on the farm, both married, plus himself and one other. The Tribunal thought one or two men from the farm should go. Shepherd was given exemption until 12 June.[149]

Howard Sinclair-Brown (34) of the Mill House, Henley, claimed to be supplying 400 farmers with flour and meal. It was decided that he was in a certified occupation and he was given conditional exemption on 24 August 1916.[150] His case came up for review before the Tribunal on 13 September 1918, when it was stated that he was 36, married and that his classification had been reduced from A to grade 3. The National Service representative, Mr Jackson, said he found that Sinclair-Brown did not appear on the list as a flour miller. Sinclair-Brown agreed, but said that he did a biggish business as a grist miller, which the Food Production Department had recognized by granting him a license for 22 gallons of petrol a month. He was

---

146 *Herald,* 18 August 1916
147 *Herald,* 20 October 1916
148 *Herald,* 24 August 1917
149 *Herald,* 19 May 1916
150 *Herald,* 1 September 1916

given two months exemption.[151] At the meeting held on 8 November 1918 he was given exemption until 1 April 1919.[152]

George Smith (36, married) acted as cowman for J H Harris of Foster's Farm, who had 42 head of cows and 21 milking cows. Smith had passed B2. He was given conditional exemption by the Tribunal at their meeting on 16 January 1917.[153]

Tom Snowden (36, married) appeared before the Tribunal on 12 January 1917. He was the only man on Camp Hill Farm, Beaudesert, owned by Mrs William Cooper. He had managed it as her bailiff since 1910. The farm comprised 31 acres of grassland and she kept 14 head of cattle and 2 horses. Mrs Cooper had two sons, but they were incapacitated. Snowden had been passed fit for general service. The military representative argued that despite the man's principal and usual occupation being a certified one, it was not in the national interest that he should be kept in civil employment and suggested that a substitute could be found for him. The Chairman said that there must be one man on the farm and Snowden was given exemption until 1 April to see if a substitute could be found.[154] Mrs Cooper pleaded for him again before the Tribunal on 27 April 1917. He was a very reliable man and she had two sons dependent on her for a living. The farm was her sole support and Snowden had managed it very successfully since 1910. The Tribunal gave him one month's exemption.[155]

John Mortimer Southern, assistant master at Beaudesert Park School, pleaded indifferent health. He had been rejected once for eyesight, but had subsequently been passed fit for garrison duty abroad following a medical at Budbrook. On 11 August 1916 he given a final exemption until 29 September.[156] His name does not appear again and it is probable that he enlisted towards the end of 1916.

William Herbert Steele (18, single) was working on his mother's farm at May's Hill, when he appeared before the Tribunal on 15 December 1916. He claimed that his knowledge of the machinery for milking, grinding and cake crushing was vital to the farm. He was given exemption until 1 April 1917.[157] His name was probably misreported and should read Wallace Herbert Steele – see his entry in the Roll of Honour.

---

151 *Herald,* 20 September 1918
152 *Herald,* 15 November 1918
153 *Herald,* 19 January 1917
154 *Herald,* 19 January 1917
155 *Herald,* 4 May 1917
156 *Herald,* 18 August 1916
157 *Herald,* 22 December 1916

William Otho Steele of May's Hill managed a farm of 367 acres for his mother and was given conditional exemption when he appeared before the Tribunal on 25 August 1916.[158] He was able to continue farming for the duration of the war.

Frank Stinson – see his entry in the Roll of Honour.

James Styles, stoker at Henley Gas Works, was granted permanent exemption by the military authorities when he appeared before the Tribunal in June 1916.[159] However, in June 1918 he wrote to the Tribunal enclosing his certificate of exemption, stating that he was no longer in a certified occupation. The military had not answered his letter of 28 May asking that he be given a medical examination; he thought he should be given one and be graded before joining up. The Tribunal agreed.[160] In 1936 James Styles was the manager of the Gas Works and living at Gas House, Beaudesert.

Herbert A Taylor – see his entry in the Roll of Honour.

Herbert Tomlin (25, single) applied for exemption through his uncle, Mr Tomlin, who farmed about 50 acres at Brook House Farm. Herbert was useful on the farm, which had 11 cows and 4 horses, and Tomlin couldn't get anyone else. He was exempted for one month, with no further leave to appeal.[161] It must be presumed that he enlisted in late 1916. He was born in Tanworth in 1890.
Possibly Private Herbert Tomlin M2/152423, Army Service Corps, who was awarded the British War Medal and the Victory Medal.

Thomas Wall – see his entry in the Roll of Honour.

Albert Waterton (39, married) was a gardener and asylum attendant for Dr Agar. He was only classified C3 and was given conditional exemption on 12 January 1917.[162] When his case came up again on 18 January 1918, it was said that he was now on munitions work in Hall Green, Birmingham. He was given three months exemption.[163]

John Valentine Watkins – see his entry in the Roll of Honour.

James C W Weetman of the Post Office in Henley was said to assist his mother on a farm at Preston Bagot. The farm had 130 acres, of which 36 were arable. He had

---

158 *Herald,* 1 September 1916
159 *Herald,* 23 June 1916
160 *Herald,* 28 June 1918
161 *Herald,* 27 October 1916
162 *Herald,* 19 January 1917
163 *Herald,* 25 January 1918

passed his medical C1 and was given exemption until 1 June when he appeared before the Tribunal on 16 January 1917.[164]

† Ernest Harrison Wheatley (1884-1917)
Private 37070, 1st Battalion Worcestershire Regiment.

Ernest Harrison Wheatley (31) the manager of six boot depots, whose address was given as Waterloo House, Henley in Arden, was granted exemption until 24 June when he appeared before the Tribunal on 12 May 1916.[165] H C Smith, the chairman of the board of T R Bird Ltd, his employers, sought further exemption for him in August. Wheatley was said to be the Secretary of the Company and the Inspector of six branches, three of which were controlled by women. Wheatley had only been passed fit for garrison duty abroad. He was given a final exemption of 14 days.[166] He took his case to appeal, but was turned down.[167]

Wheatley had been born in Belper, Derbyshire in 1884 the son of George and Elizabeth Wheatley. In 1901 he was working in Belper as a Boot shop Assistant. He enlisted in Stratford upon Avon shortly after losing his appeal and was posted to the 1st Battalion of the Worcestershire Regiment. His medical grade must have been upgraded, for on 1 August 1917 he was killed in action and is buried in Grave I K 2 of the Divisional Collecting Post Cemetery and Extension north east of Ypres. SDGW records his residence as Belper.

British War Medal, Victory Medal.

George Alfred Whitmore was a groom and male attendant for Dr Agar. The latter asked for his exemption at the Tribunal on 15 September 1916. Whitmore was then 35 and living at Blackford Hill Cottage in Henley. Dr Agar, who had a private lunatic asylum in Henley, stated that four men in his employ had already joined up. Whitmore had served 13 years as a soldier and had been discharged a year earlier. Five of his brothers were in France. The military representative wanted him back however. Charles Couchman thought it very necessary that Agar should have someone to drive him about. Whitmore was given six weeks exemption to enable Agar to get another groom.[168] He appeared again before the Tribunal on 8 November 1918, when he was given exemption until 1 March 1919.[169]

Gunner 29615 George Whitmore, Royal Field Artillery, had enlisted in Birmingham on 26 November 1902 for three years with the colours and 9 years with the reserve. In 1901 he was living with his parents George and Sarah Whitmore at 83 St George's Street, Smethwick and working as a labourer. He was the eldest

---

164 *Herald,* 19 January 1917

165 *Herald,* 19 May 1916

166 *Herald,* 18 August 1916

167 *Herald,* 8 September 1916

168 *Herald,* 22 September 1916

169 *Herald,* 15 November 1918

of seven sons and two daughters. When he enlisted he gave his age as 20 years and 3 months. His height was 5'6", his weight 133 pounds and his chest 34". His complexion was fresh, his eyes blue, his hair black and he was a member of the Church of England. His three years in the colours were served in England and he was transferred to the Army Reserve on 26 November 1905. He married Martha Jane Huish and had a daughter Gladys Martha, born on 8 February 1908. On the outbreak of war he was mobilised at Preston on 6 August 1914 and his MIC shows that he went to France on 16 August, where he served with 28th Brigade RFA. He returned to England at the end of his nine years in the reserve on 23 November 1914 and was discharged on 30 November. He was subsequently awarded the 1914 Star, the British War Medal and the Victory Medal.

John William Woodall (38), oil-dealer and small-holder of Henley in Arden, pleaded to the Tribunal in March 1916 that it would be a serious hardship if he were called up, as he had an invalid father and mother who were dependent upon him. His case was put back for 3 months.[170] He re-applied and was given a further two months.[171] When his case came up again, he was given a further six months exemption.[172]

The grounds cited for exemption were almost always that the man was in an exempt occupation or working in employment of national importance. Of the 51 men who claimed on this basis, 26 men had their claim upheld. Eight men claimed exemption on health grounds (four of whom had also claimed on the grounds of their employment): these health claims only succeeded in two cases. Two men claimed on the grounds of hardship and neither claim succeeded. There were no claims based on conscientious objection. Following the rejection of their case by the Stratford Tribunal, five men went on to the Warwick Appeals Tribunal, two being exempted and three being conscripted.

At least 15 of the 57 local men who went before the Stratford Tribunal were conscripted and their details appear in the Roll of Honour: only one of them died in the war. It is possible that up to a further 16 were conscripted as their exemption dates expired before the war came to an end: if any of them were conscripted, they survived and are unlikely to have served overseas as there are no identifiable MICs for them. Two men whose appeals were rejected and were subsequently conscripted (Jones and Wheatley) were killed in action: they have not been included in the Henley Roll of Honour because of the tenuous nature of their links with the town.

---

170 *Herald*, 17 March 1916
171 *Herald*, 16 June 1916
172 *Herald*, 18 August 1916

11. Roll of Honour 1914-1918

Beaudesert & Henley in Arden

THIS Roll of Honour includes the names of over 180 men from Henley, or closely associated with it, who served in the Great War. In July 1919 a booklet was produced for the Henley Peace Celebrations which set out to name all the men of the town who had served and died or who had served and survived. It was not, however, a comprehensive record. In this Roll of Honour the names of those who died are marked with a cross and shown in bold type; those whose names did not appear on the original memorial in St John's Church are in italics. Men with a Henley connection who served and survived but whose names do not appear in the Henley Peace Celebrations booklet also have their names shown in italics. This booklet has been the primary source of information, but it lists at best only the surnames and initials of the men and in some cases only the surname: important aids to identification such as regiment, rank and first names were not given. Another important source of names has been the *Herald*, whose Henley correspondent frequently gave details of the war service of local men.

All of the individuals who died during the war can be positively identified from the records of the Commonwealth War Graves Commission (CWGC) and the data base of Soldiers Died in the Great War (SDGW). The precise identities of those who served and survived have been more difficult and in some cases impossible to trace, because of either the absence of first names or as there are many hundreds of individuals with the same name. There are, for example, over 500 men with an MIC in the name of J Harris who served in the Royal Artillery and many more of that name and regiment who did not go abroad. Once an individual has been identified, the most important sources of information have been his Medal Index Card (MIC) and his Service and Pension records. However, MICs only exist for men who served overseas and two-thirds of the army's Service and Pension records were destroyed as the result of an air raid during the war of 1939-1945.

Just over half of the male population of the country between the ages of 18 and 49 were in the armed forces during the war, the others either being in reserved occupations or physically unfit. Many men were saved by their poor physique, failing to meet the rudimentary standards of medical fitness required. Several men from Henley passed their local medical but were rejected when they reached their units. The average height of the Henley men whose records are known was

5'6½" and their average weight only 132 lbs. The proportion of one in six of the men from Henley who served and died during the war was higher than the national average of one in eight, but this may be because not all of the men who served and survived have been identified.

Decorations
Distinguished Service Order (DSO) & bar
Brigadier-General Gerald Carew Sladen

Distinguished Flying Medal (DFM)
Corporal Leonard Albert Allen, Royal Air Force

Distinguished Conduct Medal (DCM)
Staff Sergeant Major James Perks, Royal Army Service Corps
Sergeant Mark Shelton, Royal West Surrey Regiment
Lance Corporal William Stockley, Royal Warwickshire Regiment

Military Cross (MC)
Captain Arden Cotterill Coldicott, Royal Warwickshire Regiment
Brigadier-General Gerald Carew Sladen

Military Medal (MM)
Private William Henry Bonehill, Royal Warwickshire Regiment
Private Alfred Richardson Hodgkins, Canadian Overseas Expeditionary Force
Lance Sergeant Dick Holt, Royal Warwickshire Regiment
Private Harold Ingram, Coldstream Guards
Lance Corporal William Stockley, Royal Warwickshire Regiment

Campaign Medals
The **1914 Star** was issued to all ranks who served in France and Belgium between 5 August and midnight on 22/23 November 1914. In 1919 a Bar was awarded to all of those who had been under fire during these dates.

The **1914-15 Star** was issued to men who served in any theatre of the war between 5 August 1914 and 31 December 1915 (other than those who held the 1914 Star).

The **British War Medal** was approved in 1919 for issue to men who served overseas between 5 August 1914 and 11 November 1918 for 28 days or more.

The **Victory Medal** was awarded to all those who received one of the above.

Silver War Badge
This was issued to service personnel who had been discharged due to wounds or sickness during the war to prevent them being accosted and accused of cowardice. First issued in September 1916, it was to be worn only with civilian dress. Each badge was individually numbered. It does not seem to have been awarded with any degree of consistency.

†Adkins, Albert Charles (1890-1917)

Private 21459, 1st Battalion Royal Warwickshire Regiment.

Albert Adkins was born in Knowle in Warwickshire in 1890, the eldest son of Charles Henry Adkins and his wife Amy (*nee* Holloway). In 1891 he was living in Hopwood, Alvechurch with his parents and his elder sister Eva: his father was a Manufacturer's Carter. Albert was still living there with them in 1901, as were his younger sister Ethel and his younger brother Edward. His father was now working as a Carter on a farm. In 1911, Albert was working as a Farm Labourer at Manor Farm, Lode Lane, Solihull in the employ of Horatio Morgan. He married Maud Bickley in 1916.

Albert gave his residence as Henley in Arden when he enlisted in Stratford upon Avon. The 1st Battalion was a Regular Army battalion which had landed in

France on 22 August 1914 and was part of 10th Brigade, 4th Division. It is likely that Albert was one of a draft of 199 other ranks that joined the Battalion in the first week of 1917, when it was encamped and training near Bray, between Amiens and Peronne. There was no heavy fighting at this time. On 10 February the Battalion moved to the front line north of Bouchavesnes, where activity was increased. The Battalion was relieved on 16 February and continued to move in and out of the front line over the next three months. On 8 May it relieved the 2nd Battalion Seaforth Highlanders and attacked Roeux at 7.30 pm on 11 May. There was fierce fighting for the next 24 hours until Roeux was captured. During this time the 1st Battalion lost one officer and three other ranks killed and 21 wounded, its strength being reduced to 7 officers and 141 other ranks.[173]

Albert Adkins was probably wounded in this action. His name appeared in the *Birmingham Post* on 15 June 1917 in a list of men from the Royal Warwickshire Regiment

---

173 Ashby, pp 151-2

who had been posted missing. However, it later emerged that he had been taken prisoner and had died of wounds on 13 May 1917. He is buried in grave IX E 9 in Niederzwehren Cemetery, which is some 10 kilometres south of Kassel.

Niederzwehren Cemetery

The Germans began this cemetery in 1915 for the burial of prisoners of war who died at the local camp. After the war it was decided that the graves of Commonwealth servicemen who had died in Germany should be brought together into four cemeteries, of which Niederzwehren was one. There are now 1,795 servicemen of the Great War who are buried in the Commonwealth plot at Niederzwehren.

Albert's wife Maud (whose brother Sidney Bickley (*qv*) was also killed) was left with their daughter Lilian, aged one.

British War Medal and Victory Medal.

1891, 1901 & 1911 Census; CWGC; SDGW; MIC; Mrs Carsina Goodman (his granddaughter).

Agar, Willoughby (1889-1951)

Captain, Royal Army Medical Corps.

He was baptised on 30 May 1889 in St Nicholas', the son of John James Agar, Farmer of Blackford Mill, and his wife Edith (*nee* Walsh). In 1891 he was living at Blackford Mill with his parents, a boarder and three servants. In 1901 he was a boarder at Arden House in Henley, the home of Dr Ernest Nelson, which also housed a boarding school run by Nelson's younger brother, Oswald. He was at Malvern College from 1903 to 1907 and was a House Prefect. He went up to Oriel College, Oxford in 1907 and took a 3rd Class Honours degree in Natural Science in 1911. At the time of the census he was again living in the 13-roomed Blackford Mill with his parents, his younger sister Joyce Ellen and three servants. He became MRCS and LRCP in 1915.

In October 1916 Willoughby enlisted in the RAMC. He was attached to 27th Casualty Clearing Station and served in Mesopotamia, India and Salonika. His troopship was torpedoed when arriving at Bombay and Willoughby had to swim ashore.

In July 1920 the banns were called in St John's Church for his marriage to Madeline Betty Hamilton of Beckenham: the marriage did not take place and in 1922 he married Mary Dorothy Dunn. They had two children, Ann Josephine (1923) and John Willoughby (1926). He practised medicine in Henley, where he lived at The Lawn in 1922 and at Glendossil House in 1924. He was a nephew of Dr Samuel Hollingworth Agar and helped him in the running of his private asylum at Glendossil. He was High Bailiff of Henley in Arden from 1930 to 1945 and was made an Honorary Burgess in 1946. Willoughby Agar died in 1951.

No MIC has been found, but his service entitled him to the British War Medal and the Victory Medal.

Beaudesert PR; 1891, 1901 & 1911 Census; *Malvern College Register,* p 439; *Oxford University Roll of Service,* p 125; Kelly 1924; Court Leet Minutes; John Agar (his son).

Allen, Leonard Albert DFM (1891-fl 1919)
Corporal (Aerial Gunlayer), 202615, Royal Air Force.

The son of John and Helena Allen, he was born in Balsall Heath and was living with his parents in 1901 at 2 Uplands, Hay Mill in Yardley, then part of Worcestershire. Also living with them were his elder sister Ethel Florence (12) and his younger sister Hilda (8); his parents also had an adopted son, Samuel McCracken (7). His father was an Embosser and Chaser of silver. In 1911 Leonard was still living with his parents, who had then been married for 24 years, his two sisters, and a boarder. His parents had had a fourth child who had died. The family was living at 519 Green Lane, Birmingham and Leonard was working as a Chair Maker.

Leonard Allen was awarded the DFM in September 1918. It was stated that he was from Henley in Arden and was "one of the keenest and most reliable gun-layers in his squadron. He has frequently been in action with enemy aeroplanes and has flown for 100 hours on photographic and reconnaissance flights".

DFM, British War Medal, Victory Medal.

1901 & 1911 Census; *London Gazette* 21 September 1918; *Herald* (27 September 1918).

†Andrews, George William (1897-1917)

Private 22523, 11th Battalion Royal Warwickshire Regiment.

George Andrews was born in Henley in Arden on 7 March 1897, the son of John William and Mary Ann Jane Andrews. He was baptised in St John's Church on 24 October 1897. His father was a bricklayer's labourer who was living in Henley at the time of the 1901 census with his son George, then aged 4, his daughter Elizabeth May (1) and Mary Ann Canning (57 and probably his mother in law). It is likely that his wife had died following the birth of their daughter. They lived at 54 High Street. George entered Henley Junior School on 13 June 1904 from the Infant Department (when his father's occupation was given as Painter) and left on 6 May 1910 to take up employment. In 1911 he was living with his father and step mother in a four-roomed house at 54 Henley in Arden and working as an Errand Boy for a Newsagent and Draper: his father made his mark when signing the return as head of the household and had been married for three years to his second wife Sarah Ann. Prior to enlisting George was employed by the GWR at Danzey Green Station.

George enlisted at Stratford upon Avon, joining the 11th (Service) Battalion of the Royal Warwickshire Regiment. This battalion was formed at Warwick in October 1914. In April 1915 it became part of 112th Brigade, 37th Division, which moved to France in July and August 1915. George went to France sometime after 31 December 1915. Between 6 July and 22 August 1916 112th Brigade was attached to 34th Division and fought on the Somme at the battles of Albert and the Bazentin and Pozieres Ridges. Throughout the Ancre operations of 13-18 November 1916 the Brigade served with 2nd Division, following which it rejoined 37th Division at Englebelmer. On 9 April 1917 two parallel attacks began on an area east of Arras. The southern advance was along the River Scarpe and involved 37th Division in heavy fighting until 11 April when Monchy le Preux was captured. The Division was also engaged during the 2nd Battle of the Scarpe (23-24 April) and before the end of the month fought at Arleux.

George Andrews died during the Battle of Arleux on 28 April 1917, aged 20.[174] A Memorial Service was held for him in St John's Church on 20 May. The church was crowded and the congregation included some of his former working colleagues and representatives of the Foresters' Friendly Society, of which he had been a

---

174 CWGC gives his date of death as 28 April and his age as 21. The date of 25 April and the age of 20 are given in the *Herald* of 1 June 1917: this age is confirmed by the Henley Admissions Register

member. He has no known grave and is commemorated on Bay 3 of the Arras Memorial. George is also commemorated on the GWR Memorial at Kidderminster Railway Station.

British War Medal and Victory Medal.

St John's PR; 1901 & 1911 Census; CWGC; SDGW; MIC; James, p 48; School Register; *Herald* (1 June 1917).

The Arras Memorial

†Arnold, Henry Richard (1895-1915)

Private 13058, 2nd Battalion Coldstream Guards.

Known as Harry, he was born in Henley on 3 February 1895, the eldest son of Harvey Arnold, boot and shoe maker of 251 High Street, and his wife Ellen (*nee* Mills). His father had been born in Preston Bagot and his mother in Henley.

In 1901 he was living in Henley with his parents and his elder sister Edith; he subsequently had two brothers, William and Frank. Harry was educated at the Council School in Henley, entering the Junior School on 1 May 1902 from the Infant Department. He left on 23 October 1908 to join his father's business. However, in 1911 he was the resident Domestic Gardener at Hurst House, one of Henley's lunatic asylums, with Miss Mary Agar as the head of the household. Harry

117

Arnold's shop in the High Street

was an active member of the Baptist Church and during his Sunday School days his regular attendance was proverbial. He was a member of the Henley Fire Brigade.

Harry enlisted in Birmingham on 6 October 1914, joining 2nd Battalion, Coldstream Guards. At his medical examination he was recorded as being 5'8" in height, weighing 139 lbs and having a chest of 37". His complexion was fresh, his eyes blue and his hair brown; he had two scars on the right side of his forehead; he registered as a member of the Baptist Church. He was formally appointed to the regiment on 8 October and joined it at Caterham on 9 October.

The Guards were then serving in France attached to 4th Guards Brigade, 2nd Division. They suffered very heavy casualties and Harry joined them in France on 7 April 1915. He was killed in action at Cambrin on 6 July 1915 by a rifle grenade that fell in his trench, badly wounding him in the back and his left leg. Captain H C Lloyd, commanding 3 Company of 2nd Battalion, wrote to Harry's mother on 8 July:

"I very much regret to have to inform you that your son, Private Arnold, was very badly wounded about 9 pm on Tuesday, and that he died about a quarter of an hour later. He was in a trench at the time when a rifle grenade fell into the trench very close to him, wounding him and another man. His hurts were in the leg and back…I am afraid this letter will be a great shock to you, but I felt you would wish to know the exact truth. I hope you will accept my most sincere sympathy in your great loss. Your son had not been out very long, but long enough to prove himself an excellent soldier. I had personally noticed him, and he always did his work well and willingly, and I feel that the Company has lost in him one of its best and most pleasant members. He was buried at Cambrin cemetery about four miles west of Bethune and a wooden cross, with his name and regiment, will be placed on his grave, which will be well kept."

His family also received a letter of sympathy from Corporal O J Paskin of 11 Platoon, 3 Company, which had been written on 7 July. Harry Arnold was 20 years old when he was killed and is buried in the Churchyard Extension at Cambrin, grave E 26. Cambrin is a village about 15 miles north of Arras and five miles east of Bethune, on the road to La Bassee.

A Memorial Service was held for Harry in the Baptist Church on 18 July 1915, conducted by the Revd Leonard Schofield. It was well attended: the Fire Brigade under their Captain Godfrey Hemming, the local British Red Cross Society led by Quartermaster W Dawes, and the local scout troop, were all present in their uniforms. Several of his wounded soldier friends also attended.

1914-15 Star, British War Medal and Victory Medal.

1901 & 1911 census; Henley School Admissions Register; De Revigny, Vol I, Part 1, p 10 (with photo); CWGC; SDGW; MIC; James, p 41; *Herald* (16 & 23 July 1915).

Atkins, Arthur Edward (1892-fl 1919)

Sergeant 101048, Canadian Army.

He was born in Oldberrow on 13 September 1892, the third son of Charles James and Annie Atkins, and was baptised there on 9 October 1892. In 1901 Charles James Atkins was a Farmer living in New Terrace, Oldberrow, Worcestershire, with his wife Annie and their four sons, Harold James, Percy Sellick, Arthur Edward and Frederick Charles (*qv*). In the 1911 Census C J Atkins was living in an eight-roomed house in Oldberrow with his family (other than Arthur) and described himself as an Assistant Overseer and Collector of Taxes: he became Clerk to the Wootton Wawen Parish Council on 17 April 1917 at an annual salary of £80 and also acted as Assistant Overseer for Henley.

At the time of the 1911 Census Arthur was visiting Mr and Mrs Fred Cottrell and their five children at 4 Marldon Road, King's Heath, Birmingham. He was then working as a Bank Clerk. He subsequently emigrated to Canada, sailing from Liverpool on the *Laurentic* and arriving in Quebec on 19 May 1912. When he enlisted in Edmonton, Canada on 20 July 1915 he gave his next of kin as his father, then living in Henley in Arden. Arthur had continued working as a bank clerk. According to his medical record he was 5'7½" tall, with a chest measurement of 35": he had a clear complexion, brown eyes, dark brown hair, a mole on his chest and a scar on his forehead. In June 1916 he was reported as being in the Canadian forces, serving either in the UK or France and was expected in Henley on leave. Shortly afterwards he was wounded in the leg and transferred to hospital in Woolwich. He later became an anti-gas instructor working among Canadian soldiers in England and in rapid succession was promoted to Corporal and then Sergeant. Arthur was again on leave in Henley in January 1919, when he stated that although he might have to return to Canada he hoped to have his discharge soon. After the war his parents moved to Upper Sumas Road, Abbotsford, British Colombia.

British War Medal and Victory Medal.

Oldberrow PR; 1901 & 1911 Census; Canadian Passenger Lists; Canadian Archives website; *Herald* (23 June & 20 October 1916, 15 February & 12 April 1918, 10 January 1919).

†Atkins, Frederick Charles (1894-1917)

Sapper 61782, 224th Field Company, Royal Engineers.

Fred was born in Oldberrow in November 1894, the younger brother of Arthur Edward Atkins (*qv*) and the youngest of the four sons of Charles James Atkins (see above for details of his family). He was a member of the Henley VAD before the war. In 1911 he was living with his parents and his elder brothers Harold and Percy in Oldberrow and working as a Carpenter and Builder. He was still living with his parents at 146 High Street in Henley when he joined the Royal Engineers in Birmingham on 4 January 1915. His employer Lancelot Turner, a Builder and Contractor of 204 St Vincent Street Birmingham, confirmed his trade as a Carpenter: as a proficient tradesman he received an extra 1/- a day. His mother, Annie Atkins was given as his next of kin. Fred's age was then 20 years, 2 months and 2 days, his height 5'8¾" and his chest 37": he was a member of the Church of England.

Fred joined 79th Field Company RE on 10 January and was transferred to 154th Field Company at Tidworth on 26 April 1915. His conduct was not altogether exemplary. On 16 May he was charged "whilst on active service overstaying Pass 21 hours", for which offence he was confined to camp for 2 days. He was later admonished for "Talking while on Parade". He joined the British Expeditionary Force in France on 1 August 1915. The conditions in France caused him health problems and he was admitted to 16th General Hospital on 28 February 1916 suffering from arthritis. On 24 March he was sent to the Northumberland War Hospital in Gosforth, Newcastle-on-Tyne and transferred to the strength of the Royal Engineer's Training Company in Newark. He spent 120 days in hospital and was not discharged until 21 July 1916 when he left for Newark. Fred wrote to Chaplain-Captain Revd M S Bell (*qv*) from Newark-on-Trent that he had been wounded and sent to hospital in the North of England and expected to go to France again later on. He had become a temporary member of the Army branch of the Church of England Men's Society and hoped to become a full member when he returned home. His Conduct Sheet received another entry on 2 December 1916, when he was confined to barracks for 3 days for being absent from the 7.45 parade. He was posted to the RE Base Depot in France on 13 December and was transferred to 224th Field Company on 31 December.

Fred Atkins was killed in action on Sunday, 14 January 1917, aged 22. He is buried in Delville Wood Cemetery, Longueval, Somme, grave XXVI R 8.

Delville Wood Cemetery, Longueval

His service record contains a letter from his mother, undated but acknowledged on 10 February 1917:

146 High Street
Henley in Arden
Warwickshire

Dear Sir,
If you can possibly spare a few minutes to answer this, will you kindly inform me if there is any back pay due to my laddie F C Atkins, No 61782. I thought and understood from what he said when at home last that there would be some.

I may have made a mistake, should like to know a few particulars please, as I have other sons I would like to know a little as to where I could be with regard to pay. God grant my lads will be spared to me, but one never knows.

Also is it at all likely that poor Fred's personal effects will come to us (watch etc) or have I to write to anyone about these. Thanking you in anticipation, for a little information,

> *I remain,*
> *Yours respectfully,*
> *A Atkins.*

After the war, his parents moved to Upper Sumas Road, Abbotsford, British Colombia.

1914-15 Star, British War Medal and Victory Medal.

1901 & 1911 Census; CWGC; SDGW; MIC; Service Record; *Herald* (20 October 1916).

Bayliss, Albert (1888-fl 1919)

His service cannot be positively identified, as there are 14 MICs in the name of Albert Bayliss. He was possibly Private M/298233, RASC. If so, he enlisted on 24 June 1916 and was discharged due to illness on 6 May 1919; he was issued with a Silver War Badge (B238494) on 24 July 1919.

He was born in Henley in 1888, the son of Frederick and Louisa Bayliss (see Bayliss, Raymond for details of his family), and baptised in St John's Church on 12 August 1888. In 1891 he was living in Yardley with his grandmother Emma Bayliss, aged 70, her daughters Eliza (44) and Annie Emma (32) and a cousin William Frederick Bayliss (11). In 1901 he was still living in Yardley with his grandmother Emma Bayliss, now aged 80 and her daughter Annie. He was living with his parents and elder brothers Arthur and William in a five-roomed house at 38 High Street on 2 April 1911, when he was working as a Body Maker in a Perambulator Factory. Later that year he married Lizzie Evelyn Miller of Whitnash.

British War Medal, Victory Medal and Silver War Badge.

St John's PR; 1891, 1901 & 1911 Census.

Bayliss, Arthur (1886-1951)

Driver 203255, 3rd Pontoon Park, Royal Engineers.

He was born in Henley, the son of Frederick and Louisa Bayliss and baptised in St John's Church on 11 July 1886. In 1901 he was living in the High Street (see Bayliss, Raymond for details of his family). In April 1911 he was single and living with his parents and two younger brothers at 38 Henley in Arden: he was working as a House Painter. He married Annie Elizabeth Goseley of the parish of St Alban's, Smethwick on 23 June 1911. His daughter Gladys Elizabeth was born on 14 December 1912 and baptised in St John's Church on 2 February 1913. They lived at 40 High Street. Arthur Bayliss was a plumber and painter, who worked for his father in Henley and was 29 when he applied to the Stratford Rural District Tribunal in June 1916 for temporary exemption after being called up. His father said his business would suffer seriously if Arthur went, as he had three other sons already in the forces. Arthur was granted exemption for 3 months. At the Tribunal held on 15 September he applied for temporary exemption for one month and this was granted. He was then aged 30.

His Attestation had begun on 7 December 1915, but was not completed until 30 October 1916. At his medical on 14 October 1916 at Warwick his age was given as 29 years and 180 days, his height as 5'2", his weight as 124 pounds and his chest as 36½": his medical category was A. He joined the Royal Engineers at Chatham on 14 October 1916. He had a tradesman's pay as a Painter of an additional 4d a day. Arthur embarked for France on 15 April 1917 where he went to the RE Base Depot, whence he was posted on 5 May. He went into hospital on 18 June 1917 and was admitted to 1st London General Hospital (St Bartholomew's) with appendicitis on 25 June: his appendix was removed and he was discharged on 27 July. He was with 1st Field Squadron in France from 16 January 1918 and was again in hospital from 24 to 29 March, when he returned to the RE Base Depot. He joined 3rd Pontoon Park on 20 April 1918 and was granted 14 days leave in the UK on 24 November 1918. He was demobilized on 27 January 1919.

His daughter Winifred Barbara was baptised in St John's Church on 21 September 1919. In 1936 Arthur Bayliss was a painter living at 38 High Street. He died on 15 November 1951, aged 65, and is buried in St Nicholas' churchyard.

British War Medal and Victory Medal.

St John's PR; 1901 & 1911 Census; MIC; Attestation; *Herald* (9 June & 22 September 1916).

Bayliss, Raymond (1884-1937)

Acting Sergeant T3/023216, Army Service Corps.

He was born in Henley in 1884, the son of Frederick and Louisa Bayliss and baptised in St John's Church on 11 July 1886 with his brother Albert. Frederick was a house painter, who had been born in Sutton Coldfield. In 1901 Raymond was living in the High Street with his parents, two of his brothers (Arthur and William) and two sisters (Annie and Jessie): he was then 16 and working as a house painter, probably assisting his father.

He married Ethel May Adcock in Birmingham Registry Office on 7 October 1905. On 2 April 1911 he was living in a five-roomed house at 51 High Street with his wife and their children Frederick James (born 11 February 1906), Edith Mary Louise (born 19 April 1907) and Raymond Leslie Howard (born 29 October 1910 and later baptised Leslie Raymond Howard in St John's Church). Raymond was working as a Painter and Paperhanger. His daughter Sylvia Irene was born on 25 September and baptised on 27 October 1912, when he was living at 52 High Street. He had two other sons, Eric Norman born on 1 March 1914 and George Victor born on 29 September 1916.

Raymond was reported as having left Henley in Arden to join the ASC on 24 August 1914. However, his Attestation was not completed at Birmingham until 7 November 1914, when he gave his occupation as a Wheelwright and agreed to allow one third of his pay to his wife and children. His height was recorded as 5'3¼", his chest as 37½"and his weight as 148 lbs: his complexion was fresh, his eyes grey and his hair brown. He joined the ASC at Aldershot on 9 November 1914 and was promoted to Wheelwright Corporal on 7 January 1915. Raymond landed in France on 14 September 1915, where he had a narrow escape on 23 August 1916, receiving gunshot wounds in the shoulder and scalp. On 20 October the *Herald* reported that Corporal Wheeler R Bayliss (*sic*), "one of the four soldier sons of Mr & Mrs Bayliss", was wounded by shrapnel on 22 August 1916. He found he had 53 marks, but only 15 were very bad and he was now back on duty. It would appear to be his rank as a Wheelwright Corporal, or his civilian occupation as a wheelwright, which caused him to be referred to by the *Herald* as 'Wheeler' Bayliss.

Raymond became an acting Wheelwright Sergeant on 16 December 1916. There was one blot on his disciplinary record during his service, being absent from Roll Call on 4 June 1916: his sentence cannot be deciphered. He was home on leave from 27 June to 7 July 1917 and again from 20 July to 3 August 1918. Raymond returned to England on 18 June 1919 and was demobilized on 17 July when his address was given as 30 High Street, Henley in Arden. On his demobilization he was assessed as having a 20% disability, as he suffered from giddiness in stooping (attributed to his gunshot wounds): he was given a pension of 6s.0d per week with allowances for his children of 6s.6d per week, to be reviewed after 26 weeks.

He was a member of the Fire Brigade in 1919.

1914-15 Star, British War Medal and Victory Medal.

St John's PR; 1901 & 1911 Census; MIC; Attestation; Service Record; *Herald* (28 August 1914, 20 October 1916).

Bayliss, William John (1891-1979)

Corporal T3/023511, Army Service Corps.

He was born in Henley, the son of Frederick and Louisa Bayliss, and baptised in St John's Church on 26 July 1891. In 1901 he was aged 10 and living in the High Street with his family (see Bayliss, Raymond for details). He was still living with his parents at 38 High Street, Henley in Arden in April 1911 when he was working as an Apprentice to a Shoeing Smith. The latter was John C Morris of Henley in Arden and William's apprenticeship expired on 3 January 1912.

His Attestation was taken at Stafford on 6 November 1914: he was a Blacksmith, enlisting as a Shoeing Smith. William was then 23 with a medical category of B1, his height was 5'3½", his weight 125 lbs and his chest 36": his complexion was fresh, his eyes blue and his hair dark brown. He served in England until 17 March 1915, embarking on the *Mercian* for Egypt on 18 March and arriving in Alexandria on 30 March 1915. He was attached to 89th Field Ambulance, 29th Division and promoted Corporal in April 1915, effective from 5 March of that year. William went with them to Gallipoli, where he had two spells in hospital with dysentery, the first beginning on 11 October 1915, the second on 21 October: he was discharged from hospital on 19 November 1915 and transferred to 247 Company ASC at Cape Helles. He disembarked in Alexandria from Mudros on 11 January 1916, where he was with 247 Company attached to 29th Division. When he left Egypt from Port Tewfik on 16 March 1916 he was still with 29th Division, but serving again with 89th Field Ambulance. He disembarked at Marseilles on 27 March.

William married Ada Prinold at St Mary's Church, Stafford on 28 November 1917. She was the daughter of Edwin and Harriet Prinold and in 1911 was 14, working as a Milliner and living with her parents at 21 Grey Friars, Stafford: her father was a Blacksmith.

His Service Record shows three periods of leave, from 28 November to 8 December 1916, 13 November to 7 December 1917 and 20 November to 11 December 1918. It also shows that he was twice severely reprimanded. The first occasion on 6 July 1917 was for hesitating to obey an order to put stones under wagon wheels and for insubordination to a Warrant Officer, the second on 29 June 1918 for neglect of duty in "failing to dress a mule".

On 19 April 1919 William, still with 89th Field Ambulance, signed a form in Cologne to state that he did not claim to be suffering from any disability due to his military service. His permanent address was then 16 Harrowby Street, Stafford. His medical category on discharge was B1. William returned to England on 26 April 1919 and was demobilised on 24 May. He had served in England for 151 days of his service and with Expeditionary Forces overseas for 4 years and 38 days.

1914-15 Star, British War Medal and Victory Medal.

St John's PR; 1901 & 1911 Census; MIC; Attestation; Service Record; *Herald* (7 December 1917).

Beard, Harold (1897-1957)

There are 22 possibilities from the MIC, of which Private 35081, Royal Warwickshire Regiment and subsequently Private 49008 Lancashire Fusiliers, seems to be the most likely.

Harold was born on 7 February 1897, the second son of Harry and Fanny Beard. He was baptised privately on 13 April 1897. In 1901 he was living in Henley with his parents, elder brother John Henry (*qv*) and younger brother William Ernest, his father being an agricultural labourer. Harold entered Henley Junior School from the Infant Department on 2 May 1904 and left on 17 June 1910 to take up employment. He was working as a Ploughboy and still living with his parents and five siblings in a four-roomed house at 39 High Street in 1911. Harold was a member of the Warwick Number 11 VAD and took part in its annual inspection on 6 August 1914.

In March 1917 the *Herald* reported him as being in hospital in France. In September of that year he had again been wounded and was progressing favourably in a London Hospital. His wound was evidently quite serious, as in November he had been moved to a VAD hospital in Broxbourne and in February 1918 he was expecting to receive his discharge shortly.

He was a casual helper with the Fire Brigade in 1919.

British War Medal and Victory Medal.

1901 & 1911 Census; Henley School Register; *Herald* (23 March, 28 September & 9 November 1917, 18 February 1918).

Beard, John Henry (1895-1967)

Private 47901, Royal Army Medical Corps.

Known as Jack, he was born on 13 June 1895, the eldest of the five sons of Henry (Harry) & Fanny Beard (*nee* Morral) of Henley in Arden: they also had a daughter Florence Edith (baptised in St John's on 9 October 1904). Jack was baptised in St John's Church on 8 September 1895: his father was then a labourer. His parents were living at 39 High Street when he entered Henley Junior School from the Infant Department on 1 May 1902. He left school to take up employment on 1 October 1908. In 1911 he was working as a Domestic Servant and still living with his parents in the same house. Jack was a member of the Warwick Number 11 VAD and took part in its annual inspection on 6 August 1914.

Jack Beard enlisted when he was 17, giving his age as 18 and was in France when he was 17½. His MIC shows that he landed in France on 15 May 1915. A letter from him to the Revd Michael S Bell was quoted in the *Herald* of 25 June 1915: "On Whit Monday we had 500 gas cases in a few hours". He later wrote to his parents that he was on active duty in the field. His sister Florrie said that his first job was picking heads up. In another letter to Bell in 1916 he wrote, "We are about 20 miles from the firing line, so having a good rest". He had attended a large church service the previous Sunday night in the square at which the divisional band played the music: it was the largest service he had seen. In September 1917 he spent 10 days on leave with his parents. By that time he had been on active service for 2 years and 8 months, mostly in Belgium.

Jack Beard did not marry.

1914-15 Star, British War Medal and Victory Medal.

1901 & 1911 Census; MIC; Herald (25 June & 3 September 1915, 20 October 1916, 28 September 1917, 1 February 1918); Florence Beard.

†Beard, William (1892/3-1915)

Lance Corporal 9280, 2nd Battalion Worcestershire Regiment.

William Beard was born in Pershore, Worcestershire the son of Thomas and Margaret Beard. In 1901 he was 8 and living in Priests Lane, Pershore with his parents, his two sisters (Florence and Elsie) and his two younger brothers (Ernest and Charlie). His father was a labourer in a market garden.

When William enlisted in Worcester, he gave his place of residence as Henley in Arden. He was posted to the 2nd Battalion Worcester Regiment as a private and was subsequently promoted to Lance Corporal. This Battalion was in France from 14 August 1914, when it was serving with 5th Brigade, 2nd Division; William joined the Battalion in France on 24 November 1914. They took part in the Battle of Loos, which began on 25th September and continued for some days. Loos is a small mining town between Lens and La Bassee and this was one of the Great War's bloodiest battles. 2nd Division was holding the northern sector of the British line, in the La Bassee region, and had a disastrous start to the first day, as the British gas blew back into the faces of many of its regiments. The men who were not gassed were subjected to withering machine gun fire when they attempted to attack.

William Beard died in the Battle of Loos on 26 September 1915 and has no known grave. He is among over 20,000 officers and men commemorated on the Loos Memorial.

1914/15 Star, British War Medal and Victory Medal.

1901 census; CWGC; SDGW; MIC; James, p73.

Beard, William Ernest (1899-1972)

There are 12 MICs in the name of William E Beard. It is also possible that he did not leave England, in which case there would be no MIC. His cap badge is that of the RWR.

He was known as Bill and was born in Henley on 31 July 1899, the third son of Harry Beard (see John Henry Beard for further details of his family). He was baptised in St John's Church on 10 December 1899. Bill entered Henley Junior School on 1 May 1906 from the Infant School. He was still at school and living with his parents in 1911. He left on 2 August 1912, to work as a butcher's boy.

He was reported as being on Salisbury Plain as a Private in January 1918. In letters home he declared himself well in January 1918 and safe and sound in May.

He was a casual helper with the Fire Brigade in 1919.

1901 & 1911 Census; Henley Schools Admissions Register; *Herald* (11 January, 1 February & 11 May 1918).

Beck, Percy Alwyne (1883-fl 1919)

MICs give 7 instances of Percy Beck, but none of Percy A Beck.

He was baptised on 9 September 1883 at St Nicholas', Beaudesert, the son of Thomas Edwin Beck, Returning Officer of Henley in Arden, and his wife Emily Eliza. Percy was the elder brother of Thomas Mayfield Beck (*qv*). In 1901 he was employed as a Wood Carver and was living as a boarder in Balsall Heath with Alfred Humpage, a Furniture Packer, and his wife and daughter.

He married Lilian Hough in 1919.

1901 Census.

Beck, Thomas Mayfield (1888-1960)

Canadian Overseas Expeditionary Force, Strathcona's Horse.

Born in Wootton Wawen, the second son of Thomas Edwin and Emily Eliza Beck, he was baptised in St Peter's Church on 21 May 1888. His father was described as a Relieving Officer. In 1901 he was 13 and living in Henley at 120 High Street with his parents and elder sister Irene Mary. His father was then the Returning Officer and Registrar of Births, Deaths and Marriages for the sub-district of Wootton Wawen in the Stratford upon Avon union. In 1911 he was still living with his parents and elder sister in a six-roomed house The Crofts, 120 Henley in Arden and working as a Railway Clerk.

His parents had been married for 32 years and had four children, three of whom survived. Thomas subsequently emigrated to Canada. In June 1916 the *Herald* reported that he was "now in the Canadian forces (Strathcona's Horse) and has spent a few days in the town on leave". It is likely that he returned to Henley after the war, as W G Haytree recalled that Tommy Beck lived at 120 High Street. He died in 1960.

Parish Register; 1901 & 1911 Census; *Herald* 23 June 1916; W G Haytree.

Bell, Captain Revd Michael Selwyn (1880-1927)

Reverend Chaplain, Chaplain Force.

He was born in Henley on 20 February 1880 and baptised in St John's Church by his father, the Revd George Edward Bell (1833-1924), then Vicar of Henley in Arden, on 21 March 1880. The Bells had come to Henley in 1876 (having married in 1865) and had 12 children (8 girls and 4 boys); six of their children were born in Henley, of whom one died in infancy. His mother, Mary Sophia Bell (*nee* Warren), died in Surrey in December 1917, aged 74. One of Michael's elder brothers was John Keble Bell (1875-1928), a novelist and playwright who wrote under the name of Keble Howard: he was the author of *The God in the Garden*, a novel published in

1904 and set in a thinly disguised Henley in Arden.[175] The 1881 Census shows that Michael was living at the Vicarage in the High Street with his parents, his elder brothers Robert, Stephen and John and his elder sister Monica. A governess and a general servant also formed part of the household.

Michael was educated at Christ's Hospital and Queen's College, Birmingham. In 1901 he was one of two assistant masters at a boys' boarding school in Brighton, run by Thomas Read and with some 50 boarders. He was a lay reader in Lapworth in 1905 and 1906 and in 1907 became curate of Heywood, Lancashire. In 1908 he left to become curate of Prestwich, Manchester. He then spent 2½ years in Central

America as rector of Guatemala City. Returning to England in 1912, he became curate of St Chad's, Kingswood. After what was said to be a very successful period of 21 months he left for missionary work in British Honduras, preaching a farewell sermon at St John's in Henley, where his father was still Vicar.

On 15 September 1915 Michael was appointed Chaplain to the first fully equipped Australian hospital ship, the *Kanowna*. The position carried with it the rank of Captain in the Australian Army. The ship left England on 25 September and arrived in Sydney on 25 November. It had a complement of 10 doctors, over 20 nurses and 80 Australian Medical Corps men to attend the wounded. On his return, he acted as Chaplain on a troopship carrying some 2,000 men. He was subsequently Chaplain on the *Kyarre* during its voyage from Alexandria to Marseilles, whence he reached Southampton via Paris and Le Havre. In March 1916 he was on leave, staying with his parents in Reigate, Surrey before returning to Australia as Chaplain on the *Ascasius*, taking wounded back home through the Suez Canal: these included 500 men who had been wounded in Gallipoli. The ship arrived in Sydney on 4 May after a voyage of 7 weeks. After one week's leave he was appointed to the troopship *Argylleshire*, which sailed with 1,800 men to England via the Cape. He claimed then to have completed 52,800 miles since September 1915. When billeted at the Hotel Victoria in Aldershot, he wrote to the *Herald* asking for addresses of those who had joined up from Henley and the surrounding area, "many of whom I have known personally for some years". He thought he might be able to see some personally, but would in any event drop them a line from time to time.

---

175 For further information on Keble Howard see Cooper, p109

The Australian Government awarded him the medal issued to those who had been on active service and he was given a commission in the British Army after his service with the Australians. He wrote of his experiences in a book entitled *60,000 Miles During the War*, but it does not seem to have been published. He wrote two books on local history: *Gleanings from History on Henley in Arden, Wootton Wawen and Beaudesert* and *Some Barons of Arden: an Account of the Lords of the Manor of Henley in Arden and Beaudesert 1060-1909* which were printed by T Stocks of Henley in 1902 and 1910 respectively.

In 1917 he was appointed Vicar of Over Kellet and Capernwray in Lancashire, a position he held until his death in the Royal Lancaster Infirmary on 1 October 1927. His funeral service was held in St John's: four members of the choir (R L Newcombe, H Hodges, A Bayliss and W E Hemming) had formerly been choirboys with him; his bearers (C R Herring, F E W Richards, S Hemming and Herbert Taylor) had also known him during his boyhood in Henley. He is buried in the churchyard of St Nicholas' Beaudesert. He did not marry.

His MIC shows that he applied for his medals on 27 March 1920 and that these were sent to him at Over Kellet Vicarage, Carnforth, Lancashire.

British War Medal and Victory Medal.

St John's PR; 1881 and 1901 Census; MIC; Heritage Centre; *Herald* (14 January, 17 March, 7 July & 22 September 1916, 25 January 1917 and 8 February 1918).

Benton, James (1888-1936)

Driver 10761, Royal Field Artillery, Shoeing Smith.

James was born in Henley, the son of John and Mary Benton. His father was a Domestic Gardener. In 1891 he was living in the High Street in Henley with his parents and elder brothers John and Joseph. He was still living there in 1901, though his brothers had then left home. In April 1911 he was staying with his cousin Samuel Whitehouse and his family at 44 King Street, West Bromwich. He was probably working for him at the time, as Samuel was a Haulage Contractor and James was a Carter. James married Rose Holding at Old Church, West Bromwich in 1911 and had a daughter Rose Anna who was born on 26 December 1912 but died on 21 December 1914. His wife also died, as his marital status on his Service Record was amended to widower.

James Benton enlisted at West Bromwich on 2 September 1914, aged 25 years and 319 days. He was employed as a Carter and had previously served in the Warwickshire Yeomanry where his time had expired. His medical at West Bromwich on 3 September shows that he was 5'5" tall, weighed 146 pounds and had a chest of 36", a fair complexion, blue eyes and fair hair. His religious denomination was Church of England. He was passed fit for general service and appointed to the Royal Field Artillery. His Service Record gave his wife's address as 5 Wise Street, Longton, Stoke on Trent, but his next of kin was amended to John Benton of High Street, Henley (his father).

He joined the Artillery at Hilsea on 4 September 1914 (his service dating from 3 September) and his initial posting on 12 September was as a Driver in the 16th Reserve Battery RFA. After two further postings, he was posted in the same capacity to 91st Brigade RFA on 6 January 1915 where he was appointed a Shoeing Smith on 22 April 1915. James embarked for France from Southampton on 21 July 1915, disembarking at Le Havre on the following day. On 1 June 1916, 91st Brigade became 92nd Brigade. James had three further postings in 1917 and three more in 1918: that on 14 September 1918 was to 251st Brigade. In 1918 he was on leave in the UK (via Le Havre) from 16 to 31 March and finally left France on 15 May 1918.

James Benton had a poor conduct record throughout his time in the RFA:

5 April 1915	Forfeited 2 days pay for being absent from camp without permission and for being absent from midday stables;
8 May 1915	5 days Confined to Barracks for urinating in camp;
25 May 1915	6 days Confined to Barracks for overstaying leave for 18 hours;
15 August 1915	1 day Field Punishment Number 2;
27 August 1915	5 days Field Punishment Number 2;
20 October 1915	6 days Field Punishment Number 1 and to revert to Driver;
3 February 1916	28 days Field Punishment Number 1 and forfeited 2 days pay;
4 October 1918	7 days Confined to Barracks for being absent on parade.

Field Punishment Number 1 required the offender to be shackled in irons and tied to a field gun for two hours a day: it had been introduced in 1881 to replace flogging, but was abolished in 1923. Field Punishment Number 2 was similar, but the offender was not tied to a field gun. The offences for which Benton was given these sentences are not recorded. His sentence on 3 February 1916 was a severe one and seems to have resulted in him mending his ways.

One of his elder brothers wrote a letter to the RFA at Woolwich, received there on 27 November 1918, stating that he had not heard from his brother for 6 to 8 weeks and asking to be advised if he was alright. The last address he had was Gunner J Benton 10761, 1st Army RA Reinforcement Camp, 6 Troop RFA. There is no record of any reply from the RFA.

James was posted to a Dispersal Centre on 28 July 1919 and transferred to the Z Reserve on 26 August 1919. His unit was stated to be 251st Brigade, his medical category A1 and his address 58 Railway Terrace, West Bromwich (the address from which his brother had written in November 1918). He was demobilized on 31 March 1920.

He died in West Bromwich in 1936.

1914-15 Star, British War Medal and Victory Medal.

1891, 1901 & 1911 Census; MIC; Attestation; Service Record.

Berry, A E (1883-1942)

He was probably Arthur Berry, who was living in Station Road, Claverdon in 1901, the son of John and Eliza Berry: his father was a Gardener and his mother a Laundress. The Census record shows that Arthur had been born in Claverdon, was aged 18 and working as a Bricklayer's Labourer. Two elder sisters, Emily and Ellen, were also living in the house. The 1911 Census records that his parents had been married for 49 years and had had 11 children, 9 of whom survived. Arthur was the only one of their children still living with them: he had been married, but was a widower with two children, one of whom, his son John Henry, was living with them in a five-roomed house at Station Road, Claverdon. Arthur was working as a General Labourer, as was his father (then aged 70).

The Herald reported that Mr A E Berry was elected Secretary at the annual meeting of the Henley Garden Allotment Association at the White Swan in February 1919, when he was welcomed "after much service on minesweepers in the North Sea".

He died in Birmingham in 1942.

1901 & 1911 Census; *Herald* (14 February 1919).

Berry, Eric Burton (1893-1949)

Staff Quarter Master Sergeant T/422583, Army Service Corps; formerly Lance Corporal 1919, Warwickshire Yeomanry.

Eric Burton Berry was born in Gloucester, the son of Henry Burton Berry and his wife Florence, where his father was a Chemist. In 1901 Eric was 7 and living at the Old Bull Hotel in Blackburn with his parents, his elder brother John and 16 hotel staff. His father and mother were the Hotel Manager and Manageress. In 1911 his parents were living at Chapel View, Henley in Arden, his father being a Wine and Spirit Merchant, but neither of their children was living with them on the day of the census. Eric Berry was a member of the Warwickshire Yeomanry before the war, attending the annual camp at Warwick Park in May 1914. He was a member of the Henley troop of 'D' Squadron and was also a member of Warwick Number 11 VAD. He sailed for Egypt from Avonmouth with the regiment in April 1915. His name is not recorded among those who sailed for Gallipoli in August, so he was presumably one of those who stayed behind in Egypt to look after the regiment's horses. He rose to the rank of Squadron Quarter Master Sergeant with the Yeomanry before transferring to the Army Service Corps.

1914-15 Star, British War Medal and Victory Medal.

1901 Census; MIC; *Herald* (22 May 1914).

Bickley, Peter (1898-1942)

Private 12248, Machine Gun Corps; formerly Private 821, 92nd Training Battalion.

Peter was born in Tanworth in Arden, the younger brother of Sidney (*qv*). In 1911 Peter was one of 171 inmates of the Union Workhouse in Solihull, together with his mother Annie and his younger siblings Annie (10), William (8), Florence (6), Maggie (2) and Elsie (2). Peter and Annie were both attending school. His father was evidently still alive as his mother's marital status was 'Married'. His parents had been married for 19 years and had eight children, all of whom were still living. In addition to its inmates, the Union Workhouse also acted as a Hospital, which then had 86 patients. The Union Workhouse had 20 resident staff, including the Master (George Henry Carr) and the Matron (his wife Clara Ada).

Peter was probably conscripted in early 1916 and was serving in Egypt in April 1918.

British War Medal and Victory Medal.

1901 & 1911 Census; MIC; *Herald* (26 April 1918).

†Bickley, Sidney (1896-1918)

Private 39478, 1st Battalion Royal Berkshire Regiment: formerly Private 23756, Royal Warwickshire Regiment and Private 34053, Oxfordshire & Buckinghamshire Light Infantry.

Sidney Bickley was born in Tanworth in Arden, the son of John and Annie Bickley. His father had also been born in Tanworth, his mother in Upton Snodsbury in Worcestershire. In 1901 Sidney was living in Pool Head Lane in Tanworth with his parents, his two sisters, Maud and Annie, and his younger brother Peter. His father was a Carter on a farm. In 1911 he was working as a resident Farm Labourer on the farm of James Arthur Burman at Spring Brook, Hockley Heath. When Sidney enlisted in Birmingham, he gave his place of residence as Henley in Arden.

Sidney was killed on 23 March 1918, during the Battle of St Quentin. He had been in France for about nine months. At the time of his death his battalion was part of 99th Brigade, 2nd Division. A joint memorial service for him and Owen Holt was held in St John's Church on Sunday 28 April. Sidney was 22 and is commemorated with almost 35,000 British, New Zealand and South African casualties on the Arras Memorial, Pas de Calais. He is also commemorated on the Tanworth in Arden War Memorial.

He made a verbal will at his home, 43 High Street, on 20 September 1917 in front of his mother Annie Bickley, his sister, Maud Adkins and a neighbour Dahlia Sinia Hughes of 45 High Street. This was confirmed in writing by these three individuals and their signatures were confirmed by the Revd Frank Lane, who acted as witness. All that belonged to him was to go to his mother.

British War Medal and Victory Medal.

1901 & 1911 Census; CGWC; SDGW; MIC; Will (WO Number E/550427/1); James, p 89; *Herald* (26 April 1918).

Blackwell, William (1878-1937)

Private 41921, Worcestershire Regiment; formerly Private 22422, Royal Warwickshire Regiment.

He was born on 14 February 1878, the son of William and Susannah, and baptised in St John's Church on 14 April. His father was a Painter, living in Henley. In 1881 they were living in the High Street, his father still being a Painter and his mother a Dressmaker: he had two elder sisters, Maria E and Mary A Blackwell (then 7 and 5). He began his education in the Infant Department of Henley School and transferred to the Juniors on 30 March 1885. His parents' occupations were unchanged in 1891 and he was then living with them, his elder sister Mary and his two younger brothers John and Thomas (aged 9 and 1). William left school on 28 May 1891 to go to work. In 1901 William was 23 and living with his mother, who was a Dressmaker, his sister (Mary Annie) and two younger brothers (John and Thomas Francis) in the High Street: his father was then dead. William was working as a servant for a grocer. He married Sarah Ann Ward of the parish of St Peter's, Handsworth in 1910. In 1911 they were living in a three-roomed cottage at Littleworth, 220 Henley in Arden and William was working as a Drayman for a brewery.

William Blackwell did not go overseas until at least 1916, as no date appears on his MIC.

William Blackwell was a blacksmith and had a forge in the High Street opposite the Yew Trees.

British War Medal and Victory Medal.

St John's PR; 1881, 1891, 1901 & 1911 Census; MIC; Arthur O'Donnell.

Bonehill, William Henry MM (1884-1948)

Private 9940, 15th Battalion, Royal Warwickshire Regiment.

William was born in Henley in 1884, the sixth of the nine children of Emma Bonehill (*nee* Pratt), who had herself been born in Henley in about 1852. She was living in Tanworth as a servant aged 9 in 1861 and in 1871 was a servant in the King's Head in Henley. At the time of the 1881 census she was living with her husband Alfred and three daughters Florence, Sofia and Amelia in Beaudesert. The 1891 census shows her living as a housekeeper, together with seven of her children including William then aged 5 and a scholar, with James Keasey, a widower, in Ullenhall. She was herself recorded as a widow, although her husband Alfred did not die until 1912. When William Henry Bonehill was baptised privately in St

John's Church in Henley on 20 July 1887, he was stated to be the illegitimate son of Emma Bonehill. The 1901 census records Ellen as still living in Ullenhall with James Keasey, but gives her relation to him as "Mistress": William was one of three of her children still living with her: he was then 16 and an Agricultural Labourer. It is possible that William attended the Council Schools in the High Street, but unfortunately the best source for this information, the Register of the Junior School, is missing for the years 1891 to 1901: he may, however, have gone to school in Ullenhall. In 1911 William was living in Beaudesert Street with his wife Minnie Leah (32), his stepdaughter Ethel Leah Steedman (9) and his daughter Minnie Muriel (9 months). William's occupation was given as Railway Carman. Charles Bertram Lloyd, a Railway Porter, was also living with the family as a boarder.

William had been employed as a groom when he joined the 1st Battalion of the Royal Warwickshire Regiment as a regular soldier on 19 February 1904, his age being given as 18 years and 6 months. His Soldier's Small Book records that he was 5'3½" tall, with a fresh complexion, grey eyes and brown hair. He enlisted for 3 years, with 9 years in the reserve, so that he left the army for the first time in 1907. He was then employed by the Great Western Railway as a carman at Henley in Arden, delivering parcels in the local area.

William married Minnie Leah Steedman (*nee* Neal and born in Ullenhall), then a widow, who already had a daughter Ethel. They had five children of their own: Minnie Muriel (known as Muriel, baptised in St Nicholas' Church on 4 September

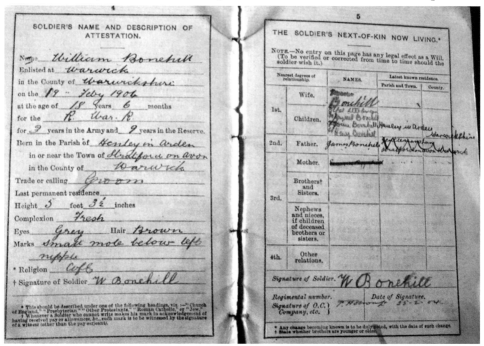

William Bonehill's Small Book

William Bonehill and family, Beaudesert Lane, c 1920

1910), Florence, William Henry (known as Bill), Denis Albert (known as Denis, baptised in St Nicholas' on 3 September 1916) and Thelma (born in 1924, later Thelma Briedens). The family lived in Beaudesert Lane until they moved after the war (most reluctantly on Mrs Bonehill's part) to 14 Cherry Orchard, as the Council felt that the family was overcrowded in their two bedrooms in Beaudesert Lane.

Being a reservist, William was called up into the Royal Warwickshire Regiment on 5 August 1914, the day after war was declared. It is not known which of the two regular battalions of the Royal Warwickshire Regiment he was posted to. The 1st Battalion landed in France on 22 August 1914 as part of 4th Division, while the 2nd Battalion landed at Zeebrugge on 6 October 1914 as part of 7th Division. Whichever battalion he was with, William was in the firing line very quickly and was wounded in the right foot by shrapnel on 9 November 1914. This brought him back to Henley where, being one of the first from the town to return home wounded, a subscription of £2.10s.0d was raised for him. He returned to France and was attached to the grenade company of his battalion. On 30 July 1915 he was again wounded, having a narrow escape when he was shot in the thigh by a sniper while carrying grenades. William was sent to hospital in Dublin to recover. Writing home from there, he said that he was hoping to see his wife and children in Beaudesert very soon. His letters showed him to be "his usual cheerful self". He came home on another occasion after suffering in a mustard gas attack.

It is not known precisely when he joined the 15th Battalion, which had been formed as the 2nd Birmingham Battalion of the Royal Warwickshire Regiment in September 1914. It landed at Boulogne on 14 January 1916, moving to Italy in

December 1917 and returning to France in April 1918. It was then part of 14th Brigade, 5th Division.

William was awarded the Military Medal in 1918 for "gallantry and devotion to duty". On 20 July 1918 "2nd Lieutenant W Farrimond and 23 other ranks carried through a successful raid on the enemy trenches. Zero hour was fixed for 1.30 am but the party moved into No Man's Land half an hour before. At zero hour the barrage opened on the enemy trench and lifted at zero plus one minute, when the party entered the trench. They bombed 14 occupied shelters, destroyed two machine guns and brought back one prisoner (for identification purposes) and one machine gun. They returned at 2.00 am having had only two men slightly wounded".[176] The *Herald* of 23 August 1918 reported that Private Bonehill had killed nine of the enemy and captured a machine gun. He was one of three men presented with the Military Medal on 6 August by Lieutenant-General Richard Haking, commanding XI Corps. His award was listed in the *London Gazette* on 13 November 1918. The 15th Battalion was relieved on 30 July and was disbanded on 6 October, its men being transferred to the 14th and 16th Battalions. The battalions remained in France after the Armistice, most of their men being demobilised between January and April 1919.

William Bonehill was one of the Old Contemptibles and was at the front, except for the three occasions when he was wounded, for virtually the entire war.

Rats were one of the enemies soldiers had to fight in the trenches and William carried on his war with them after his demobilisation. He was an enthusiastic member of the Henley Rat Club and appears on most of the Club photographs.

Military Medal, 1914 Star with clasp, British War Medal, Victory Medal.

His MIC records that the clasp and roses for his 1914 Star were issued to him on 13 January 1920.

1891, 1901 & 1911 Census; Soldier's Small Book; MIC; *Herald* (13 August & 3 September 1915, 23 August 1918); Mrs Thelma Briedens (his daughter).

Bourton, Percy George (1888/9-1947)

Private 670, Royal Warwickshire Regiment.

Percy was born in Budbrooke, the son of George Bourton, an agricultural labourer, and his wife Eliza. In 1901 he was 12, living in Budbrooke with his parents, two brothers (Walter and George Henry) and his younger sister Nellie. In 1911 he was living in a three-roomed cottage at Hampton on the Hill (in the parish of Budbrooke) with his parents George (61) and Eliza (48), and his younger brothers George Henry (11) and Frank Sidney (9). His parents had been married for 29 years and had had nine children, of whom 3 had died. Percy was working as a Waggoner on a farm. By the beginning of the war he was living in Beaudesert

---

176 Bill, p 139

and is recorded as being in the army in September 1914. He went to France on 16 June 1915 and was discharged from the Army on 29 February 1916.

1914-15 Star, British War Medal and Victory Medal.

1901 & 1911 Census; MIC; *Herald* (25 September 1914).

Bullock, Farmer (1886-1971)

Driver 671576, 65th Divisional Ammunition Column, Royal Field Artillery.

He was baptised privately on 1 February 1886, the son of Farmer and Jane Bullock of Henley. In 1891 he was living on the west side of the High Street with his parents, elder brother (Edward John) and four elder sisters (Mary Ann, Emily Esther, Martha W and Kate Elizabeth). In 1901 he was 15 and living in the High Street with his parents, Farmer and Jane, his sisters Kate E, Alice O and Nellie May and his younger brothers Thomas Edwin (*qv*) and Francis H. His father was a Carpenter and Joiner. His mother was born in Beaudesert and his father in Upton Snodsbury, Worcestershire.

In 1911 he was living in two rooms at 67 Oxford Street, Swansea with his wife Martha, whom he had married in 1910 and who had been born in Swansea: he was working as a Harness Maker. His MIC shows that he enlisted on 18 August 1916, was discharged on 16 April 1917 and applied for a Silver War Badge on 25 September 1917. His address was then 32 Western Street, Swansea. He seems to have applied for some compensation as a result of his discharge, as there is a note on his Discharge Card "Ineligible unless re-examined etc". He did not serve overseas.

He returned to Henley after the war, and was a carpenter and joiner living at 90 High Street in 1924. He died in Swansea in 1971.

Silver War Badge B343875, (issued 12 December 1919).

St John's PR; 1901 & 1911 Census; MIC; Discharge Card; SWB; Kelly 1924.

Bullock, George Frederick (1886-1957) or (1894/5-fl 1919)

Corporal 305863, Royal Warwickshire Regiment.

He enlisted in the RWR on 11 November 1914 and was discharged at the age of 39 on 22 October 1918, having been wounded. He was issued with a Silver War Badge (number B33454) on 8 November 1918 and had served overseas. There were two men of this name living in the vicinity of Henley, but neither was 39 in 1918. There is the possibility that the age given on his SWB record was incorrect.

The first was the son of George F and Mary A Bullock, born on 7 January 1886 in Bevington, in the parish of Salford Priors and baptised in Salford Priors on 11 July of that year: this would have made him 32 in 1918. In 1891 his parents were living in Aston with their two sons, Charles W and George F, and their three daughters, Mary A, Priscilla and Olive E. The father was a Farm Wagoner. In 1901 George was still living with his parents, his elder brother Charles and a younger sister Susanna: he was aged 15 and working as a Plumber and Gas Fitter. In 1911 he was working on his own as a Plumber and living with his wife Elizabeth in a five-roomed house at 38 Dridge Road, Erdington: they had been married in the last year.

The second was the son of George Frederick and Caroline Bullock, his birth being registered in Solihull in 1904. In 1901 his parents were living in Yardley, then part of Worcestershire, with their two children May (8) and George Frederick (6), which would have made the latter 23 in 1918. Also living with them was William Whiting, aged 24 and a Professional Golf Player. The father was a Market Gardener, but he was dead by the 1911 Census. At that time the remainder of the family was living in a five-roomed house at 6 The Elms, Lakey Lane, Hall Green. His widow Caroline was Stewardess at a Golf Club, May was a Waitress at a Golf Club, George Frederick was an Assistant Golf Professional and living with them was Alfred Vincent Tunley, a Golf Professional. Caroline had been born in Kings Norton and both of her children in Yardley. The Golf Club concerned is likely to have been the Robin Hood Golf Club in Hall Green.

The connection of either with Henley is not known.

British War Medal, Victory Medal and Silver War Badge.

1891, 1901 & 1911 Census; MIC; SWB.

Bullock, Thomas Edwin (1893-fl 1919)

There are MICs for Private 92188 Thomas E Bullock, Nottinghamshire and Derbyshire Regiment and for Private 51775 Thomas E Bullock, Gloucestershire Regiment.

Neither of these has been positively identified as the Thomas Edwin Bullock who was baptised in St John's Church on 28 February 1894, the son of Farmer and Jane Bullock and a younger brother of Farmer Bullock (*qv*). In 1901 he was 7 and living in the High Street (see Bullock, Farmer for details of his family). In 1911 he was living with his parents (who had been married for 35 years and had 13 children, two of which had died), two elder sisters and a younger sister, three of his parents' grandchildren and a boarder, in an eight-roomed house at 64 High Street. Thomas was then working as a Railway Porter.

St John's PR; 1901 & 1911 Census.

†*Burden, William Oliver (1891-1918)*

Private 45996, 2nd Battalion Worcestershire Regiment.

William Burden was born in Henley in Arden, the elder son of William Oliver and Mary Ann Burden. In 1901 he was living at 58 Severn Street, Birmingham with his parents, younger brother and three younger sisters. His father was a railway porter and evidently moved a lot, as each of the five children was born in a different place in the Midlands. By 1911 the family had moved to a five-roomed house at 27 Blucher Street, Birmingham and the number of children had increased to seven (two other children had died). At this time William was working as a Labourer.

William joined the Worcestershire Regiment at Birmingham and is recorded as living there at the time: the date of his enlistment is not known. The 2nd Battalion was a battalion of the Regular Army. It landed at Boulogne on 14 August 1915 and on 20 December became part of 100th Brigade, 33rd Division. William's MIC shows that he did not serve overseas before 1916. The Division was in the Bethune area at the outbreak of the Battle of the Somme on 1 July 1916 and entered the Somme offensive on 12 July, incurring heavy casualties in an attack on Bazentin Ridge on 14 July. It saw action at High Wood at the end of the month and was then withdrawn from the line until 25 October. In April 1917 it was involved in the 2nd Battle of the Scarpe and in May was successful in taking some of the German front line trenches on the Hindenburg Line. At the end of July the Division moved to the coast of Flanders for rest and training. It moved to the Ypres Salient on 15 September and from 24 to 27 September took part in the great battles of the Menin Road Ridge and Polygon Wood. In April 1918 the Division was involved in the battles of Messines, Hazebrouck, Bailleul and Kemmel Ridge. The Bailleul operations on 13 to 15 April included a gallant defence by 100th Brigade of Neuve Eglise. On 18 September the Division fought in the Battle of Epehy, followed by operations on the St Quentin Canal on 29 September, on which day William was killed in action.

He is buried in Pigeon Ravine Cemetery, Epehy, grave I C 15.

Pigeon Ravine Cemetery, Epehy

CWGC records his age at death as 32, although the 1901 Census gives his age as 9 and his birth was recorded in the first quarter of 1891, which would make him 27 when he died. William did not marry: at the time of his death his parents were his next of kin (they were then living at 1 Roseberry Avenue, George Street West,

Birmingham). His medals were not claimed, as on 7 March 1922 his MIC records a request for authority to dispose of them.

British War Medal, Victory Medal.

1901 & 1911 Census; CWGC; SDGW; MIC; James, p73.

Chambers, Albert Thomas (1892–1943)

Lance Corporal 7893, Royal Warwickshire Regiment and Lance Corporal 187128, Labour Corps.

Albert was born on 29 May 1892, the son of Thomas and Emma Chambers and was baptised in St Peter's Church, Wootton Wawen on 26 July 1892, his father being a Labourer. No record of the family in the 1901 census has been found, but the census of 1891 shows his parents living in Alcester Road, Wootton Wawen with his elder brother and two sisters. His father was a Horse Carter, who had been born in Wilmcote, while his mother was born in Bretforton.

In 1911 he was living at the Crown Inn, Claverdon as a servant, his occupation being given as a Farm Labourer. He was subsequently employed for about 14 months as a Labourer at the Rudge-Whitworth Company in Coventry.

He joined the Royal Warwickshire Regiment at the Town Hall in Birmingham on 9 September 1914 at the age of 23 years and 4 months, his occupation being given as Labourer and his religion as C of E. His Medical Certificate of the same date records that he was 6'0" in height, weighed 152 pounds with a chest of 36½": his complexion was sallow, his eyes and hair brown and he was passed fit for General Service (when examined at Parkhurst on 17 February 1917, his complexion was stated to be dark, his eyes blue and his hair dark brown). His next of kin was given as his mother, Emma Chambers Mason of 59 High Street, Henley in Arden.

Albert was posted to 10th Battalion, RWR which formed part of 57th Brigade, 19th Division. This was training in England on Salisbury Plain and around Tidworth, until it first went to France on 18 July 1915. He was appointed an unpaid Lance Corporal on 9 August 1915. He was wounded in action on the Somme on 22 July 1916, with gun shot wounds to his arms and legs. His major wound was in the right hand, with his right thumb broken; he also had a flesh wound on the inner side of his forearm. It was not until 8 September that the *Herald* recorded, "The name of Lance Corporal A E Chambers [sic] 7893 of Henley in Arden is included among the wounded of the RWR".

Albert suffered a compound fracture of his right thumb, which a medical report stated to be foreshortened and permanently stiff and useless. Rather than being caused by a gun shot wound, the same report said that is was caused by a piece of High Explosive shell. He was sent to the Stourbridge Section of 1st Southern General Hospital, where he was treated from 26 July 1916 to 6 January 1917 and then moved to the Longfield Auxiliary Hospital, Sutton Coldfield. On 6 February 1917 he appeared before a Special Invaliding Board at Parkhurst on the Isle of Wight and was reclassified as C2. While at Parkhurst he was charged for disciplinary offences on three occasions: on 5 March 1917 for being absent from Reveille (reprimanded); on 28 March for being improperly dressed on parade (admonished) and on 10 May for being absent from Parade (admonished).

He was transferred to the 3rd Labour Battalion of the Labour Corps on 17 May 1917 and was discharged as unfit for war service on 23 June 1917. He was then said to have "no power of grip in his right hand, thumb is quite useless, hand always perspiring". Albert had served for a total of 2 years and 288 days, of which 1 year and 8 days were spent in France. When his discharge was being considered, Albert said he would like light employment in the vicinity of Coventry. A medical report from Parkhurst dated 26 February estimated that his capacity "for earning a full livelihood in the general labour market" was reduced by a half: a medical report from Plymouth dated 2 June reduced this to still further to three-quarters.

His Discharge Certificate (AFB 2079) and Character Certificate (AFB 2067) were posted to him at Oldbarrow Cottage, Henley in Arden on 15 June 1917 and he acknowledged their receipt on 18 June 1917. He received his King's Certificate (number 772) on 14 July 1918, his address then being 208 Burbury Street, Lozells, Birmingham. His rank on discharge was Lance Corporal and his character was said to be Very Good.

1914-15 Star, British War Medal and Victory Medal.

1891 and 1911 Census; Attestation; Pension Record; MIC.

†Clare, William Louis (1893-1917)

Private 41103, 1st Battalion Royal Inniskilling Fusiliers.

William Clare was born in Liverpool in 1893, the elder son of Edward and Jessie A Clare. In 1901 he was living at 51 Cadogan Street, Wavertree with his parents, his elder sister Jessie and younger brother Edward Malcolm. His father was a General Labourer. By 1911 his mother had died and he was living with his father (now described as a Dock Labourer), his sister and brother in a four-roomed house at 16 Pensby Street, Birkenhead. William was working as a Butcher's Assistant.

His connection with Henley has not been established: presumably he was living in the town when he was posted to the Royal Inniskilling Fusiliers after enlisting in Birmingham, probably at some time in 1916. The 1st Battalion of the Royal Inniskilling Fusiliers was a regiment of the Regular Army. It was in India when war was declared and arrived back in Avonmouth on 10 January 1915. There it joined the 87th Brigade of the 29th Division. Training and mobilisation took place in the Midlands, in the Warwick-Leamington-Nuneaton-Rugby area. The Battalion then embarked with the Division from Avonmouth to the Mediterranean. On 25 April 1915 it was among the first troops to land on Gallipoli. Following the failure of that campaign it left Gallipoli in early January 1916 and landed in Egypt. It arrived in Marseilles on 18 March 1916.

William must have joined the Battalion after it arrived in France. It fought in the Battle of Arras from 9 April to 15 May 1917. William was killed in action on 19 May, aged 24. He has no known grave and is commemorated on the Arras Memorial. At the time of William's death his next of kin was his elder sister, Mrs Jessie Dickinson, living at 13 Evelyn Road, Somerville, Wallasey, Cheshire.

British War Medal and Victory Medal.

1901 & 1911 Census; CWGC; SDGW; MIC.

†Coldicott, Arden Cotterell MC (1897-1918)

Captain, 15th (Service) Battalion Royal Warwickshire Regiment.

Known as Cotterell or Cottie, he was the elder son of the nine children of Arthur Cotterell Coldicott and his wife Annie, of the Rectory, Beaudesert. He was baptised on 17 April 1897 in Stratford upon Avon. He was not with his parents

when the 1901 census was taken: they were then living in Brook House, Ullenhall but with only one of their children namely Cecil, then aged 11 months. There were also two servants living in the house. There were ten children in all, the youngest being named Decima. In 1911 the family was still living at Brook House, Ullenhall now with all of their 8 surviving children and two different servants: his father was described as an Estate Agent, and was managing the estate of H R Newton of Barrells.

Cotterell attended King Edward's School Birmingham from 1909 to 1915, and was a cadet in the Officers' Training Corps. He was commissioned as a 2nd Lieutenant in the Special Reserve of Officers on 22 May 1915 and was attached to the 3rd Battalion, Royal Warwickshire Regiment.[177] This was a reserve battalion and he left it in May 1916 to join the 2nd Battalion, which was with 22nd Brigade, 7th Division in France. He took part in the Battle of the Somme on 3 July at Mametz Wood and was wounded by a sniper in an attack north of Bazentin-le-Grand Wood on 16 July 1916. When he returned to France in October, he was posted to the 15th Battalion. This was one of the Birmingham Pals battalions (the 2nd Birmingham) and was then with 13th Brigade, 5th Division. He was appointed acting Captain on 24 May 1917.[178] On 16 July 1917 he was wounded slightly in a successful trench raid undertaken by 26 men from B Company, which he led, on the German lines north of Oppy Wood.

> "In the early morning of the 16th July the raiding party left our lines... fighting resulted in attacking the enemy at sight with revolver, bomb and bayonet. A party of three or four Germans were bombed in one

---

177 *London Gazette*, 21 May 1915
178 *London Gazette*, 13 July 1917

place without hope of escape and several more were known to have been bayoneted. The raiding party remained in the enemy line for about twenty minutes and penetrated to his second line before withdrawing …By this time an intense enemy protective barrage was being put down on our own front line and Coldicott decided to dispose his party in No Man's Land until things quietened down. He himself came in to report the situation and then rejoined his men…The raid was highly successful, eight or ten of the enemy being known to be killed and one prisoner taken."[179]

Cottie Coldicott was awarded the MC for his part in this action, his citation reading:

"For conspicuous gallantry and devotion to duty when commanding a raiding party. Although the original scheme had to be altered at a moment's notice, his resource and skilful leadership saved any confusion. During the raid he accounted for two of the enemy himself, and afterwards withdrew his party in good order, and brought them safely and skilfully through an intense hostile barrage back to our own lines. His enthusiasm and personal example kept his men in high fettle throughout, and contributed greatly to the success of the raid".[180]

He lost his acting rank of Captain on 7 June 1917, when he ceased to command a company, probably due to the return to service of its former commander.[181] However, he was re-appointed as an acting Captain on 20 July 1917.[182] He took part in the 3rd Battle of Ypres and in the action at Polderhoek Chateau. In November 1917 he was posted with his Battalion to Italy and took part in the crossing of the River Piave before the German Spring Offensive brought about his return to France in April 1918. He was wounded for the third time in Operation Borderland, an attack on a three-mile section of the German front line opposite Nieppe Forest and was initially reported killed, but it later emerged that he had been badly wounded and taken prisoner on 28 June. He was in hospital in Lille and later in St John's Hospital, Dortmund, where he died of his wounds on 14 August 1918.

Bill wrote of him that "he was an officer of sterling worth, utterly fearless, and greatly liked and respected by all ranks of the Battalion".[183]

He is buried in Cologne Southern Cemetery (known in Germany as Sudfriedhof, Zollstock), grave XV B 26. At the time of his death he was engaged to be married to Marjorie Hawkes, a younger sister of 2nd Lieutenant J A Hawkes

179 Bill, p 98
180 *London Gazette*, 9 January 1918
181 *London Gazette*, 8 August 1917
182 *London Gazette*, 11 October 1917
183 Bill, p 135

Cologne Southern Cemetery

(*qv*) of Henley in Arden.[184] He left a will with effects of £203.2s2d and probate was granted to his father on 9 January 1919. An entry on his MIC reads, "Medals not required".

Military Cross, British War Medal and Victory Medal.

1901 & 1911 Census; CWGC; SDGW; MIC; Heath, p 31; Carter, pp 227-9, 257-8.

Coldicott, Cecil Underhill (1900-fl 1939)

2nd Lieutenant, 2/8th Gurkha Rifles.

Cecil was the younger brother of Arden Cotterell Coldicott (*qv* for details of his family). He was born in Ullenhall on 15 April 1900 and baptised there on 20 May 1900. Cecil was educated at King Edward's School, Birmingham from 1910 to 1918, when he left to become a cadet at Hipswell Camp, Catterick. From September 1918 to April 1919 he was at the Royal Military College, Quetta. He was commissioned on 15 April 1919 and appointed to the Indian Army on 2 May 1919. The *Indian Army List 1929* records him as Adjutant of the 2nd Battalion, Gurkha Rifles and as having been appointed Captain on 15 April 1915. The *Indian Army List 1939* shows him as a company commander in the regiment, having been appointed Major on 15 April 1937.

He was married in a Dublin registry office in 1933.

1901 & 1911 Census; Heath, p 32.

---

184 Mrs J L Palmer (*nee* Hawkes)

†Collins, William (1887-1916)

Corporal 462, 1st Battalion Royal Warwickshire Regiment.

William was baptised in St John's Church on 28 August 1887, the youngest son of George and Ann Collins of Henley. His father was a labourer. The family was living in the High Street at the time of the 1901 census. William was then 14 and had two brothers (Jacob and John) and two sisters (Elizabeth and Matilda): he was working as an under boy on a farm. He was living in Wootton Wawen when he joined the Royal Warwickshire Regiment at Warwick as a regular soldier. In 1911 he was serving as a Private with 1st Battalion in Bombay. He subsequently became a Corporal in 1st Battalion, which served in France with 10th Brigade, 4th Division from 22 August 1914. William went to France with them on that date.

In October 1916 the Battalion was in the line at Guillemont, where they were heavily shelled on 10 and 11 October. William was killed in the course of an attack that the Battalion made on 12 October.

> "The attack began with a creeping barrage, under cover of which all the companies left the assembly trenches and moved across no man's land with little or no loss…The initial advance gained over 300 yards, and the men dug-in. By mid-evening, however, it was obvious that other elements of the attack had not been so successful. Without flanking support the 1st Battalion was forced to reorganize and consolidate."[185]

William has no known grave and is commemorated on the Thiepval Memorial.
1914 Star with clasp, British War Medal and Victory Medal.
St John's PR; 1901 & 1911 Census; CWGC; SDGW; MIC; James, p48; Ashby, pp 141 & 194.

---

185 Ashby, p 141.

Cooke, Howard D (1872-1967)

Sergeant 615018 (previously 614980), Royal Engineers; formerly Sergeant 11866, 19th Battalion Welsh Regiment.

Howard Cooke was born in Cinderford, Gloucestershire on 1 January 1872. He began his education at Hereford Blue Coat School and transferred to the Junior Department of Henley School on 13 February 1882. His father was Leonard Cooke, then a baker of Henley. In 1891 Howard was 19 and boarding in a court in All Saint's Parish, Birmingham (his occupation is indecipherable). In 1901 Leonard Cooke was living in the High Street in Henley with his wife Sarah and two daughters: it is likely that Howard was then serving in the army. His first theatre of active service was Gallipoli, where he landed on 16 June 1915. On 23 March 1917 the *Herald* reported that Sergeant H D Cooke, son of Mr & Mrs Cooke of The Gables, High Street, had been wounded on 25 February. He was sent home and ultimately came to the VAD Hospital in Henley, where he made a good recovery. Howard was mentioned in dispatches by Sir Douglas Haig.

His MIC records his address after the war as c/o Pontypridd PO, Glamorgan. He died in Birmingham in 1967 at the age of 95.

Mentioned in Dispatches, 1914-15 Star, British War Medal and Victory Medal. 1881, 1891 & 1901 Census; MIC; Herald (23 March 1917, 10 January 1919).

Coppage, George (1883-1943)

He was born in Henley in March 1883 and baptised in St John's Church on 8 April. He was the second son of Walter Francis Coppage and his wife Mary. He first attended the Infant Department of Henley School and moved to the Juniors on 27

May 1889. His father was a bricklayer and George left school on 25 February 1897 to begin work as a bricklayer himself. In 1901 he was living in Henley at 79 High Street with his parents, his elder brother Frank and his younger brother Walter. He was then employed as a House Painter. The photograph shows him as a member of the Henley Quoits Club in 1905. He married Minnie Maud Higgins of Henley in St John's on 5 February 1910 and in 1911 they were living in a six-roomed house at Bank View, 101 High Street: Minnie had been born in London. George was a member of Warwick Number 11 VAD and scored 65% in the examinations held in the autumn of 1914.

In 1916, aged 33 and described as a jobbing builder, undertaker, plumber etc of Henley in Arden, he appeared before the Stratford Rural District Tribunal to apply for exemption from the forces. His grounds were that he had recently succeeded to the business of his uncle, which would cease if he were taken. He was granted exemption until 12 August.[186] He then applied for a further exemption, as he had been unable to find a suitable person to take over if he were called up. He was given a final exemption to 29 September.[187]

As there is no further record of appearances, it seems that he enlisted in late 1916. The *Herald* reported on 15 February 1918 that he had recently been home on leave. No MIC in his name has been found and it is therefore likely that he did not serve overseas.

He was living at 277 High Street when his son entered the Junior School in 1919 and was still living there in 1936. He was a builder and also acted as an undertaker. George Coppage built the houses at Barley Close to provide an income for his son, who was blind. He died on 23 June 1943 and is buried in St Nicholas' churchyard.

St John's PR; 1901 & 1911 Census; Florence Beard; W G Haytree.

Cox, D

It has not been possible to identify him.

†*Crompton, George Valentine (1889/90-1918)*

Lance Bombardier 836409, Royal Field Artillery; formerly Gunner 3012, Royal Horse Artillery.

George Crompton was born in Henley in Arden. In 1891 he was one and visiting 9 Heath Street, Rotton Park, Birmingham with his mother (*nee* Fawcett) and elder brother William. The 1901 Census records his name as Valentine George Crompton: he was then 12 and living with his parents William and May Compton at 92 Yew Tree Road, Aston Manor. His elder brother William, two younger brothers and four younger sisters were also living with them. His father was a postman and had been born in Henley, as were all of George's siblings. In 1911 the family was living in a six-roomed house at 11 Charles Road, Aston Manor, Birmingham, there being four sons (of whom George was the eldest) and four daughters. His parents had been married for 22 years and had 9 children, of whom one had died. George was employed as a Printer Compositor. He married Mabel Gertrude Hunt in Aston in January 1912: they were living at 1 Wilton Place, Wilton Road, Aston when he enlisted in Birmingham. He served with the Territorial Force, initially with the Royal Horse Artillery, but was with 'B' Battery, 307th Brigade of the Royal Field Artillery when he died of wounds on 6 November 1918.

He is buried in Awoingt British Cemetery, grave III E 22.

British War Medal and Victory Medal.

1891, 1901 & 1911 Census; MIC; CWGC; SDGW.

---

186 *Herald,* 19 May 1916
187 *Herald,* 18 August 1916

Awoingt British Cemetery

Davis, Abel Frank (1880-1953)

Frank was born on 30 August 1880, the son of Abel Davis, a bricklayer of May's Hill, and his wife Rhoda (*nee* Bliss). He was baptised in Wootton Wawen on 19 September 1880. Frank began his education at Wootton Catholic School and transferred to the Junior Department of Henley School on 16 March 1891. He left school on 15 September 1893 to begin work as a labourer. In 1901 he was still living with his parents in Wootton Wawen and working as a Bricklayer. He married Charlotte Emily Leck in Wootton Wawen on 12 March 1905. By 1911 they had three children, Dora Emily Selina (5), Lilian Rhoda (baptised in St John's 29 March 1908) and Frances Annie (baptised 2 January 1910). Frank was working as a Bricklayer and he and his family were living in Henley at 233 South End. They subsequently had four other children, Alfred Edward (baptised 11 June 1911), Albert Frank (baptised 8 December 1912), Lydia Eliza (baptised 22 January 1915) and William Ernest (baptised 6 October 1918). The eldest child was born in Wootton Wawen, the others all in Henley.

The *Herald* of 1 February 1918 reported that Private Frank Davies (*sic*), an old Henley boy who was with the GWR, had been met by Private F Stinson (*qv*) in January 1918, though it does not say where.

Frank died on 221 August 1953 aged 72 and is buried in St Nicholas' churchyard.
1901 & 1911 Census; *Herald* 1(1 February 1918).

Duggan, Leslie Archibald (1899-1972)

Sergeant, 16th Battalion Royal Warwickshire Regiment.

Leslie was born in Gloucester on 30 May 1899, the only son of John Ernest and Annie Elizabeth Duggan: he had a younger sister, Kathleen. In 1901 his father was a tailor, then aged 42, working from their home in 37 London Road, Gloucester. His father is likely to have died early as, when Leslie entered Henley Junior School on 1 May 1906 from the Infant Department, he was described as the son of Mrs Duggan of Glendossil, Henley in Arden. Leslie left on 11 May for Burman's House and was subsequently educated at Solihull School. In 1911 his mother was resident at Glendossil with her daughter Kathleen and working as the Matron at the lunatic asylum there. Leslie was also living in Henley at this time, as a boarder with Mr & Mrs Vernon Russell of 263 South End, .

While at Solihull School, Leslie served four years in the OTC, becoming a sergeant in charge of the armoury. He joined 13th Battalion, RWR when he left in July 1915 and trained in the Isle of Wight. Leslie became a Lance Corporal immediately and the *Herald* reported in April 1916 that he was now a Corporal, aged 17 and stationed at Blandford in Dorset. He was a Sergeant in the 16th Battalion of the Royal Warwickshire Regiment in August 1918. He probably had a training role and did not leave the UK as there is no MIC for him.

He died in Birmingham in 1972, aged 73.

1901 & 1911 Census; Henley School Admissions Register; *The Shenstonian* (December 1915 & August 1918); *Herald* (7 April 1916).

Dyer, David Henry (1895-fl1920)

Rifleman Y1331, King's Royal Rifle Corps.

The Census of 1901 shows that he was living in Wootton Wawen with this father Thomas (a Wagoner on a farm), his mother Mary Ann and his sister Jane (3). He had been born in Henley. He enlisted in Birmingham on 31 August 1914 and was working as a Farm Labourer. He gave his next of kin as his mother Mary of New Inn House, Wootton Wawen. His height was 5'3½", his weight 123 lbs and his physical development was Very Good. He was a Wesleyan.

David joined the KRRC at Winchester and was posted to Sheerness, where he joined the 14th Battalion on 30 October 1914. He served in two other locations in the UK before moving to France on 20 August 1915 where he joined the 11th Battalion. His only injury during his service in France was a broken nose, resulting from a fall from a bicycle on 5 February 1918: he was then with the 12th Battalion. He served in France until 16 January 1919, going home on leave from 26 January to 9 February 1918.

He wrote from Hunger Hill that he had civil employment waiting and requesting his release. Mrs Steele of Mayswood Farm wrote that she had employed Dyer of the 12th Battalion KRRC before 4 August 1914 and was prepared to offer him employment as a Farm Labourer immediately on his return to civil life.

Neither letter was dated. David was discharged from Number 1 Dispersal Unit, Crystal Palace on 17 January 1919 and transferred to the Army Reserve on 14 February 1919.

1914-15 Star, British War Medal and Victory Medal.

1901 Census; MIC; Service Record.

Dyer, Walter (1873-1936)

Saddler Sergeant 420120, Royal Army Service Corps, formerly Saddler Sergeant 268641, 3rd Battalion Royal Warwickshire Regiment and Saddler Sergeant 1290, Warwickshire Yeomanry.

Walter Dyer was born in Alcester. In 1891 he was living with his parents William and Sarah Dyer at Arrow, near Alcester. His father and elder brothers were blacksmiths; Walter was 18 and working as a saddler.

Walter took the oath in Warwick on 4 June 1906, joining the Warwickshire Imperial Yeomanry on 24 June 1906. He had a medical on 17 July in Henley, when he was declared fit by Dr Samuel Agar. Walter signed on for a further two year term at Henley in Arden on 29 April 1908, his attestation certificate being signed by Lord Brooke. Walter was then 35 and working as a saddler in Henley. At his medical examination in Warwick on the following day his height was given as 5'10½" and his chest as 35": he was declared fit for military service. He did not own a horse, but said he could obtain one. He re-engaged for further service annually from 1910 to 1914 inclusive. Each year he did two weeks training with the Warwickshire Yeomanry as follows:

28 May to 12 June 1908	Warwick Park
19 May to 2 June 1909	Perham Down, Salisbury Plain
7 May to 21 May 1910	Windmill Camp, Salisbury Plain
16 May to 30 May 1911	Warwick Park
17 May to 31 May 1912	Combe Park
10 May to 24 May 1913	Bulford Camp
25 May to 6 June 1914	Warwick Park

His next of kin was his wife of 97 High Street, Henley (he had married in 1911). He served in the Henley troop of 'D' Squadron and was promoted to Lance Corporal in 1910 and to Saddler Lance Corporal in 1912.

He began war service on 5 August 1914 and signed his agreement to serve overseas at Newbury on 18 October 1914 before Lieutenant-Colonel T A Wight-Boycott, then commanding the 1/1st Warwickshire Yeomanry. He was promoted Acting Saddler Corporal on 1 October 1915, paid acting Saddler Sergeant on 8 April 1916 and confirmed in the rank of Saddler Corporal on 1 October 1916. His service had been continued under the Military Service Act on 24 June 1916. On 21 February 1915 he was admitted to hospital in Norwich suffering from congestion in both lungs: he was recommended for 10 days leave.

He was given a medical examination in Colchester on 23 November 1917 and graded B1. On 5 February 1918 he was in hospital for 8 days with bronchitis. He was transferred to the 3rd (Reserve) Battalion of the Royal Warwickshire Regiment at Dover on 8 February 1918 and thence to Number 2 Remount Depot Army Service Corps at Woolwich on 11 May 1918. He was medically examined on Woolwich on 21 October 1918 and downgraded to B2. On 20 February 1919 he was allowed a bounty of £15 under Army Order 209 of 1916 when with 50 Squadron of the RASC Remounts Service at Woolwich and was given one month's leave. His final transfer was to the RASC Remounts Depot at Romsey on 20 April 1919 and from there he was discharged from the Army on 27 July 1919 at the age of 46. He had been classified as A1 when he enlisted in 1906 and left with a medical category of B2 in 1919.

On his discharge he did not claim to be suffering from any disability as a result of his military service.

He married Dora Elizabeth Biggadike at the St Peter's Church, Balsall Common on 4 June 1900. Their daughter Ivy Dora was baptised in St John's Church on 24 July 1904 (Walter then being described as a Saddler of Henley). In 1911 the family was living at 97 High Street together with an Aunt, Mary Anne Forley. He was a saddler and harness maker living at 97 High Street in 1924.

Walter Dyer, saddler & harness maker, was still living at 97 High Street in 1936. He died at his home in Stratford Road, Warwick on 1 January 1957 and is buried in Warwick Cemetery.

1891 & 1911 Census; Service Record; Interment Record.

East, William Henry Martin (1895-fl 1919)

Private M2/194486, Royal Army Service Corps.

William was born in Thurlestone, Devonshire, on 9 November 1895, the son of William and Gertrude S East. In 1901 his parents were living in Thurlestone, his father being described as "Living on Own Means": both had been born in Warwickshire, his father in Salford and his mother in Bidford. He had a younger brother John Eric Gordon (born in Henley) and a younger sister Ivy. William was initially educated privately and then moved to Henley Junior School on 8 December 1902, only to leave it again due to illness on 24 December. He re-entered on 15 April 1907, having been educated in the meantime at Burman's House. He left on 16 December 1909 to go to commercial school. By 1911 his father had died and he was living in a six-roomed house at 109 High Street with his mother, younger brother and a domestic servant.

British War Medal and Victory Medal.

1901 & 1911 Census; MIC.

Edgington, Frank (1886-fl 1919)

Sapper 253457, Royal Engineers; formerly Driver 57054, Royal Horse Artillery.

Frank was born in Henley in 1886, the son of Henry and Hannah Edgington. In1901 he was working as an Assistant to a Cycle Agent and living with his brother-in-law Thomas Whiting at 40 Ely Street, Stratford upon Avon. He enlisted in the Royal Horse Artillery in Birmingham on 24 May 1909, joining them at Cosham on 24 May. His height was 5'5¾" and his weight 135 lbs. He was a member of the Church of England. Frank served for a total of 9 years and 284 days as follows:

Home	17 May 1909 to 12 October 1910
South Africa	13 October 1910 to 7 February 1913
Home	8 February 1913 to 4 October 1914
France	5 October 1914 to 25 January 1919
Home	26 January 1919 to 24 February 1919

He married Annie Shelley in Suffolk on 28 January 1915. He had given his father Henry Edgington of 224 Tanyard Terrace, Henley as his next of kin when he enlisted but amended this to his wife Annie Edgington of 395 Wharstead Road, Ipswich after his marriage.

He was posted as a Driver in the Royal Horse Artillery on 29 July 1909, where he was described as "a steady man who works fairly well". He gained a 3rd Class Certificate of Education on 26 June 1909 and a 2nd Class on 23 March 1910. He joined 44 Brigade as a Driver on 11 September 1914. Frank transferred to the Royal Engineers on 28 April 1917, initially serving as a Driver with 4th Army Signalling Company. On 24 July 1918 he was "remustered" as a Harness Maker being given a "proficiency rate" of 1/- a day. He was serving with 62 Division Signalling Company when he was discharged from the army on 24 February 1919 "being surplus to requirements having suffered impairment since entry into the service". His disability was assessed as 40% and he was given a pension of 11/- from 30 May 1919 to 2 September 1919, rising to 16/- from 3 September 1919 to 7 December 1920. He was issued with a Silver War Badge (485587) on 17 August 1920.

1914 Star with Clasp, British War Medal, Victory Medal and Silver War Badge.
1901 Census; MIC; Service Record.

Edgington, Harry (1900-1951)

In 1901 he was one and living with his father Harry Edgington, timber feller, in the High Street together with his younger brother Roland and five others. The household was a smaller one in 1911, Harry (11) living with his father (61 and a widower), his sister Lily (17) and his brother Roland (10) in a three-roomed house at 224 Tanyard Terrace, Henley. He was one of "several Henley boys" together on Salisbury Plain in January 1918.

He married Beatrice Lilian Sanford on 27 May 1921. He was Arthur O'Donnell's grandfather.

There are several MICs in the name of Harry Edgington and variations on this, but it seems likely that he did not go overseas and thus did not qualify for a medal. 1901 and 1911 Census; *Herald* (11 January 1918).

Elvins, Samuel (1895-1956)

Private 16245, 11th Battalion Royal Warwickshire Regiment.

Samuel was the son of Samuel and Hannah Elvins (*nee* Cross) and was baptised in Solihull on 9 June 1895. He was living with his parents in Elmdon Heath, Solihull at the time of the 1901 Census: also living with them were two other sons, John and Isaac, and their daughter Fanny. All had been born in Solihull, except his mother who was born in Rowington. His father was a Labourer, working for the Rural District Council. In 1911 the family was living in a five-roomed house in Drury Lane, Solihull: his parents had been married for 20 years and his father was now a Foreman with the District Council. They had had 7 children, of whom 4 had survived: John was 19, Samuel 15, Fanny Elizabeth 12 and William 5. Samuel was working as a Gardener in a Nursery.

He enlisted on 7 December 1915, at which time he was living in Broomfield Avenue, Solihull. He was a Gardener, aged 20 years and 221 days and was unmarried, giving his next of kin as his father. He was 5'3¾" tall, with a chest of 32½". Samuel was mobilised on 26 January 1916 where his height was given as 5'4", his weight as 105 lbs, his chest as 33" and his physical development described as good, though he had a very slight goitre. He was posted to a depot at Blandford. On 19 May 1916 he embarked from Folkestone and arrived in Etaples on 20 May, where he was posted to 'D' Company of 11th Battalion Royal Warwickshire Regiment. The battalion had been in France as part of 112th Brigade, 37th Division since 30 July 1915. Between 6 July and 22 August 1916 the Brigade was transferred to 34th Division, a move which was necessitated by the 34th Division having lost 6,380 casualties on the first day of the Somme – the most lost by any division. During its time with 34th Division, 112th Brigade fought on the Somme at the battles of Albert and the Bazentin and Pozieres Ridges. It was evidently during this time (as recorded in a medical report in March 1917) that a trench in which Samuel Elvins was serving was blown up and he was buried.

On 14 October 1916 he was sent sick to a Field Ambulance, which he left on 21 October to rejoin his battalion. On 19 November he was diagnosed as suffering from shell shock, but rejoined his battalion on 22 November. He was again sent to a Field Ambulance on 16 December and was transferred to England suffering from a nervous breakdown on 19 December 1916. He was in Tooting Military Hospital with shell shock from 20 December 1916 to 20 January 1917. A medical report from 4th London General Hospital at Denmark Hill dated 12 March 1917 recorded his disability as Neurasthenia (shell shock). His problem resulted from his experiences in the Somme, his Pension Record stating, "In August 1916 while in trenches was blown up and buried; sent to Base Hosp 3 days and then to another

Hosp at Boulogne for 3 weeks and was several times sent back to trenches but always broke down". Samuel was complaining of headaches, broken sleep and bad dreams, with a general feeling of weakness, especially in his legs. The Medical Officer in charge of his case reported that he showed "some mental enfeeblement is very dull and apathetic and has no initiative. He does not improve and there is no prospect of his being fit to resume his military duties". It was recommended that he be discharged "as permanently unfit for army service but could be employed on the land. His trade is a gardener". A Special Medical Board on 14 March 1917 duly recorded his disability as being due to shell shock sustained on active service. His disability was not regarded as permanent but as having a probable minimum duration of six months. His capacity for earning a full livelihood in the general labour market was estimated to be reduced by three quarters, but his disability was such that it would not obviously "cause him to be rejected by an Approved Society under the National Insurance Act". Samuel was discharged as no longer physically fit for war service on 9 April 1917. He had spent 225 days of his military service in England and 215 days in France. He was given £30 in lieu of nine months' pension and issued with a Silver War Badge (155096) on 10 April.

Samuel went on to be employed by Dr Samuel Agar of Henley as a gardener. Agar was living in Hurst House and was then in his late eighties. He was evidently unaware of Samuel's war record and wrote to the District Tribunal suggesting that Samuel might be better engaged in the army. The Tribunal agreed with this at a meeting in May 1917. Samuel's medical history of apathy and lack of initiative seem to have resulted in his military record not being drawn to the Tribunal's attention. He was not called upon to re-enlist.

British War Medal, Victory Medal and Silver War Badge.

1901 & 1911 Census; Attestation; MIC; Pension Records; *Herald* (18 May 1917).

England, Howard John Thomas (1887-1956)

Sapper 214618, Royal Engineers; formerly Private 35854, Worcestershire Regiment.

He was born in Henley in Arden on 24 August 1887, the fourth son of Martin and Jane England (*nee* Pettifer). In 1891 he was living in Henley with his parents and his three elder brothers, Frank (11), Walter (8) and David (6): his father was a Labourer. Howard was still living there in 1901 with his mother Jane (who was employed as a Charwoman) and his elder brother David: his mother was Head of the household and Howard was employed as a Hotel Yard Boy. In 1911 Howard was working as a Boot Maker and living with his mother (then 66 and working as a Laundress) in a three-roomed house at 24 Henley in Arden: his father was in Stratford upon Avon Workhouse, where he died on 10 April 1924. Howard played in goal for the Forest of Arden football team and was a postman in Henley after the war. He did not marry and died in December 1956.

British War Medal and Victory Medal.

1891, 1901 & 1911 Census; MIC; Douglas Wilkes (his great-nephew).

England, William G

Private 66285, Royal Army Medical Corps.

The birth of William George England was registered in King's Norton in the first quarter of 1878, but no census records relating to him have been found.

British War Medal and Victory Medal.

MIC.

† *Evans, Percival Thomas (1886-1918)*

Lance Corporal 198906, 57th Signal Company Royal Engineers.

Percival Evans was born in Aston in 1886, the son of Thomas and Mary Evans. In 1891 he was living with his parents and two younger sisters (Elsie Hilda and Clementine) at 39 High Street, Dudley: his father was a Sporting Gun Finisher. By 1901 the family had moved to 346 Green Lane, Aston, his father now being a Confectioner Dealer. In 1911 the family were living at 52 Oakfield Road, Balsall Heath: his parents had been married for 25 years and his father was a Gun Maker. Percival was a Telegraphist with the Post Office. He became a member of the Territorial Army, his original number being 165.TF and was a Sapper in the Royal Engineers when he was called up on the outbreak of war. He went to France on 10 October 1914. Percival Evans died in England on 6 August 1918 and was buried in St Nicholas' churchyard on 10 August, aged 32. The register records him as being of Henley in Arden. His tombstone reads:

Sacred
to the memory of
Percival Thomas Evans RE
only son of
Thomas and Mary Ann Evans
of Beaudesert
who died for his country August 6 1918
Aged 32 years
Peace perfect peace

1914 Star, British War Medal and Victory Medal.

1891, 1901 & 1911 Census; MIC; CWGC; SDGW; Beaudesert PR.

Farr, A W

There are two MICs with this name, Corporal 27517, Hampshire Regiment and Corporal 4171, MGC.

The *Herald* of 8 February 1918 reported that he had worked at the local branch of the London City and Midland Bank. He recently visited Henley after being discharged from the army having been severely wounded in the left arm about 18 months ago. His wound was slow to heal. He was now resting prior to taking up another clerical appointment.

The birth of Albert William Farr, born in Welford-on-Avon, was registered in Stratford upon Avon in the first quarter of 1886. In 1911 he was living with his father (a blacksmith) in Herefordshire and was working as a Farm Labourer. It seems very unlikely that he was the individual referred to in the above paragraph, but no other candidate has been found.

British War Medal and Victory Medal.

MICs; *Herald* (8 February 1918).

Finch, Bert (1891/2-fl 1919)

Private 412604, Labour Corps; formerly Private 99434, Machine Gun Corps.

He appears in the 1901 Census as "Berty" (see George Finch below for details of his family). Bert was born in Nethby, Yorkshire. He was living with his parents and some of his siblings at 227 High Street in Henley in 1911 and working as an Agricultural Labourer. He married Gertrude Shepherd, also of Henley, in 1919. A daughter Eileen Drusilla was baptised in St John's Church on 18 March 1921, when he was described as a Labourer living at 217 High Street.

Bert enlisted on 7 August 1916. His transfer to the Labour Corps suggests that he had been wounded or was not otherwise fully fit and his SWB record shows that he was discharged due to sickness on 25 June 1919. He was issued with his SWB (B243561) on 24 July 1919.

British War Medal, Victory Medal and Silver War Badge.

1901 & 1911 Census; MIC.

Finch, George H (1888/89-1958)

Private 120988, Machine Gun Corps; formerly Private 310126, Corps of Hussars and Private 1883, Warwickshire Yeomanry.

He was born in Crowedge, Yorkshire and in 1891 was living there with his parents, Thomas and Elizabeth, two elder brothers Frederick and William and two elder sisters Mary and Nelly. His father was a Coal Pit Labourer. The family had obviously moved about a lot, as all of the children had been born in a different location. In 1901 he was living in the High Street, Henley. His father was absent, as his mother is shown as Head of the household, but also as a Wife. His elder brother William and elder sister Mary were still living at home, as were two younger brothers Bert (*qv*) and Christopher and a younger sister Maud. The younger members of the family had again been born in different locations. In 1911 he was living in a six-roomed house at 227 High Street with his parents, brothers Bert (19) and Sidney (10) and sisters Nellie (26), Maud (14) and Ivy (4): his parents had been married for 35 years and had 10 children, 9 of whom had survived. The three men in the household were all working as Agricultural Labourers.

He was a member of the Warwickshire Yeomanry before the war, attending the annual camp with them at Warwick Park in May 1914. He sailed from Avonmouth to Egypt with the regiment, arriving there on 28 April 1915. He remained behind in Egypt when the greater part of the Warwickshire Yeomanry left for Gallipoli on 14 August 1915.

1914-15 Star, British War Medal and Victory Medal.

1891, 1901 & 1911 Census; MIC; *Herald* (22 May 1914).

Finch, Sidney Christopher (*1900-fl 1919*)

Private 535324, Labour Corps.

Sidney was the son of Thomas and Elizabeth Finch (see George Finch for details of his family). He was born in Henley in 1900 and was 18 when he enlisted in Coventry on 2 June 1918 at which time he was working as a Polisher. He was the smallest man from Henley to join the armed forces, being 4'11¾" in height and weighing 85 lbs. He was given a medical category of Grade II and reported to Cowley Barracks in Oxford on 9 September 1918. Sidney served with 364th Reserve Employment Company, but only for a short time. He was returning from leave in Henley to his Depot at Codford in Wiltshire on 9 November 1918 and reported to the 3rd Southern General Hospital in Oxford on his way there. He was diagnosed as suffering from influenza and was subsequently transferred to the Red Cross Hospital in Banbury. He was not discharged from hospital until 27 January 1919: he was given 28 days leave and was demobilized on 15 February 1919.

1901 and 1911 Census; Service Record.

†Findon, William Sutton (1882-1917)

Private 430157, 7th Battalion, Canadian Infantry (British Columbia Regiment).

William was the son of James and Hannah Sutton Findon (*nee* Bartlam) of Henley in Arden, who were married in St John's on 26 March 1878. He was born in Henley on 20 September 1882 and baptised on 15 October 1882 in St Nicholas' Church, Beaudesert. His father had a butcher's shop beneath the present Guild Hall. His father died early, as the 1901 Census records William as living with his mother (now Hannah Sutton Stokes), his sister (Mary Hannah Sutton Findon), and his half brothers Francis Stokes (*qv*) and Roland Stokes. William was then working as an Assistant Baker, presumably with his mother who was head of the household and gave her employment as a Baker. In 1911 he was living in the High Street in the six-roomed house of Miss Harriet Mary Bartlam (now the Guild Hall),

and working as a Butcher. Also living there were Alfred Edward Stokes (41), who was the managing Butcher; Frank Stokes (18), a Butcher; Roland Stokes (17) an Assistant Butcher and Mary H S Findon (29) a Bookkeeper. It is not known precisely when he emigrated to Canada, but the Henley Electoral Roll of 1914 gives his address as 199 High Street and shows that he held a freehold house and land in Beaudesert.

He married Frances Mary Meyrick in Celista on 24 July 1914. She was a granddaughter of James Argyle, who was a stationer in Henley. When he enlisted in Victoria, British Colombia on 3 March 1915 he gave his next of kin as his wife and her address as Celista, Notch Hill, British Colombia. His medical examination gave his height as 5'5" and his chest as 43". He had a dark complexion, grey eyes and brown hair.

In June 1916 the *Herald* reported that he was now serving with the Canadian forces either in the UK or France and had recently been in Henley for a short visit while on leave. He had emigrated to Canada in about 1913. William made other visits to Henley, where he was warmly welcomed, while he was training in England.

William died on 4 July 1917, aged 34, his death being reported in the *Herald* of 13 July. There was much sympathy for those bereaved by his death, particularly as his sister Miss E S Findon was seriously ill, having been thrown out of a trap just outside Wootton Hall while going on a bread round for Mr Welch, who was short of men. William Findon is buried in Bruay Communal Cemetery Extension in the Pas de Calais, grave H 7.

Bruay is a large village 6 kilometres south west of Bethune. The Canadian Corps occupied this part of the line early in 1917 and almost half of the graves are of their casualties during that year. William left a widow, Frances Mary Findon, of Toronto, Notch Hill, British Columbia. The government of Canada also awarded a Cross of Sacrifice to the mother and widow of man who lost his life during the war: each received a cross if both were alive.

British War Medal and Victory Medal.

1901 & 1911 Census; Canadian Archives website; CWGC; *Herald* (23 June 1916 &13 July 1917).

Bruay Communal Cemetery Extension

Ford, A

There are too many military records in this name to make a positive identification.

He was possibly Albert Ford, born in Reading in about 1883, who was a lodger at 176 High Street in 1911 and working as a Railway Engine Cleaner.

Arthur Ford was reported as joining the Hussars at Colchester, leaving Henley in Arden on 24 August 1914 and A Ford was reported as having been a member of the VAD before joining the colours.

1911 Census; *Herald* (28 August 1914 & 28 January 1916).

Franklin, Ralph (1888-1972)

Sergeant 86041, Royal Field Artillery.

Ralph Franklin was born in Ullenhall. In 1891 he was living at Perry Mill Cottage, Ullenhall with his parents Charles and Amy, his elder brother Albert Mark, his elder sister Sarah Jane and his younger brother Herbert John. His father was an Agricultural Labourer, who had been born in Tanworth; his mother was born in Ullenhall. The family was still living there in 1901. By 1911 Charles Franklin had taken over the farm at Perry Mill and was living there with his family. Ralph was then described as a Farmer's son employed on the farm.

He enlisted at Stratford upon Avon on 25 January 1915 at the age of 26 years and 122 days: the Recruiting Officer was Major Bairnsfather. Ralph's occupation was given as Postman. His height was 5'8¼" and his chest measurement 38". Ralph was unmarried and his father was presumably dead, as he gave his mother as his next of kin. He joined the RFA at their Number 3 Depot at Hilsea on 28 January. He was appointed to 105th Brigade on 20 April and promoted to Acting

Bombardier on 28 December 1915. He was subsequently promoted to Bombardier on 30 April 1917 and to Sergeant later in the same year. On 6 February 1919 he was at the RFA Dispersal Centre at Chiseldon and was given 28 days leave three days later, on the termination of which he was to cease wearing his army uniform: he was also given a £2 advance of pay. Not only had he survived, but he had done so with a medical category of A1. He was demobilised on 9 March 1919.

Ralph Franklin served 222 days of his military service in England, 2 years and 76 days in France and 345 days in Italy. He also had 10 days leave in England while on service in Italy.

He was mentioned in dispatches (Sir Douglas Haig's dispatch of 7 November 1917, *London Gazette* 11 December 1917) and sent two oak leaves to wear on his medals as a result (receipt acknowledged in May 1920). Sergeant R Franklin, RFA, Henley in Arden was awarded the Belgian *Croix de Guerre* in 1918 (*London Gazette* 15 April 1918) and acknowledged its receipt in May 1920: he signed an acknowledgment of his receipt of a Diploma to the *Croix de Guerre* in February 1922. He was awarded the Italian *Croce de Guerra* on 29 November 1918.

Mentioned in Dispatches, 1914-15 Star, British War Medal and Victory Medal (with oak leaves), Belgian *Croix de Guerre* and Italian *Croce de Guerra*.

1891, 1901 & 1911 Census; WW1 Service Records; MIC; *London Gazette* (11 December 1917 and 15 April 1918); *Herald* (19 April 1918).

Franklin, Joseph William (1892-fl 1919)

Private 18122, 1st Battalion Coldstream Guards.

Joseph William Franklin was born in Beaudesert and baptised at St Nicholas' Church on 27 November 1892, the son of Joseph William and Bessie Franklin. In 1901 his father Joseph was a Gas Stoker, aged 34 and his mother, who had been born in Chipping Campden, was 36: they were living in Beaudesert Street with their children Frances (12), Ada (10), Joseph (8), Fanny (3) and Annie (1). In the 1911 Census Joseph's name is given as William Joseph Franklin. He was then living at Hall End in Ullenhall in a three-roomed house with his parents Joseph William (then a Farm Labourer) and Bessie, who had been married for 24 years and had six children, all of whom were surviving. Living with them were his two younger sisters, Fanny Ellen and Annie and his younger brother Thomas Edward (7). William was a Stockman on a farm.

When he joined the Coldstream Guards in Birmingham on 23 November 1915 he gave his name as William Franklin, but signed himself as William Joseph Franklin. He was then living at 748 Warwick Road, Tyseley, Birmingham and working as a Packer with the GWR. His next of kin was his father, of Hall End, Ullenhall. William was 5'9" tall with a chest of 40½" and weighed 160 lbs. He was passed as fit, subject to dental treatment, for service in the field at home or abroad. William was mobilized on 18 February 1916 and posted to the Guards Depot at Caterham. Other than short spells of a month with 2nd and 4 months with 3rd Battalions, he served with 1st Battalion. He served in the UK from 23 November 1915 to 11 December 1916, and sailed from Southampton to join the BEF in France on 12 December.

William was wounded by shrapnel in his right thigh on 9 October 1917 and after some local treatment was sent back to England on 18 October. He was in Mill Road Infirmary, Liverpool from 20 October to 5 November and was then transferred to Sherlock St Hospital, Liverpool, where he remained until 30 November. He spent some time at the London Command Depot in Shoreham before embarking from Southampton again on 1 April 1918, when he was posted to 2nd Battalion but after a few days in the Base Depot he was transferred to 3rd Battalion on 15 April. He rejoined 1st Battalion on 27 August. On 4 November he was shot in the left side of his neck while deepening a trench at Fille St Paul. He was treated initially in 4th Field Ambulance, then at 38th Casualty Clearing Station and at 32 Stationary Hospital in Boulogne. On 24 November he was transferred to Huddersfield War Hospital in England. At his medical board in Huddersfield on 7 January 1919 it was stated that the wound was "soundly healed" and that there was "no loss of function or usefulness in the affected part" and he was placed in Category A. William was demobilised on 5 February 1919.

British War Medal and Victory Medal.

St Nicholas' PR; 1901 & 1911 Census; Attestation & Service Record; MIC.

Ghee, Thomas William (1894-1973)

Gunner 37851, Royal Garrison Artillery.

He was known as Tom and was born in Henley on 16 September 1894, the son of Frederick William Ghee, a painter, and his wife Harriet Ellen. He was baptised in St John's on 9 December 1894. In 1901 he was living in Henley with his parents and three sisters (Edith, Polly and Lydia). The family surname was then recorded as Gee and his father's occupation was given as Painter and Paperhanger. Tom and his wife Dora had a son Thomas William baptised at St Nicholas' on 7 August 1921. He was then described as a Labourer, of Beaudesert.

He first served in Egypt, arriving there on 14 July 1915.

Tom lived at 9 School Road.

1914-15 Star, British War Medal and Victory Medal.

1901 Census; St John's PR; MIC; W G Haytree.

Goodyear, Howard (1894-1976)

Sergeant 53078, Machine Gun Corps.

He was the son of Walter and Mary Goodyear, who were living in West Bromwich in 1901. His father was a Baker and Confectioner. They had six children including Howard, then aged 6, and his younger brother Sidney, then aged 4. In 1911 the family was living at The Shrubbery, Stanford on Teme in Worcestershire. His father was still working as a Baker, as were Howard and his elder brother Walter.

Howard's daughter Betty was baptised at St Nicholas' on 13 September 1922 at which time he was a toolmaker living at 25 High Street. His wife's name was Ada. Howard Goodyear lived in Warwick Road and his son Peter is said to have served in submarines in the Royal Navy in WW2. He died in Solihull in 1976.

British War Medal and Victory Medal.

St Nicholas' PR; 1901 & 1911 Census; MIC; W G Haytree.

Goodyear, Sydney (1897-1972)

Royal Flying Corps or Royal Air Force.

Sydney was the third son of Walter and Mary Goodyear (see Howard Goodyear above). In 1911 he was living with his parents, two elder brothers and a younger sister, at The Shrubbery, Stanford on Teme and was still at school.

No details of his war record have been found.

He married Helen May Badger, also of Henley, the banns being called in St John's Church in September 1921: their daughter Janice Jane was baptised in St John's on 14 October 1928. Sydney Goodyear was then a mechanic and was living at 2 Cherry Orchard.

St John's PR; 1901 & 1911 Census.

Green, A

No military record can be identified.

He is possibly Arthur Green, born in Wantage, Berkshire in 1893 and working as a male attendant at Glendossil in 1911.

1911 Census.

Greening, Arthur (fl 1910-1919)

Air Mechanic 2nd Class 7115, Royal Flying Corps & Royal Air Force.

Arthur married Florence Ellen Malins, the sister of Edward John Malins (*qv*), on 15 January 1910 in St John's. They had three children, all baptized in St John's: Florence Henrietta on 18 September 1910 (Arthur being described as a Labourer of Grimsby); Randolph Robert Arthur, baptised 28 April 1912 (Labourer of 283 High Street) and Stanley William, baptised 26 April 1914.

He went to France on 17 November 1915, but later served in the Sudan.

1914-15 Star and the Sultan's Sudan Medal (if awarded this medal the recipient was not eligible for either the British War Medal or the Victory Medal).

St John's PR; MIC.

Hadley, Cecil Tom (1894-1970)

Served in the RN or RNVR.

He was born on 17 October 1894 and baptised in St John's Church on 10 February 1895. Tommy was the son of Jane Hadley of Henley, a widow and was recorded as illegitimate. In 1901 he was living in the High Street with his mother, his elder brothers Walter and Fred and his elder sister Catherine. His mother and sister were Laundresses and his brother Walter was a Bricklayer. By 1911 he was the only one still living with his mother at 78 Henley in Arden and was working as a Telegraph Messenger: his mother was still working as a Laundress.

He married Ivy Alberta (surname unknown) and was described as a Sailor of 78 High St when their daughter Barbara May was baptised in St John's Church on 10 June 1917. Tommy Hadley lived in School Road.

St John's PR; 1901 & 1911 Census; W G Haytree.

Hadley, G

Possibly George Hadley, L/Cpl Devonshire Regiment; formerly Private, Royal Warwickshire Regiment.

MIC.

Harris, A (1898-fl 1919)

Private 22528, Royal Warwickshire Regiment.

Arthur Henry Harris was born on 7 March and baptised in St John's Church on 17 April 1898. He was the son of Arthur William and Mary Elizabeth Harris and was living with them, aged 13, at 170 Henley in Arden in 1911.

He enlisted on 15 May 1916. In April 1918 the *Herald* reported that Private A Harris had been wounded recently.

Arthur was discharged on 12 May 1919 because of his wound and was awarded a Silver War Badge (B208849) on 13 June 1919.

British War Medal, Victory Medal and Silver War Badge.

1901 & 1911 Census; SWB; *Herald* (12 April 1918).

Harris, Eustace Lionel (1896-1957)

Private 5873, Leinster Regiment; formerly Private 161777, Army Service Corps.

He was born in Henley and baptised in St John's Church on 17 January 1896, the son of Frederick William Harris (*qv*) and his wife Alice. In 1901 he was 5 and living with his parents in the High Street, Henley. He served with the Warwickshire Yeomanry for some years before the war.

He died in Rugby in 1957.

British War Medal and Victory Medal.

St John's PR; 1901 Census; MIC.

Harris, Frederick Archie 1884-fl 1919

Private S/295135, Royal Army Service Corps.

Frederick was born in Clent, Worcestershire in 1884 and living at 83 High Street, Henley when he enlisted in Stratford upon Avon on 14 February 1917. He was living and working with his uncle Frederick William Harris (*qv*). He was 5'3½" tall and weighed 150 lbs: his physical development was good and he was classed B2 but he suffered from varicose veins. He applied to join the Machine Gun Corps, but since he worked as a Slaughterman he was sent to join the RASC as a Butcher.

Frederick served in Salonika from 26 June 1917 to 9 April 1920. He embarked at Southampton on 26 June and disembarked at Cherbourg on 27 June. He then travelled by train to Taranto in southern Italy, sailing on the SS *Saxon* on 10 July 1917, arriving in Salonica on 15 July. He joined 3rd Base Horse Transport Depot, the first of a number of units he served with in Salonika. On 25 September 1918 he was charged with being drunk on duty and was given 14 days Confined to Barracks and forfeited 5 days pay. He disembarked in Constantinople on 22 February 1920 and left on HMT *Czar* on 10 April. He was demobilized on 23 April 1920.

British War Medal and Victory Medal.

1911 Census; MIC; Service Record.

Harris, Frederick William (1861-1924)

Squadron Sergeant Major 541, Warwickshire Yeomanry.

Known as Fred, he was born in Henley, the son of Samuel and Jane Harris (*nee* Bishop) on 14 July 1861. In the Census of 1881 he gave his age as 18 and was living with his wife Alice (28), in the High Street. He was a Farmer and Butcher. They had married in 1880 and their eldest son William Albert Frederick was born in May 1881.

At the date of the 1891 Census they had five sons living with them, namely Leonard Samuel (born 1883 *qv*), Harold Arthur (1884 *qv*), George Roland (1887), Ralph Leslie (1888) and Harry Selwyn (1890) and a daughter Jessica Alice (1886). His wife Alice died suddenly in 1899. In 1901 Fred was a Butcher and Farmer, living with his three younger sons and two daughters, Ethel Agnes (born 1893) and Lilian Beatrice (born 1895) and another son Eustace Lionel (born 1896 *qv*): his sister in law Sarah Hill was living with him as his Housekeeper. Later that year Fred married Catherine Cecilia Mathias (*nee* Hall, born in 1887), a widow who had been managing the Swan Inn at Aston Cantlow. His sons Ralph and Harry emigrated to Canada in about 1909.

The 1911 census shows Fred and Catherine living at 83 Henley in Arden, Fred being described as a Butcher and Auctioneer. Catherine was assisting him in his business and their sons Norman Beckwith (8) and Dennis Bernard (7) were living with them. Fred's daughter Jessica (now Mrs Pring) was staying with them, together with her recently born daughter, Irene Jessica Aubrey Pring. A nephew Archie Frederick Harris was also living with them and working as an Assistant Butcher. Catherine died in December 1915 and on 26 November 1916 Fred married for the third time, his wife being Lucy Jane Quinn of Earls Court, then a 49 year old spinster.

Fred Harris had joined the Warwickshire Yeomanry on 22 August 1899 and retired from it in 1912, having risen to become Squadron Sergeant Major of 'D' Squadron with proficiency badges for the rifle and the sabre.

His three eldest sons William, Leonard and Harold were also in the Yeomanry for some years before the war. Two of his younger sons, Ralph and Harry, and his

daughter Lilian emigrated to Canada where Harry died at Battle Lake, Alberta in 1913.[188] Lilian died in 1923.

In 1913 the Yeomanry were training at Bulford on Salisbury Plain and Fred was invited to join them to enable a presentation to be made to him by its commanding officer, Lt-Col Frank Dugdale. The event was reported in the *Herald* of 30 May 1913, but the nature of the gift was not specified. Fred rejoined the regiment on the outbreak of war and HNW recalled him leaving Henley in charge of the Henley contingent of the Yeomanry. Adderley records Sergeant F Harris as leaving Egypt for Gallipoli on 14 August 1915 and HNW also recalled that Fred Harris went to Gallipoli with Percy Hawkes and Joseph Steele. He was discharged by 1917 (probably on the grounds of his age as he was then about 54), as on 14 November of 1917 he participated in a meeting of the Court Leet in his capacity as Town Crier (1917-1924). He also served as a Brook Looker from 1917-1921. In April 1917 he was a member of the Footpaths Committee and of the Fire Engine Committee of the Parish Council (he had previously served as Captain of the Fire Brigade, resigning in 1907).

Among Fred's other activities, he ran auctions at the back of the White Swan. He was a Past Provincial Grand Master of the Oddfellows. On the sporting front he captained Henley Cricket Club and the White Swan Bowling Club. He was secretary of the White Swan Bowling Club in 1919.

---

188 *Herald,* 14 November 1913

He committed suicide on 30 November 1924 at the age of 63, the inquest finding that he was temporarily insane due to bereavement and insomnia.

1914-15 Star, British War Medal, Victory Medal and Territorial Force Efficiency Medal (awarded 1 October 1909).

1891, 1901 and 1911 Census; MIC; Adderley, p 22; *Herald* (31 October 1919); Court Leet Minutes; H N Welch; Mrs Bibby Barrett (his grand-daughter).

Harris, Harold Arthur (1883-1928)

His military record cannot be identified with any degree of certainty.

Harold was born in Henley on 10 September 1883 and baptised in St John's Church on 26 November, the son of Frederick William Harris (*qv*) and his wife Alice. He went to the Infant Department of Henley School, transferring to the juniors on 8 June 1891 and leaving on 31 May 1897 to begin work as a butcher, no doubt in his father's business. He was aged 17 working as a butcher with his elder brothers William and Leonard at 712 Stratford Road, Sparkhill, Birmingham in 1901.

He married Lucy Emily and was described as a Dairyman from Warwick Road, Greet when his son Harold Frederick William was baptised in St John's Church on 25 September 1910. In 1911 he was working as a Dairyman and Butcher and living with his wife and son and a resident Domestic Servant at 630 Warwick Road, Greet.

Harold was a well-known local sportsman. In September 1904 he took part in a cycling competition, riding the 110 miles from Acocks Green to Weston super Mare in 6 hours 40 minutes. The following year he won prizes at Acocks Green Athletics' Sports and won a shooting competition at Shottery. He was then serving as a trooper in D Squadron of the Warwickshire Yeomanry.[189]

Harold died on 30 August 1928 aged 45 and is buried in St Nicholas' churchyard.

1891, 1901 & 1911 Census; St John's PR; Mrs Bibby Barrett.

Harris, James (1887-fl 1919)

Gunner 43867, Royal Garrison Artillery.

James was born in Ullenhall and baptized there on 12 June 1887, the son of Alfred and Elizabeth Harris. His father was a Labourer. James, then 13, appears in the 1901 Census as the adopted son of William and Mary Elizabeth Tomlin, who were living at Irelands Farm (then in Lapworth). In 1911 James was living as a boarder in the house of Frederick George Maine (*qv*) in Beaudesert and working as a Tree Feller.

---

189 *Herald,* 23 Sep 1904 and 18 August 1905

He had joined the Warwickshire Battery of the Royal Horse Artillery in Henley in Arden on 29 April 1908, his Attestation being witnessed by F W Harris (*qv*) and signed by Major Lord Brooke as the Attesting Officer. He was then 20, 5'6" tall with a 37" chest, and had good vision and physical development. He was medically examined in Henley on 4 May and declared fit for the Territorial Force. He attended a camp in Warwick from 19 May to 2 June 1909 but was discharged on 11 March 1910 as being "not likely to become an Efficient Soldier": no further details were given.

The *Herald* reported that he was one of nine men who left Henley on 24 August 1914 to begin their military service, James being one of three joining the Royal Artillery at Portsmouth. He enlisted on 29 August 1914 and was discharged through Sickness on 2 June 1919. A Silver War Badge (B239283) was issued to him on 23 July 1919.

British War Medal, Victory Medal and Silver War Badge.

1901 and 1911 Census; Service Record; MIC; SWB; *Herald* (28 August 1914).

Harris, Leonard Samuel (1882-fl 1919)

Sapper 275054, Royal Engineers.

Known as Leonard, he was baptised in St John's Church on 26 November 1882, the son of Frederick William Harris (*qv*) and his wife Alice. He was living with them in Henley in 1891. In 1901 he was living and working at 712 Stratford Road, Sparkhill with his brothers William and Harold. All were working as butchers, though Leonard was also described as a Carpenter. By 1911 Leonard had been married for four years and was living with his wife Elizabeth and daughters Lillian (4) and Winifred (8 months) at 30 Mickleton Road, Coventry. Both his daughters had been born in Coventry. He was working as a Carpenter and Joiner.

He was a member of the Warwickshire Yeomanry for some years before the war. Leonard enlisted in the Royal Engineers on 24 March 1917 and was discharged on 2 February 1918 at the age of 35 on the grounds of Sickness. He was issued with a Silver War Badge (323406).

British War Medal, Victory Medal and Silver War Badge.

1891, 1901 & 1911 Census; St John's PR; MIC; SWB; Mrs Bibby Barrett.

Harrison, Edward Richard (1884-fl 1919)

Private, 16th Battalion Royal Warwickshire Regiment.

He was born in Henley on 1 March 1884, the son of William Harry and Sarah Elizabeth Ann Harrison and was baptised in Temple Balsall on 13 April. In 1901 he was 17 and living in the High Street with his parents and two younger sisters, Frances Annie (14) and Amy Ellen Elizabeth (4). His father was a House Painter and Decorator and Edward was a Painter. He married Emily Jane (surname unknown) and was living with her at 159 Henley in Arden when their 9 month old daughter Frances was baptized in St John's in 1911, and he was working as a Carpenter. They had two other daughters, Edith Nancy (baptised in St John's on 26 October 1913) and Emily Grace (baptised on 16 May 1915, when he was described as a Carpenter of 16 High St).

He was 32, a jobbing builder and plumber in the High Street, when he applied for exemption before the Stratford Rural District Tribunal on 25 August 1916. He stated that he had several contracts on hand and his father was unable to give assistance: he would have to sell the business and suffer financial loss. He was also a member of the local Fire Brigade. He was given exemption to 29 September, with no further leave to appeal.[190] However, he took his case to the Warwickshire Appeal Court in October. Although he had been passed for general service by the military medical board, he had a certificate from Dr W E Nelson stating that he was not fit for work of any kind due to lead poisoning. He was referred to the Medical Board in London.[191] There he was told that his present condition was not permanent and he was passed fit for general service. Dr Nelson had seen the man the day before the Appeal Court and said that he was unable to follow his employment. Edward's appeal was dismissed and he was given 14 days to arrange his affairs.[192]

On 13 September 1918 the *Herald* reported that Private E R Harrison of 16th Battalion Royal Warwickshire Regiment had been wounded in the shoulder and was in Fushill War Hospital, Carlisle. He had been on active service since early November 1917. He had also been wounded in April last, but did not then get back to England.

British War Medal and Victory Medal.

Temple Balsall PR; 1901 & 1911 Census; *Herald* (13 September 1918).

†Hastings, Stephen (1878-1918)

Private S/407351, 2/4th Field Bakery, Army Service Corps.

Stephen Hastings was born in Coleshill in 1878, the son of Charles and Charlotte Hastings. In 1881 he was two and living in Back Lane, Coleshill with his parents and five brothers, four of whom were older than him: his father was an Agricultural Labourer. In 1891 he was 12 and living in Parkfield Road, Coleshill with his parents, an elder brother Arthur and a younger brother William: Stephen was described as a Farmer's Boy. In 1911 he was living in the High Street, Hampton in Arden with his wife Rose Anna, his son Charles Edwin (7) and his daughters Margaret (3) and Olive (2). Stephen was then working as a Journeyman Baker. His son Christopher John was baptised in St John's Church on 21 May 1916, when Stephen was described as a Baker of 10 High Street.

---

190 *Herald*, 1 September 1916
191 *Herald*, 13 October 1916
192 *Herald*, 17 November 1916

He was 38 and the bread baker for Mr J Welch of Henley, when the latter appeared before the Stratford Rural District Tribunal on 25 August 1916 and said that Hastings was indispensable to his business. Asked as to another employee, Welch said that Hastings was the man he could least afford to lose. Stephen was given seven days exemption to see if the other man joined up. At an appearance before the tribunal on 1 December 1916, Welch stated that the other man had now joined the Colours. Stephen Hastings was married with 4 children. He was given conditional exemption until the military could find a proper substitute. At the District Tribunal held on 18 January 1918, Welch said that Hastings was the backbone of his baking business. It was suggested that as Welch only baked 20 sacks of flour a week he was overstaffed, as there was another man as well as the employer. Hastings was given three months exemption, and Welch was to try to find a substitute in the meantime.

Stephen was living at 10 High Street, Henley when he enlisted at Leamington some time shortly after the end of April 1918, when he became a baker in the Army Service Corps. He died of bronchial pneumonia on 8 November 1918 in Le Havre and is buried in Ste Marie Cemetery, grave Div 62 II T 1.

Ste. Marie Cemetery, Le Havre

His widow received a letter from his commanding officer, Captain H C Bradshaw, who was writing on behalf of his fellow officers and men: Stephen was very popular with his comrades, over 100 of whom had voluntarily attended his funeral.

He had been associated with the Baptist Church in Henley and a memorial service was held for him there on Sunday, 1 December 1918. He left a widow and four children. He is also commemorated in the Baptist Church and on his wife's headstone in St Nicholas' churchyard.

British War Medal and Victory Medal.

1881, 1891 & 1911 Census; MIC; CWGC; SDGW; *Herald* (1 September & 8 December 1916, 25 January, 15 & 29 November & 6 December 1918).

Hawkes, Harry Percy (1891-1973)

Warrant Officer Class II 360607, Labour Corps; previously Squadron Quartermaster Sergeant 1462, Warwickshire Yeomanry.

He was known as Percy and was born on 7 February 1891. At the census of 1891 he was two months old and living with his parents and his grandmother

in the High Street. He was the eldest child of Harry Hawkes (1859-1952) and his wife Mary Jane (*nee* Aston) and was baptised in St John's Church on 9 June 1891: his father was then described as a Butcher. In 1901 he was living at 116 High Street, his father then being described as a Farmer, Butcher and Coal Merchant. The household had expanded considerably, comprising his parents, his sisters Dorothy Mary and Marjorie Joyce and his brother Jack (see Hawkes, John Aubrey), his grandmother and two servants. Harry Hawkes was described as a Butcher and Farmer in 1911 and Percy was described as assisting in the business. His father had served for 12 years in the Warwickshire Yeomanry and his grandfather had also served in the regiment. Percy Hawkes had two other sisters, Christine Monica and Edna Rosalind.

In November 1914 he was a Corporal in the Warwickshire Yeomanry, serving in Cromer. He left Egypt for Gallipoli with the regiment on HMT *Saturnia* on 14 August 1915, being then a sergeant. The photograph shows him in Egypt on Christmas Day, 1915. By December 1915 he was a Squadron Quarter Master Sergeant. In May 1916 he was on leave, "looking well and hardy after his exciting yeomanry experiences". When he returned to his regiment, he was wounded in action at Romani on 9 August 1916[193]. It is likely that he was transferred to the

---

193 Adderley, p 77

Labour Corps when he recovered from his wounds. He was discharged on 18 April 1919.

1914-15 Star, British War Medal and Victory Medal.

He was a butcher in the town. Percy had a real empathy with horses. His niece Mrs Jean Palmer described how she had held a horse's head while he stitched up its wounds inflicted by barbed wire when hunting: the horse remained completely still.

St John's PR; 1901 & 1911 Census; MIC; *Herald* (27 November & 10 December 1915, 19 May 1916); Mrs J L Palmer.

†Hawkes, John Aubrey (1894-1918)

2nd Lieutenant, 7th (Service) Battalion Leicestershire Regiment.

He was known as Jack and was baptised in St John's Church on 6 May 1894, the second son and the third of the six children of Harry and Mary Jane Hawkes (see Hawkes, Harry Percy for details of his family). Jack Hawkes was a great friend of A C Coldicott (*qv*).

He was a member of the VAD before enlisting. Jack Hawkes was described as a Bank Clerk at the time of the 1911 Census and was on the staff of the London City and Midland Bank in Selly Oak when war began. Shortly afterwards he joined the Warwickshire Yeomanry, being a Lance Corporal in November 1914 and rapidly being further promoted to Corporal and Sergeant. He was with the second line of the regiment, which moved to the Eastern Counties on 21 June 1915, the first line having sailed for Egypt two months earlier. Sergeant Jack Hawkes was serving with the Warwickshire Yeomanry on the East Coast in December 1915. He was a riding instructor and, despite frequent attempts to go on active service, he was retained in England due to his exceptional training ability. He also became a master of the art of musketry and was appointed an instructor in the same. Still wishing to go on active service, he stated his intention of joining the regular army as a private. His commanding officer then strongly recommended him for a commission, which he received in due course. He was posted to the 7th Battalion of the Leicestershire Regiment and went to France on 15 June 1918.

The battalion had been formed at Leicester in September 1914, as part of K2. At the time of the German Spring Offensive in March 1918, it was part of 110th Brigade, 21st Division. The Division had been engaged in confronting the enemy around St Quentin from 21 to 23 March 1918 and fought at Bapaume on the following day. During the German offensive in Flanders from 9 to 29 April, the Division fought at Messines, Bailleul, Kemmel Ridge and Scherpenberg.

Between 27 and 30 May the Division fought at the Battle of the Aisne and during the allied advance fought at Albert and Bapaume. This was followed by fighting on the Hindenburg Line in September.

After a short but eventful period of active service, Jack Hawkes was severely wounded while leading his men and died of his wounds on 11 September 1918, aged 24. His parents were advised of his death on 12 September. On 14 September his commanding officer, Lt-Col G H Sawyer told his parents by letter that Jack was wounded when leading his company and died a few hours later: the doctors did not think he suffered any pain.

"I cannot speak too highly of the work he has done while with the battalion and only quite recently I had selected him to command a company." Another letter received from Captain H R Horne of the 7th Battalion testified to his cheerfulness and efficiency. Jack Hawkes was described as being of an unassuming modesty and cheerful disposition. He made his way by his own natural abilities and everything he took up was done with thoroughness and concentration of effort.

A memorial service was held at St John's on Sunday, 22 September that was "well attended and exceedingly impressive" and was conducted by the Rector, the Revd F D Lane. The congregation was fully representative of the life of the town and included wounded soldiers and Red Cross nurses from the local hospital, under the command of Dr Nelson. He is buried in Fins New British Cemetery, Sorel-le-Grand, Somme, grave VIII B 10. An obelisk in his memory was erected in the churchyard of St Nicholas', Beaudesert, with an inscription that reads:

In ever loving memory
of
John Aubrey Hawkes
(2 Lieut Leicestershire Regiment)
killed in action in France
September 11th 1918
Interred in Fins New
British Cemetery S E of Bapaume
"Greater love hath no man than this,
that a man lay down his life for his friends"

This quotation from St John's Gospel was the text used by the Rector for his address at Jack's memorial service.

At the time of his death Jack was engaged to be married to Nancy Izod of Hall Green, Birmingham (above).

British War Medal and Victory Medal.

St John's PR; 1901 & 1911 Census; CWGC; SDGW; MIC; Adderley; James, p 60; *Herald* (10 December 1915 & 28 January 1916); Mrs L J Palmer; Mr & Mrs H N Welch.

†Hayward, William Eardley (1890-1918)

Ordinary Seaman Clyde Z/8730, Royal Naval Volunteer Reserve.

William was born in Warwick in 1890, the second son of Stephen Eardley Hayward and his wife Anne. In 1891 he was 8 months old and living at 1 Church Street, Warwick with his parents, his elder brother Benjamin and a general servant: his father was a Fancy Draper and his mother (who had been born in Henley) was a

Milliner. By 1901 the family had moved to 29 High Street, Warwick: his father was now running a Registry Office for Servants, while his mother's millinery business had expanded as she now had an Assistant Milliner living in and she had moved into hairdressing, with an assistant hairdresser also living in. By 1911 William had left home, was boarding at 57 South View Road, Sheffield and working as a Journalist.

Reporting his death, the *Herald* of 12 April 1918 recorded that William had a career in newspapers, beginning with the *Warwick Advertiser* and finishing with important positions on the editorial staff of the *Dundee Advertiser* and the *People's Friend*. He had many friends in Henley and died on 3 April 1918 in London. His health had not been good for some time and broke down under the strain. Two days after he died, his name was announced as a successful candidate for a commission. He left a widow and son. The burial service was held in the Baptist Church in Henley on Monday, 8 April 1918 and he is buried in its churchyard. Mourners included his widow, his parents and his brother Lance Corporal Benjamin Hayward.
1891, 1901 & 1911 Census; CWGC; *Herald* (12 April 1918).

Hemming, Edwin Percy (1877-1965)

512642, Canadian Army Service Corps.

He was known as Percy and was born in Henley on 18 December 1877, the son of William Hemming, a Wheelwright, and his wife Betsy. In 1881 he was living in the High Street with his parents, his brother Frederick and his sisters Ellen and Alice. In 1901 he was living at Burman House in the High Street with his parents, his brother and another sister, Gertrude. His occupation was a Wheelwright, so he was no doubt assisting his father in his business. He married in York, Ontario on 27 December 1913.

When he enlisted in the Canadian Overseas Expeditionary Force on 11 March 1916, he gave his father as his next of kin: Percy was then a widower and was employed as a Traveller. He had already served four years in the Imperial Yeomanry in England. His address at the time of his enlistment was 92 Prust Avenue, Toronto. His medical shows that he was 38, 5'6" tall and had a chest of 35". His complexion was medium, his eyes and his hair brown. He had several distinguishing marks, including a birthmark on his left forearm, several moles and a scar at the side of his right eye. The *Herald* reported in June 1916 that, having emigrated to Canada, he was serving with the Canadian forces at home or in France and had been able to pay a short visit to Henley.

He died in the UK in 1965.
1881 & 1901 Census; Canadian Attestation Paper; *Herald* (23 June 1916).

Hemming, Horace Frank (1891-fl 1919)

Private 6609 and 242168, Worcestershire Regiment.

He was born in Henley in 1891, the son of Frank R Hemming and his wife Mary Elizabeth. In 1901 Horace was nine and living in the High Street with his parents and younger sister Lilian. His father was a Tailor and Clothier and had also been born in Henley.

British War Medal and Victory Medal.

1901 Census; MIC.

Heraper, Albert James (1898-1973)

Private 39102, 2nd Battalion Loyal North Lancashire Regiment; formerly Private, Army Service Corps.

Albert Heraper was born in Birmingham on 18 April 1898, the son of George Arthur Heraper. In 1911 he was living at Rose Cottage, 22 Henley in Arden, with his grandparents Harry and Kate Brown, who had been married for 22 years. Albert was 12 and his elder sister Rose Emily (23) and younger sister Dora Evelyn (10) were also living with them. Albert was a member of the Warwick Number 11 VAD and took part in its annual inspection on 6 August 1914.

His next of kin was given as his father, George Arthur Heraper, of the George Inn, High Street, Henley when Albert had his medical at Warwick on 17 August 1916. He gave his age as 18 years and 120 days. He was a Gardener, 5'8" tall, had a 33½" chest and weighed 130 pounds. His eyesight was good, but he had a flat left foot. He joined the Army Service Corps and was posted initially to Woolwich. His early service was in the UK, being posted to Saxmundham on 25 October 1916, Basingstoke with 821 Company, 71st Divisional Train on 28 November and Colchester on 7 March 1917. He transferred to Park Royal on 6 April 1917. He sailed for Egypt on HMT *Saxon*, disembarking at Alexandria on 4 August 1917. There he was transferred to 2nd Battalion, Loyal North Lancashire Regiment. He left Egypt from Port Said on 18 May 1918 and disembarked at Marseilles on 27 May. He was admitted to hospital with severe diphtheria on 19 June 1918 and was sent back to England.

He went to Netley Hospital on 1 August 1918, where he developed influenza on 30 September. He had "several attacks of nervous tremor spreading up the body & accompanied by signs of Cardiac Distress believed to be purely of nervous origin and not of the nature of minor epilepsy or due to structural disease of the heart". On 8 October he left Netley and was transferred to Barnfield Hospital at Weston, Southampton, leaving there on 29 October 1918.

He was then posted to the Command Depot of the Loyals at Heaton Park, Manchester on 4 November and was transferred to Class Z of the Army Reserve on his demobilisation at Preston on 20 January 1919. His medical category was C2 (the same grade as when he enlisted) and his address was given as Bridge View, New Road, Henley in Arden.

He married Emma Louis Houghton at Claverdon on 12 August 1922. They emigrated to the USA in 1925, sailing from Liverpool on the *Montclare* on 17 July. He was then working as a Chauffeur. Their daughter Betty Mar was born in Seattle on 7 April 1930. He took American citizenship on 25 January 1936, when his address was 4528, 50th Avenue, Seattle. Albert returned to the UK at least twice, arriving in Southampton on the *Empress of France* on 6 June 1930 and in Liverpool on the *Empress of England* on 7 July 1958, sailing from Montreal on each occasion and travelling on his own. He lived at 98177 Seattle, Washington and died there in August 1973.

British War Medal and Victory Medal.

1911 Census; Pension Records; MIC; Passenger Lists; USA Petition for Citizenship.

Herring, Charles R (1884/85-1964)

Sapper T/1895 (formerly 562934), Royal Engineers.

Born c 1885, died in Birmingham 1964.

In 1936 Charles Richard Haden Herring was a shopkeeper at 4 High Street.

British War Medal and Victory Medal.

MIC.

Herring, Cyrenius Robert (1878-1955)

Private 467308, Labour Corps; formerly Private 2208, Warwickshire Yeomanry.

Known as Cy, he was born in Henley in Arden on 3 November 1878, the son of Robert Herring, a draper, and his wife Charlotte Anne. He was baptised at Burton Dassett on 28 September 1879. He attended the Infant Department of Henley School and transferred to the Juniors on 1 June 1885, leaving on 1 July 1892. In 1891 he was 12 and living on the west side of the High Street with his parents, two sisters, Alice Minnie (17) and Ina Margaret (14), and his elder brother Arthur William (15). Ten years later he was still living with his parents, his father being a House Agent (born in Nottinghamshire) and his mother a Draper (born in Gloucestershire): Cy was a Commercial Traveller and also living with them were his brother and two sisters: two servants, both recorded as Dressmakers, also formed part of the household.

Cy joined the Warwickshire Yeomanry before the war. He was reported safe after the torpedoing of the *Wayfarer* (he was with the main part of the regiment on the *Saturnia*) and arrived in Egypt on 11 April 1915. He is not recorded in Adderley as one of those who sailed for Gallipoli on 14 August 1915, so that he stayed in Egypt to look after the regiment's horses, as the Yeomanry went to Gallipoli dismounted. His transfer to the Labour Corps suggests that he became unfit for active service at some time.

He married Fanny Hodgkins in early 1918. They lived at North Rookery, Lowsonford (where Norman Welch stayed with them as a boy), James' Farm, Ullenhall and finally retired to a bungalow in Ullenhall.

1915 Star, British War Medal and Victory Medal.

1891 & 1901 Census; Burton Dassett PR; MIC; *Herald* (16 April 1915); H N Welch.

Hewins, William George (1885/6-fl 1919)

There are MICs for Sapper 139591, Royal Engineers and Driver 130465, Army Service Corps but it is not known which (if either) is applicable.

William was born at Clerkenwell in London, the son of George and Susannah Hewins. In 1901 he was 15, living in Upper Brailes and serving as an apprentice to a Shoeing Smith. He married Alice Mary Hunt of Brailes on 8 June 1908. They were living in a three-roomed tenement at 49 High Street, Henley in Arden in 1911. He was then 25, his wife was 26 and William was working as a Milk Man.

He founded and owned Tudor Dairies after the war and established Henley's reputation for ice cream.

British War Medal and Victory Medal.

1901 & 1911 Census; Brailes PR; MIC.

Hicks, C

Norman Welch suggested the name Clyde Hicks, but no further information has been found.

†*Hobbins, Howard (1899-1918)*

Private 44904, 2nd Battalion Royal Berkshire Regiment (Princess Charlotte of Wales's); formerly Private 42579, Hampshire Regiment.

Howard Hobbins was born in Walcote, Haselor, the son of William and Ellen Hobbins. He was one year old at the time of the 1901 census and was living in Haselor with his parents, his elder brothers Sidney (14) and Wallace (7) and his elder sister Amy (12). His father was a Quarryman. In 1911 he was the only one of their children still living with them in a three-roomed house at Ettington, near Stratford upon Avon. His parents had by then been married for 33 years and had had 9 children.

When he enlisted in Birmingham, probably in 1917, his place of residence was recorded as Henley in Arden: he lived in Mayswood Road. His battalion was serving with 25th Brigade, 8th Division. Howard died of wounds on 27 April 1918 near Villers-Bretonneux. This village in the Somme, on the road between Amiens and St Quentin, was the scene of fierce fighting when the German advance on Amiens ended in its capture by them on 23 April 1918. On the following day, 4th and 5th Australian Divisions, with units of 8th and 18th Divisions, recaptured the village.

It seems likely that Howard Hobbins was mortally wounded during its recapture. He was officially reported wounded between 20 and 27 April and only in July were his parents officially informed that he had died of his wounds. He was within a few days of his nineteenth birthday.

Howard is buried in Crucifix Corner Cemetery, Villers-Bretonneux, grave V A 8. He is also commemorated on the memorial in the Baptist Church in Henley and on his parents' gravestone in Wootton Wawen churchyard.

British War Medal and Victory Medal.

1901 & 1911 census; CGWC; SDGW; James, p 89; MIC; *Herald* (31 May & 19 July 1918).

Hodges, Donovan Thomas (1898-1970)

Private 200666, South Staffordshire Regiment.

Donovan was baptised on 1 May 1898 in St Nicholas', the son of James Edward Hodges, baker of Henley in Arden, and his wife Caroline Jane (*nee* Griffiths). In 1901 he was living in Henley with his parents and his elder brother William (*qv*), his father being described as a Baker and Confectioner; the family was still together at 257 Henley in Arden in 1911 when Donovan was at school.

He enlisted on 15 September 1914 at the age of 16½ and joined either the 2/5th or 2/6th Battalion (Territorial Force) of the South Staffordshire Regiment. Both formed part of 176th Brigade, 59th Division; they were in the Luton area in January 1915, moving to the St Albans area in July; in April 1916 they moved to Ireland, serving in Dublin and the Curragh. They saw active service in

the Easter Rebellion. The Brigade moved to Salisbury Plain in January 1917 and landed in Le Havre on 25 February 1917. On 8 November 1918 it was reported that Donovan had been wounded and missing since 3 October. His parents did not learn that he was alive until January 1919: he had been wounded in the leg and had been a POW in Germany, but was now in France and hoped to be home soon. He was discharged from the army as a consequence of his wounds on 12 April 1919 and given his Silver War Badge (B270447) on 19 August 1919.

His MIC is in the name of Private 200666, Donovan Horace Hodges of the South Staffordshire Regiment, as is his SWB.

After the war he moved into his father's business as a baker at 145 High Street. His first marriage was registered in Stratford in 1924 and his second in Worcester in 1949. His death was registered in Evesham in September 1970.

British War Medal, Victory Medal and Silver War Badge.

1901 & 1911 Census; MIC; SWB; *Herald* (11 August 16, 8 November 1918 & 17 January 1919).

Hodges, Edgar Harry (1896-1968)

Private 65065, Royal Warwickshire Regiment (MIC Edgar Hodges).

He was baptised Harry Edgar in St John's Church on 6 December 1896, the eldest child of Joseph Henry (known as Harry) and Laura Elizabeth Hodges. His birth was registered in the name of Henry Edgar Hodges. His father was a gardener, living in Henley. In 1901 Edgar (no other forename is given) was four and living in Henley with his parents and younger sister Mildred. In 1911 he was living with his parents, two younger sisters Mildred (12) and Laura (8) and his younger brother Osborne (6). The family was living at 110 Henley in Arden and also had four boarders. Edgar was working as an assistant in a butcher's shop.

The Hodges family c 1915

| | Osborne | | Laura | |
| Edgar | Laura Elizabeth | | Harry | Mildred |

On 22 September 1920 he married Beatrice Alice Wells in Sheffield: he was then 23 and Beatrice was 22. Edgar was described as a Railway Porter of 110 High Street when their son Edgar was baptised in St John's on 8 February 1921. This son did not survive, nor did their daughter Alice. Three children did survive: George Henry (born 1925), Jean (1926) and Ruth (1929). Edgar worked with the railways until he retired on 11 October 1961 after 48 years' service. He died on 27 February 1968 aged 71 and is buried with his wife in St Nicholas' churchyard.

No further details of his military service are available.

British War Medal and Victory Medal.

St John's PR; 1901 & 1911 Census; MIC; Mrs Ruth Zakis (his daughter).

†Hodges, Lawrence John Arden (1897-1917)

Able Seaman J/28634, HMS *Vala*, Royal Navy.

Lawrence Hodges was the son of Charles Samuel and Margaret Maud Hodges of High Hurst Cottages, Henley in Arden. He was born on 6 April 1897 and baptised in St John's on 16 May, his father then being a soldier. His father had died by 1911 and Lawrence was living at High Hurst with his mother (an Army Pensioner), four younger sisters and a younger brother. His mother (36) had been born in Nagpur, India; his sisters Hilda (12) and Maud (10) in Mandalay, Burma; his sister Julia (9) in Madras, India; his brother Bertie (5) in Rangoon, Burma and his youngest sister Olive (1) in Henley in Arden. Lawrence was 14 and working as

a Solicitors Clerk, but when he joined the navy was employed as a Groom and Gardener.

He joined the Royal Navy at the age of 16 on 4 November 1913 and was on the training establishment HMS *Impregnable* until 13 July 1914. The photograph shows him as a Boy on his first ship, HMS *Endymion*, a cruiser of 7,350 tons, completed in 1894, on which he served from 14 July to 27 November 1914. He subsequently served on the *Veredo* and *Cordelia*. The latter was a C-Class light cruiser launched in 1914 in which he served from 5 January to 17 June 1915. He was made an Ordinary Seaman on 4 March, when his height was 5'10", his chest 36", his hair light brown, his eyes grey and his complexion fair. Lawrence enlisted for 12 years on 6 April. After two months on *Vivid I* (a training establishment) he served on *Marlborough* from 1 October 1915 to 30 June 1916. This was an *Iron Duke*-class battleship launched in 1912, its main armament being ten 13½" guns. She fought in the Battle of Jutland, as part of the

6th Division of 2nd Battle Squadron, flying the flag of Vice Admiral Sir Cecil Burney: the other ships in the Division were *Revenge*, *Hercules* and *Agincourt*. *Marlborough* was hit by a torpedo from the German light cruiser *Wiesbaden*, which in turn was hit by gunfire from *Marlborough*. The torpedo killed two and injured two of *Marlborough's* crew.

HMS Marlborough

Lawrence was promoted to Able Seaman on 10 November 1916.

When he was killed on 21 August 1917, he was serving on HMS *Vala*, a totally different ship. *Vala* was of 1,016 tons, built in 1894 and had been a collier: she was taken over by the navy in 1915 as one of its Special Service Ships, commonly known as Q Boats. They were armed, but were to all appearances small merchant ships: they hoped to lure a U Boat to the surface where they could sink it by gunfire. In the later stages of the war U boats became suspicious of small merchant ships sailing on their own. Lawrence served on *Vala* from 1 May 1917. She was torpedoed and sunk by the German submarine UB 54 on 21 August, some 120 miles south west of the Scilly Isles on a voyage from France to Queenstown (its last reported position being latitude 47° North, longitude 9°.32' West). News of this did not reach Henley for some time: the *Herald* reported on 21 September that his mother had been informed by the Admiralty of the feared loss of the merchant ship on which he was serving and that nothing definite was yet known of his fate.

His conduct throughout his time in the navy was Very Good. He is commemorated on the Plymouth Naval Memorial, Panel 21. He was 20 years old.

1914-15 Star, British War Medal and Victory Medal.

St John's PR; 1911 Census; RN Service Record; CWGC; Tennant, p 206; *Herald* (21 September 1917).

Hodges, William James (1892-1961)

Private 1754, 14th (Service) Battalion Royal Warwickshire Regiment (1st Birmingham Battalion), later Private 352613, Labour Corps.

William was baptised on 13 November 1892 in St Nicholas' Church, the son of James Edward Hodges, baker of Henley in Arden, and his wife Caroline Jane (*nee* Griffiths). In 1901 he was living in Henley with his parents and younger brother (see Hodges, Donovan Thomas), as he was in 1911. By the latter date he was assisting in his father's business, as was his mother.

William enlisted on 18 November 1915 and "rendered much useful service in France". He was wounded in the neck and arm by shrapnel on 30 July 1916 and was sent to the Wellington Road Hospital in Liverpool. As a consequence of this he was transferred to the Labour Corps and was honourably discharged from the army on 20 October 1917. He was awarded the Silver War Badge on 20 December 1917 (283947).

He subsequently took over the bakery business from his father.

British War Medal, Victory Medal and Silver War Badge.

1901 & 1911 Census; MIC; SWB; *Herald* (11 August 1916 & 8 November 1918); W G Haytree.

Hodgkins, Alfred Richardson MM (1892-1977)

Private 435828, Canadian Overseas Expeditionary Force Infantry Battalion.

He was known as Fred and was born in Market Drayton in 1892, the only son of Alfred Henry and Fanny Margaret Hodgkins. In 1901 he was living with his parents and three sisters at Ridgwardine, Market Drayton: his father was a Farmer. By 1911 he was living with his parents and two sisters, Bertha (22) and Alice (20) at the six-roomed Park Farm in Beaudesert. Fred was assisting his father on the farm.

He later emigrated to Canada. Fred enlisted in Edmonton on 16 August 1915 at the age of 23, giving his occupation as a Farmer and stating that he had served for two years in the Warwickshire Imperial Yeomanry. He was not married, his next of kin being his father, who was living in Henley in Arden. His medical record gives his height as 6'2" and his chest measurement as 38"; he had a dark complexion, blue eyes and brown hair. He was a member of the Church of England. The *Herald* reported in June 1916 that he was serving with the Canadian forces either in the UK or in France: he had recently visited Henley, having had a few days leave. Fred was an Acting Lance Corporal in an Infantry Battalion of the Canadian Contingent when his award of the Military Medal appeared in the *London Gazette* of 16 February 1917. This award was noted in the Beaudesert Parish Meeting of 26 March 1917 and a letter of congratulation was sent by the Chairman, Revd Frank Lane.[194]

Fred went back to Canada for a short time after the war before returning to England. He sailed from Quebec on the *Victorian* of the Canadian Pacific Line and arrived in Liverpool on 19 May 1920. Fred died in Cheltenham in 1977.

Military Medal.

1901 & 1911 Census; Canadian Attestation Paper; UK Incoming Passenger List; *LG* (16 February 1917); *Herald* (23 June 1916).

Holt, George (1893-fl 1920)

Private A1419, King's Royal Rifle Corps.

George Holt was baptised in St John's Church on 5 August 1893, the son of Richard and Ellen Jane Holt (*nee* Ricketts). His father was then a labourer, living in Henley. He was living at 232 High Street in 1914 (see Holt, Harry Hugh for further details of the Holt family).

His Attestation shows that he signed up for three years with the colours at Birmingham Town Hall on 20 August 1914. At that time he was working as a Labourer (Timber Feller) in Henley. He was 5'2¼" tall and weighed 124 pounds, with a florid complexion, grey eyes and brown hair: his age was given as 20 years

---

194 Warwickshire County Record Office, CR1098/1

and 4 months. The *Herald* reported that he left Henley on 24 August, to join the KRRC. Although he was said to be fit for service when he enlisted in Birmingham, he only served for eight days, as when he reached the KRRC depot at Winchester he was declared unfit for military service and was discharged on 27 August. In May 1915 he was employed in a gun factory in Birmingham. He applied for a Silver War Badge in July 1920, but his application was not successful.

St John's PR; 1901 Census; Attestation; WW1 Pension Records; *Herald* (28 August 1914 & 21 May 1915).

†Holt, Harry Hugh (1890/1-1917)

Driver 62128, D Battery, 38th Brigade, Royal Field Artillery.

Harry Holt was born in Preston Bagot, the son of Richard and Ellen Jane Holt (*nee* Ricketts). His father was a general labourer, born in Beaudesert, his mother being born in Stratford upon Avon. In 1901 they were living in the High Street, Henley in Arden, with four of their five sons and two daughters. All five of their sons served in the Great War, Harry's youngest brother Owen also being killed (see Holt, O V C). In 1911 Harry was 21 and living at 232 Tanyard, Henley with his parents, Richard (69) and Ellen (51), his younger brother Owen (13) and younger sister Bertha (8). His parents had been married for 30 years and had 10 children, all of whom had survived. Harry was working as a Coal Carter.

Harry married Mary Edgington of Henley on 11 June 1914. He was described as a Labourer of Henley when their son Hugh Wilfred was baptised in St John's Church on 9 August 1914. He enlisted in Stratford upon Avon and was killed in action on 10 September 1917, his age being given as 28. His widow received letters from his Battery Major, his Chaplain and a comrade, testifying to the high esteem in which he had been held. He took ammunition up to the trenches on 10 September and was about to return when he was killed instantaneously by a shell: his two horses were also killed. He had joined up just after the outbreak of war and had served in France for about one year and seven months. He was expected home on leave in the same week that news was received of his death.

He is buried in Brandhoek New Military Cemetery 3, Vlamertinghe, Ypres, grave I G 9. The first cemetery at Brandhoek had opened in May 1915 and closed in July 1917, the second opened in July 1917 and closed the following month. The third cemetery opened in August 1917 and when it closed in May 1918 contained almost 1,000 burials. Brandhoek was the site of the 32nd and 44th Casualty Clearing Stations.

British War Medal and Victory Medal.

His widow was living at 61 High Street at the end of the war and subsequently married John (Jack) Robinson.

1901 & 1911 Census; MIC; CWGC; SDGW; *Herald* (21 September 1917); A O'Donnell.

Holt, J

He left Henley in Arden on 24 August 1914, to join the KRRC but no further information on him has been found.

Herald (28 August 1914).

†Holt, Owen Victor Cornelius (1897-1918)

Driver 1558, B Battery, 84th Brigade, Royal Field Artillery.

Owen Holt was born in Henley, the son of Richard and Ellen Jane Holt. He was baptised in St John's Church on 26 September 1897. His father was a general labourer, born in Beaudesert, his mother being born in Stratford upon Avon. In 1901 they were living in the High Street, Henley in Arden, with four sons and two daughters. All five of their sons served in the Great War, Owen's elder brother Harry also being killed (see Holt, Harry Hugh). In 1911 Owen was living with his parents, his brother Harry and his sister Bertha at 232 Tanyard, Henley: he was still at school.

Owen enlisted in Birmingham early in 1915 at the age of 17. In the spring of 1915 he was with the RFA on Salisbury Plain. He first went to France on 26 July 1915 and saw continuous action thereafter. He died on 11 April 1918. The first news received by his parents was a letter from his Battery Major stating that he had been seriously wounded by several pieces of shell, mostly in his chest. A later letter announced his death from wounds at 23rd Casualty Clearing Station. He is buried in Lapugnoy Military Cemetery in the Pas de Calais grave VII C 16. It was begun in September 1915 and until April 1918 the dead were brought from the Casualty Clearing Stations at Lapugnoy and Lozinghem (chiefly the 18th and 23rd). This cemetery commemorates almost 1,500 casualties of the Great War.

A joint memorial service for him and Sidney Bickley was held in St John's Church on Sunday 28 April. He was unmarried.

1914-15 Star, British War Medal and Victory Medal.

1901 & 1911 Census; MIC; CWGC; SDGW; *Herald* (21 May 1915 & 26 April 1918).

Holt, Richard MM (1896-1955)

Lance Sergeant 1705, Royal Warwickshire Regiment.

He was born in 1896 and registered as Dick, with which name he was also baptised in St John's Church on 6 June 1896, the son of Richard and Ellen Jane Holt. His father was then described as a labourer of Henley.

In his military records he is recorded and signs himself as Richard. His medical examination was in Warwick on 11 August 1914, when he was passed fit for service. He was an Agricultural Labourer, 18 years and 90 days old. His physical development was fair, and he was 5'3¼" tall, with a chest of 35". He was a member of the Church of England. On 14 August 1914 he joined the 3rd (Reserve) Battalion, Royal Warwickshire Regiment and moved to Parkhurst on the following day. He joined the 2nd Battalion with the BEF in France on 1 April 1915 after training on the Isle of Wight with the 3rd Battalion.

He had a gunshot wound in the left arm on 25 September 1915 when serving as a Maxim gunner and was treated in Number 1 General Hospital at Etretat on 27 September, leaving on 29 September for Le Havre. He rejoined his battalion on 13 October and was promoted to unpaid Lance Corporal on 19 October. He received another gunshot wound on 16 November 1915, this time in the left shoulder. He was treated initially in 22nd Field Ambulance and transferred to 6th General Hospital in Rouen on 19 November. The *Birmingham Post* of 7 December 1915 reported that he had been wounded.

On 1 January 1916 he was posted to the 7th Battalion Depot in Le Havre. On 10 March he was sent to Cinder City, a base unit of about 100,000 men near Calais: it was so named as the land on which it was built was formed by dumping the cinders from steamships onto a marsh. Later that month he was serving with 7th Battalion in France and was wounded again. On 6 August 1916 he was posted to the 16th Battalion of the Warwicks where he was made a paid Lance Corporal on 1 December. On 6 April 1917 he was sent to 23rd Casualty Clearing Station, suffering from foot problems and moved to 7th Canadian General Hospital on 8 April. After a period of recuperation in Rouen he rejoined his battalion on 1 June. He went on leave to the UK on 31 August 1917, rejoining his battalion on 14 September.

The 16th Battalion was serving with 15th Brigade, 5th Division and moved into the line on 5 October, in trenches immediately to the north of the Ypres-Menin road. Dick was promoted to Corporal in the Field on 6 October 1917. The Battalion was to go on the offensive on 9 October. Fighting was intensive. The War Diary of the Battalion notes on 7 October, "1.15 am Dressing Station blown in, killing nearly all Aid Post staff and RAMC bearers". The Battalion relieved the 1st Norfolks in the line that night, during which time one officer was killed and 39 other ranks were casualties. On 8 October they began an attack on Polderhoek Chateau, with three companies in the attack and one in reserve as a counter-attacking company. The formation of the attack was detailed: "Assaulting companies will move in three waves, the 1st wave consisting of two lines extended (normal formation), if strength does not permit, in one line. The 2nd wave will consist of sections in file in artillery formation, 50 yards behind the 1st wave. The 3rd wave preceded by Company HQs in artillery formation 75 yards behind 2nd wave." Further detailed instructions followed, including "Supplies – There will be a double issue of rations tonight".

Zero hour was 6.20 am on 9 October. Despite the thorough planning the attack failed because of the strength of the German resistance. Lt-Col Deakin commanding the Battalion wrote in the War Diary, "7.05 am – I proceeded forward to the front line and discovered that the Battalion was back in the front line from which it jumped off. It appeared that there had been heavy casualties to officers and NCOs from MGs firing from pill boxes behind the Chateau and also from the direction of Gheluvelt....Another factor in the situation was the condition of the men – they had been five days without any hot food, soaked to the skin by the heavy rain which fell and owing to the state of the ground and the constant heavy shelling, very little rest or sleep had been possible for them."

The Battalion was relieved by the 7th Battalion of the Rifle Brigade at 12.45 am on 10 October and withdrew to Ridge Wood. It had a strength of 20 officers and 514 other ranks on 5 October: by 10 October 13 officers and 291 other ranks were casualties. Dick Holt was one of ten other ranks who were awarded the Military Medal "for gallantry & devotion to duty during the operations Oct 5-10th".[195]

Dick Holt's award was published in the *London Gazette* of 25 January 1918. He was appointed a paid Lance Sergeant on 10 July 1918. He had three gold wound stripes, having gunshot wounds in the arm on 25 September 1915, in the shoulder on 16 November 1915 and in the abdomen on 23 August 1918. The last, caused by a machine gun bullet, was the most serious: he was treated first at 3rd Casualty Clearing Station, then in 2nd Canadian General Hospital before being shipped to England on the *Esscouibo* on 12 September: he was in Gatesgrove Hospital, Reading from 18 September to 4 November 1918 and was posted to the Command Depot at Prescot on 12 November 1918.

On Army Form Z22 (Statement as to Disability) completed at Number 1 Dispersal Unit, Chiseldon, his disability was given as a gunshot wound in the abdomen. It was stated that no documents were available relating to his disability. He had a scar twelve inches long extending to the left from his umbilicus. The scar itself was fair, but his abdominal muscles were generally weak; he had a slight hernia near the wound in the umbilical region. He complained of being unable to lift anything. His appetite was good, his bowels regular and his general condition was good. The degree of his disability was assessed as 20%. He had been involved in farming before joining the army and his last employer was Mrs Beechman of Henley. His next of kin were his parents of 232 High Street and his elder brother William of Moreton Morrell.

Dick was transferred to the Special Reserve on demobilisation on 2 March 1919 with a "Very Good" character, being "a sober, honest and reliable NCO". He was given a gratuity of £15 and an award of £37 for the gunshot wound in his abdomen.

He was a member of the Fire Brigade in 1919. Two daughters were baptised at St Nicholas' in the early 1920s, when he was a labourer with the GWR and living at 61 High Street. His wife was Daisy Irene. He was killed in a railway accident on 12 April 1955 and is buried in St Nicholas' churchyard.

---

195 Lt-Col G Deakin, *War Diary of 16th Battalion Royal Warwickshire Regiment 3 – 10 October 1917*

Military Medal, 1914-15 Star, British War Medal and Victory Medal.

St John's PR; 1901 Census; Service Record; MIC; *Herald* (21 May & 1 October 1915, 24 March 1916 & 26 April 1918).

Holt, William Richard (1883-fl 1919)

Royal Army Medical Corps.

William was the eldest son of Richard Holt, Labourer of Whitley, and his wife Ellen Jane. He was baptised on 28 January 1883 in St Nicholas, Beaudesert. In 1901 he was living in the household of John Mitchell, a Brewer of Rowington, and serving as a Groom. By 1911 he was a Domestic Chauffeur, one of ten servants living in The Stables, Moreton Hall, Warwickshire.

The *Herald* recorded that he had volunteered his services and that he was with the RAMC. He was serving in England in April 1918. As no MIC has been found for him, it is likely that he did not leave the UK.

St Nicholas' PR; 1901 & 1911 Census; *Herald* (21 May 1915 & 24 March 1916).

†Hopkins, Edward (1894-1915)

Private 11466, 9th (Service) Battalion Royal Warwickshire Regiment.

Edward Hopkins was baptised in St John's Church on 13 August 1894, the second son of John and May Ann Hopkins of 21 High St, Henley in Arden. His father was a farm labourer, aged 34 in 1901 and his wife was ten years older; their elder son James (*qv*) was two years older than Edward. In 1911 Edward was living with his parents and was working as a Boot Maker's Apprentice. He was a member of Warwick Number 11 VAD and scored 80% in the examinations held in the autumn of 1914. He was also a member of the choir of St John's Church and of the Society of Foresters. Prior to joining the army, he was apprenticed to Oliver James (*qv*), who had a boot and shoe shop in Henley.

Edward enlisted at Stratford upon Avon. He was a member of D Company, 9th Battalion, Royal Warwickshire Regiment. The 9th Battalion was formed at Warwick in September 1914. It was initially stationed on Salisbury Plain as part of 39th Brigade, 13th Division. After brief periods at Basingstoke and Blackdown, near Aldershot, it sailed from Avonmouth for Gallipoli on 24 June 1915. 13th Division arrived in Gallipoli in July and relieved 29th Division at Helles. It moved back to Mudros at the end of July, but on 5 August returned to Gallipoli via Anzac Cove.

Edward Hopkins died of wounds on 8 October 1915, aged 21, on board HMT *Nevassa* and was buried at sea. He is commemorated on the Helles Memorial, which lists the names of over 20,000 men who have no known grave or who were buried at sea.

He was "a smart, promising and courteous young fellow and had deservedly won many friends by his good qualities". A Memorial Service was held for him in St John's Church on Sunday, 24 October 1915. The church was crowded and a wreath was hung in his former place in the choir stalls. Those attending the service

included the High Bailiff (Dr Nelson), members of the Henley Detachment of the Red Cross Society, members of the Society of Foresters and several soldiers from the local hospital.

He had made his will on 8 August 1915, leaving "the set of volumes of *The Great War* also my watch and the photographs of myself and writing desk to my fiancée Miss G Smith, New Cottage, Warwick Road, Stratford on Avon....and I give the remaining part of my belongings to my mother Mrs J Hopkins, 21 High Street, Henley in Arden".

1914-15 Star, British War Medal and Victory Medal.

1901 & 1911 Census; MIC; CWGC; SDGW; Will; *Herald* (22 & 29 October 1916).

Hopkins, James (1892-fl 1919)

Possibly Private 201993, Royal Warwickshire Regiment.

There are 108 MICs in the name of James Hopkins, so it has not been possible to identify his army record with any certainty.

James was born in Henley in 1892. In 1901 he was 8 and living with his family in Henley (see Hopkins, Edward for details of his family). He was reported as serving his country in October 1915.

The above Private Hopkins is the likeliest of the possible candidates, as he was in the same regiment as his younger brother and would have been, as was the above soldier, 25 when he was discharged from the army on 18 March 1918. He had enlisted on 11 December 1915 and was discharged after being wounded. He was issued with the Silver War Badge (371237).

British War Medal, Victory Medal and Silver War Badge.

1901 Census; *Herald* (22 October 1915).

Horsley, Walter Geoffrey (1899-1963)

Private 44917, Royal Berkshire Regiment; formerly Private 42846, 2nd Battalion Hampshire Regiment.

Known as Geoff, he was born in Henley. In 1901 he was living there with his parents Walter John and Louisa Anne Horsley: he was still doing so in 1911 when they were living at 112 Henley in Arden (see Horsley, Walter John for details of his family). He went to school in Henley from 1906 to 1912, when he went to work as a Garden/Yard Boy, being paid three shillings a week and his food. He later worked for Johnson's Coaches as a driver. When he moved to Coventry, he worked for the Coventry Gauge and Tool Company in that capacity.

Geoff enlisted on 18 April 1917 and was home on leave in November 1917. He was one of "several Henley boys" on Salisbury Plain in January 1918. In August 1918 he was seriously wounded. He was reported as progressing favourably in September, but was going to be bed-ridden for some considerable time. He was treated in the Royal Canadian Hospital in Tapslow, Buckinghamshire and subsequently moved to Stratford upon Avon Hospital. Mrs Horsley stated that he had a wound in his thigh big enough to put your fist in. He was discharged on 19 August 1919 and given his Silver War Badge (B286861) on 18 September 1919.

Geoff had some rehabilitation as a carpenter. He married Claudia Russell in St Mark's Church, Coventry in 1926. They lived in Coventry, where they had two daughters, Kathleen (born 1927) and Margaret (1929). He never limped, but even at the seaside he would not be seen without his trousers.

British War Medal, Victory Medal and Silver War Badge.

1901 & 1911 Census; MIC; SWB; *Herald* (30 November 1917, 11 January, 30 August & 20 September 1918); Mrs Horsley (his niece by marriage); Mrs Kathleen Dunkley (his daughter).

Horsley, Walter John (1872-1941)

Private 360605, Labour Corps; formerly Private 2116, Warwickshire Yeomanry.

Walter John Horsley was born in Wootton Wawen in 1872, the son of John and Mary Ann Horsley. In 1891 he was living with his parents on the west side of the High Street in Henley; his father was a Gardener and he was employed as a Butcher's Labourer. In 1901 he was living in Henley with his wife Louisa Anne (whose maiden name had also been Horsley), their daughters Florence and Gladys and their son Walter Geoffrey (*qv*). He was then a Wine & Spirits Warehouseman. In 1911 he was living at 112 Henley in Arden with his wife, their son Walter

Geoffrey, their daughters Gladys Evelyn (10), Louisa Ethel (2) and their other sons Ernest Edward (8), Harold John (6) and Herbert James (4): he was then working as a Groom at a Livery Stable and had been married for 14 years. He was described as a Labourer of Henley when five of his children were baptised in St John's Church on 15 October 1913 (Gladys Evelyn, Harold John, Herbert James, Louisa Ethel and Stephen George). They had ten children in all, the last being born in 1920.

John was a member of the Warwickshire Yeomanry. He was part of the main body of the regiment which embarked from Avonmouth on HMT *Saturnia* on 11 April 1915, arriving in Alexandria on 24 April 1915. He left Alexandria with the regiment for service in Gallipoli on 14 August of that year. Adderley records that he was the cook. His name does not appear in the casualty lists in Adderley, so that it is likely to have been his age which resulted in his transfer to the Labour Corps.

John Horsley, his wife and nine children outside their house in the High Street before he left to go to Egypt in April 1915. His eldest son Geoffrey is standing at the back on the right

He was a member of the Henley Fire Brigade in 1919. He died at 215 High Street in 1941.

1914-15 Star, British War Medal and Victory Medal.

St John's PR; 1891, 1901 & 1911 Census; MIC; Adderley; Mrs Kathleen Dunkley (grand-daughter).

†Horsnett, Maurice Edward (1898-1917)

Private TR/8/1449, 13th Battalion Royal Warwickshire Regiment.

Maurice Horsnett was born in Fulbroke, Hampton Lucy, the youngest son of Edward and Eliza Horsnett. In 1901 the family was living at Sherbourne Hill, Hampton Lucy, his father being a Carter on a farm. Maurice (spelled Morris in the census record) was the youngest of three boys (his elder brothers being Ernest and Harry) and had six older sisters (Emma, Elizabeth, Ellen, Kate, Ruth and Beatrice). He has not been found in the 1911 Census, by which time his mother had died. His widowed father was then working as a Farm Labourer and living with his daughters Kate and Ruth at Blackhill in Snitterfield. Maurice became a member of St John's choir and of the Boy Scouts in Henley and gave his residence as Henley when he joined the 13th (Reserve) Battalion of the Royal Warwickshire Regiment at Stratford upon Avon. The 13th Battalion had been formed as a Service battalion in February 1915 and in April 1915 became a 2nd reserve battalion in 8th Reserve Brigade, located at Swanage in May 1915 and at Blandford in October. On 1 September 1916 it became 33rd Training Reserve Battalion in 8th Reserve Brigade at Wool. Maurice died on Salisbury Plain, where he had been training, on 8 April 1917 at the age of 18. His body was sent home at the request of his relatives and he is buried on the south side of St Nicholas' Church, Beaudesert. His tombstone reads:

TR8 1449 Private
M Horsnett
33rd Training Reserve Bn
8th April 1918 Age 18
Come unto me ye weary
and I will give you rest

A full choral service was held in St John's when he was buried on 15 April. Mourners included his father (his mother seems to have died by this time) Private and Mrs Payne (sister and brother-in-law), three other sisters and one brother. 1901 census; CWGC; SDGW; James, p 48; Herald (20 April 1917).

†Huggard, Charles Evan (1877-1915)

Sergeant 5768, 3rd Battalion East Yorkshire Regiment.

Charles was born on 22 October 1877 in Quanby, Leicestershire the second son of Evan and Charlotte Huggard. In 1881 Charles was living with his parents at Wykeham near Scarborough and in 1891 they were living at Dingley near Market Harborough. At the time of the 1911 Census Charles was staying with his parents in a four roomed house in Beaudesert, was 34 and was one of three of their seven children to have survived. He was described as a Colour Sergeant in the Army. His father Evan died in Henley on 27 June 1914 at the age of 67; he had been gardener to the Misses Knight at "their interesting new residence" of Brook End, New Road, and had at one time been gardener to the Marquis of Hertford at Ragley Hall.

Charles was a professional soldier, having enlisted on 14 July 1898 in the 1st Battalion of the East Yorkshire Regiment. He served in the South African campaign and held the Long Service and Good Conduct Medals. In 1914 Charles was serving with the 3rd Battalion (a reserve battalion) and was stationed at Hedon near Hull. He contracted pneumonia while on service and died in hospital at Killingbeck, Leeds on 10 May 1915, aged 38. He was buried in Leeds (Lawns Wood) Cemetery. His widowed mother was then living at The Limes, Ella Street, Hull.

Queen's Medal with two clasps, King's Medal with two clasps, Long Service Medal and Good Conduct Medal.

Census 1881, 1891 & 1911; CWGC; SDGW; de Revigny Vol 2, p 174; *Herald* (3 July 1914 & 28 May 1915).

Huggard, Cyril Godfrey (1894-1923)

Sergeant 3516, 2nd South Midland Field Artillery Brigade; formerly Sergeant 9632, 1st Battalion East Yorkshire Regiment.

Cyril was born in Henley in Arden, the son of Sydney Godfrey Huggard and his wife Sarah Ann (see Huggard, Leslie Sydney for details of his family). He was baptised at St John's Church on 25 March 1894. In 1911 he was living at 235 Henley in Arden with his parents, elder sister Winifred and younger brother Gordon and was working as a Builder's Clerk.

He joined the East Yorkshire Regiment as a regular soldier on 26 April 1911. The 1st Battalion of the East Yorkshire Regiment was with 18th Brigade, 6th Division and landed at St Nazaire on 10 September 1914, making him one of the Old Contemptibles. Cyril was seriously wounded shortly afterwards and returned to hospital in England. He had suffered a severe bullet wound in the right arm, while carrying dispatches under trying conditions. The wound was above the elbow and his arm had to be amputated.

He progressed slowly, the severity of his wounds being such that careful nursing was required before he could feel anything like his old self. He was visited by his immediate family and friends. After a long and tedious convalescence his health improved, but he was discharged from the East Yorkshire Regiment on 10 May 1915 as a consequence of his wounds. He joined the 2nd South Midland Field Artillery Brigade as an instructor on 1 July 1915.

In August 1915 he married Gladys Mary Plummer, formerly of Henley in Arden, in Southam: the wedding had been postponed because of the war, as the banns had been read in St John's Church in July 1914.

Cyril was discharged from the army at Bulford on 29 September 1916, "being no longer physically fit for further War Service". He was then 24, 5'8" tall, with grey eyes and black hair. His military character was "Very Good"; he was a clerk by trade and was intending to live at Poplar View, Henley in Arden.

A Silver War Badge (714) was issued to him on 10 October 1916 as a result of his discharge from the East Yorkshire Regiment. He was given another Silver War Badge (21961) on 10 February 1917 following his discharge from the RFA.

In 1921 he applied for the position of Clerk to the Parish Council at a salary of £130 per annum and was one of three candidates interviewed by the Council.

He was unsuccessful, losing on the casting vote of the Chairman (Councillor G Busby), the position being given to Mr F Collins of Stratford upon Avon (Minutes 11 and 18, April 1921).

Cyril died on 28 December 1923 in Warneford Hospital, Leamington Spa shortly before his 30th birthday. He had been living at the Post Office in Southam and left an estate of £1,207.2s.6d. Probate was granted to his executors, John Plummer groom and Frederick Plummer commercial clerk (probably his brothers-in-law) on 6 February 1924.

1914 Star with clasp, British War Medal, Victory Medal and Silver War Badge (2). 1901 & 1911 Census; Pension Records; MIC; SWB; National Probate Calendar 1861-1941; *Herald* (6 November & 11 December 1914, 9 July & 13 August 1915).

Huggard, Gordon Cuthbert (1897-1952)

Flying Officer, Royal Air Force; formerly 2nd Lieutenant, Oxford & Bucks Light Infantry.

He was baptised in St John's on 28 February 1897, the son of Sydney Godfrey Huggard and his wife Sarah Ann (see Huggard, Leslie Sydney for details of his family). Gordon was living with his parents, elder sister Winifred and elder brother Cyril at 235 Henley in Arden in 1911 and was working as a Cycle Repairer. He enlisted in the 15th Battalion of the Royal Warwickshire Regiment in October 1914 and was transferred to the Oxford & Bucks Light Infantry when he was commissioned in 1915. He was best man at the wedding of his elder brother Cyril Godfrey Huggard in August 1915. The *London Gazette* of 2 April 1918 noted his transfer as a Flying Officer to the RFC.

He applied for his war medals on 12 February 1921, possibly also for the 1914-15 Star, for which his MIC specifically notes that he was ineligible. At that time he was serving with 31 Squadron RAF at Mhow in India.

He died in Gosport, Hampshire in 1952.

British War Medal and Victory Medal. 1901 & 1911 Census; MIC; *LG* (2 April 1918); *Herald* (6 November 1914 & 13 August 1915).

Huggard, Leslie Sydney (1892-1960)

Private 8991, 1st Battalion Coldstream Guards.

He was baptised in St John's Church on 20 November 1892, the eldest son of Sydney Godfrey Huggard (born in the Isle of Wight) and his wife Sarah Ann (born in Henley). His father was a postman. In 1901 he was living in Henley with his parents, three elder sisters and two younger brothers (see Huggard, Cyril Godfrey and Huggard, Gordon Cuthbert). His parents were then operating a laundry business from their home. His father had died by the beginning of the war.

Leslie was in the Regular Army and in 1911 was stationed at the Guards' Depot in Caterham. He went to France with his Battalion on 13 August 1914, being part of 1st Guards Brigade, 1st Division. One of the Old Contemptibles, he was wounded in the left thigh at the Battle of Mons and in November 1914 was in hospital in the Midlands, where family and friends visited him. His brother Cyril was wounded at about the same time. Leslie's wound healed relatively quickly and he hoped to be able to return to the front at the end of January or in early February 1915. The *Herald* reported that he had returned to barracks in January 1915. He was soon back in the front line, as he was wounded again (shot through the jaw) in July 1915. The Regimental Archivist of the Coldstream Guards has been unable to find his records.

He married Florence Chesters in Watford in 1918 and was a Police Constable in Henley in Arden when their son Norman Leslie was baptised on 6 November 1921 in St Nicholas'.

Leslie died in Scarborough in 1960.

1914 Star with clasp, British War Medal and Victory Medal.

St John's PR; 1901 & 1911 Census; MIC; *Herald* (6 November & 11 December 1914, 22 January & 9 July 1915).

†Ingram, Harold MM (1891-1918)

Private 8242, 2nd Battalion Coldstream Guards.

Harold Ingram was born in Henley, the second son of Joseph Thomas and Clara Ingram. They were living in the High Street at the time of the 1901 Census. Joseph Ingram was a carpenter, aged 47, and had been born in Stratford upon Avon. His wife Clara was also 47 and had been born in Walsall. They had five daughters, Clara (13), May (12), Annette (7), Ada (5) and Grace (3) and three sons, Cyril (10), Harold (9) and Albert Edward (2 months) all of whom were born in Henley.

Harold Ingram was a regular soldier, enlisting in the Coldstream Guards on a short Service engagement (3 years with the Colours and 9 years in the Reserve). He joined in Birmingham on 4 January 1909, when he was 18 years and 2 months old: he had worked as a Brass Filer. He had his medical on the same day, his height being just over 5'8½", his weight 136 lbs and his chest fully expanded was 36". Other details gave his complexion as fresh, his eyes grey, his hair brown and he was a member of the Church of England. He went to the Guards Depot at Caterham Barracks on 12 January 1909. He was awarded a 3rd Class Certificate of Education on 5 February 1909 and passed a class of instruction in swimming in 1910. On 14 October 1910, he extended his period of service with the Colours to 7 years. The 1911 Census found him serving with the 2nd Battalion in Marlborough Lines, Aldershot.

Harold served in the UK until 11 August 1914, being made a Lance Corporal on 8 August, just before he left the UK. He then served with the British Expeditionary Force in France and Flanders from 12 August 1914 until his death. He was a member of the 2nd Battalion Coldstream Guards, which landed at Le Havre as part of 4th Guards Brigade, 2nd Division. He was thus one of the Old Contemptibles. On 20 August 1915 his battalion transferred to 1st Guards Brigade, Guards Division.

His initial record with the battalion was very successful, as he was promoted to Corporal on 7 April 1915, to Lance Sergeant on 14 April 1915 and to Sergeant on 17 October 1915. His final promotion was to Acting Company Quarter Master Sergeant on 20 September 1916. Harold won the Military Medal for bravery in the field in 1916 (*London Gazette* 16 November 1916). He ceased to be Acting CQMS on 4 September 1917 and on 12 February 1918 he was reduced to the rank of Private for inefficiency. It may well be wondered what brought this about, but it is quite likely that after 3½ years in a front line regiment which had suffered heavy casualties, he was mentally and perhaps physically shattered. The majority of the men with whom he had gone to France in August 1914 had by this time been killed or maimed. Harold served a further 7 months with the regiment in France before he died of wounds received in action on 27 September 1918, only some six weeks before the end of the war.

Although his military record gives his date of death as 27 September 1918, the Commonwealth War Graves Commission gives the date as 28 September. He is buried in Grevillers British Cemetery, grave XIV A 19. Grevillers is in the Pas de Calais, three kilometers west of Bapaume.

Grevillers British Cemetery

A war cemetery had been established there in March 1917, but in March 1918 the village was lost to the Germans during their Spring Offensive. Grevillers was recaptured on 24 August 1918. In September, the 34th, 49th and 56th Casualty

Clearing Stations came to the village and used the cemetery again. Harold Ingram died in 56th CCS. His parents must have died by this time, as his next of kin were his brothers Joseph, James, Cyril and Harry and his married sister Clara Daykins, the address given being 72 Dugdale Street, Dudley Road, Birmingham.

Military Medal, 1914 Star with clasp, British War Medal and Victory Medal.

1901 & 1911 Census; CWGC; SDGW; MIC; James, p 41; Army Form B217 (Coldstream Guards Archives); *LG* (16 November 1916).

James, Oliver (1882-fl 1934)

Private 436506, Labour Corps, formerly Private 21291, Coldstream Guards.

He was born in King's Heath (then in Worcestershire) in March 1882 and in 1901 was living with his parents at 375 Ladypool Road, Balsall Heath: his father was away, as his mother Sarah is shown as head of the household. Also living there were his elder brother Ernest and elder sister Beatrice. He was married in the Registry Office, King's Norton and by 1911 had been married for 9 years: he was living and had his business at The Old Bank House, 115 High Street with his wife Elizabeth Minnie James; also living with them was Frederick W P Hemming, a Law Clerk. Oliver was then a Bootmaker. He was an occasional singer of comic songs at entertainments held in the Public Hall. A member of the Warwick Number 11 VAD, he scored 70% in the examinations held in the autumn of 1914.

In 1914 he was still a Bootmaker at The Old Bank House in the High Street. He was first attested at Stratford upon Avon on 18 November 1915 when he stated that he had served 4 years with the Warwickshire Yeomanry. His was then 33 years and 234 days old, his height 5'9", his chest 38". He was transferred to the Army Reserve on that date. He asked for exemption in May 1916 at the Stratford Tribunal, through his employers Messrs T R Bird and Co. Oliver was said to be mainly responsible for boot repairing and for maintaining the machinery. The Chairman, Charles Couchman, asked if it would be better if people bought new boots rather than have them repaired. Oliver was given exemption until 30 June 1916. His employers appealed again in September. Oliver had presented himself for service in accordance with the Tribunal's earlier decision, but had not been passed and had been told to present himself again in three months. Having done so, he had been passed for general service, although he was in the same condition as he had been previously.

A director of the firm presented two medical certificates in respect of James and his case was adjourned *sine die* to allow him to go before the Medical Appeal Board in London. The Board classified him as fit for general service and when his case came before the Tribunal again in November 1916 Mr F J Whitely of Redditch appeared for T R Bird Ltd claiming that repairing boots and shoes was a certified occupation. Bird's had purchased the business, which originally belonged to James, and the shop was managed by Mrs James. James' time was taken up almost entirely in repair work, repairing 80 to 90 pairs each week. It was stated that there were three other boot repairers in Henley. James was granted two week's exemption and Whitely stated his intention to appeal.

There is no record of the appeal and Oliver enlisted at Warwick on 3 January 1917, his medical category being A (despite having failed to pass a medical the previous year). He was posted to the Coldstream Guards at Caterham on 11 January, but after spending 32 days in hospital at Caterham from 27 June to 28 July 1917 suffering from DAH (Diffuse Alveolar Haemorrhage) he was discharged to light duties. He was transferred to the Labour Corps on 3 November and posted to 620 Agricultural Company of the Labour Corps at Budbrook Barracks, Warwick on 23 November 1917. At Fovant in Wiltshire on 24 March 1919 he stated that he did not claim to be suffering from any disability due to his military service and was given 28 days leave prior to being discharged. He was demobilized at Nottingham on 22 April 1919 with a good character and again transferred to the Army Reserve. When he returned from the war, he went back to the boot and shoe business.
1901 & 1911 Census; Army Service Record; *Herald* (2 June, 29 September & 24 November 1916).

Jamieson, William Casildo (1878-fl 1919)
Corporal M2/223359, Royal Army Service Corps.

He was born in Landport, Hampshire, the son of William J Jamieson, a Seaman, and his wife Sarah. In 1881 he was living at his maternal grandmother's with his parents and two younger sisters. His name has not been found in the 1891, 1901 or 1911 census. He married Florence Emma Small at King's Norton Register Office on 5 November 1898.

William was attested at Stratford upon Avon on 12 November 1915 when his age was given as 37 years and 213 days, his address as the White Swan Hotel, Henley in Arden and his occupation as Licensed Victualler (to which Driver was subsequently added). His height was 5'7" and his chest 38½".

In August 1916 he was the licensee of the White Swan and asked for conditional exemption on the grounds that serious hardship would ensue if he were called up. The military representative thought he should go, but Jamieson said the house would be difficult for his wife to manage. He admitted his wife had done so during his own illness, the Chairman commenting that this had been at the busiest time of year. He was given a final exemption of one month. In October he appeared before the Henley Bench, applying for the transfer of the licence for the White Swan into the name of his wife, Florence Emma Jamieson, as he had been called up for military service.

He joined the Army Service Corps on 18 September 1916. William was given a Medical Category of A1 and sailed from Southampton on the SS *Viper* on 12 January 1917, arriving in Rouen on 16 January. He was posted to the 2nd ASC Repair Shops on 28 January, re-classified as a Wheeler Class I on 10 February and transferred to 1st Base Motor Transport Depot on 12 February. He had a number of postings within the RASC in 1917 and was on leave from 6 to 20 January 1918. On his return he was promoted to paid Acting Corporal and subsequently to Corporal on 20 May 1918. He had another period of leave from 1 to 15 December 1918, later extended to 26 December. In April 1919 he was in 44th Casualty Clearing Station in Cologne suffering from Impetigo. On 11 July 1919 at Cologne he acknowledged that he was not suffering from any disability due to his military service. He was transferred to Class Z Army Reserve from Number 1 Dispersal Unit at Fovant on 13 August 1919 after a month's leave with a military character of Very Good: he was regarded as sober, reliable and intelligent.

After the war he became Captain of the Fire Brigade in 1919: it had been stationed at the White Swan for some years. He was elected as the member for Henley to the Stratford Rural District Council on 8 December 1919, in a straight fight against H Sinclair Brown.

British War Medal and Victory Medal.

1881 Census; Service Record; MIC; *Herald* (12 December 1919).

Johnson, Herbert Winford (1891–fl 1919)

Private 20068, Royal Warwickshire Regiment.

He was born in Loughborough in 1891 and was living at 137 High Street when he signed his Attestation at Stratford upon Avon on 5 December 1915. Herbert was working as a Book Keeper and was put on the Army Reserve, not being mobilized until 21 June 1916.

He served in the UK until he went to France on 30 November 1916 and was posted to the 10th Battalion of the RWR on 11 December. He served in France until 15 April 1917 when he returned to the Home Depot. He was transferred to the 3rd Battalion on 9 July 1917 and to the 9th Battalion on 10 August when he left for Mesopotamia. Herbert served there until 26 December 1918 when he returned to the UK. He was posted back to the 3rd Battalion on 19 February 1919 and demobilized on 26 September of that year.

British War Medal and Victory Medal.

MIC; Service Record.

Jones, Ernest

He left Henley in Arden on 24 August 1914, to join the Army Service Corps at Woolwich, but no further information on him has been found.

Herald (28 August 1914).

Lane, Kenneth Westmacott (1893-1954)

Lieutenant, Royal Engineers; formerly 2nd Lieutenant, 1/2nd South Midland Battery, Royal Field Artillery (TA).

He was born in Oxford on 16 July 1893, the only son of the Revd Francis Dalrymple Lane and his wife Annie Elizabeth Graham Lane. In 1901 the family was living in Kidderminster: it moved to Henley when Francis Lane became Rector of the joint parish of Beaudesert and Henley. His father then moved to Clifton on Dunsmore and Kenneth was living at the Vicarage there in 1911 with his parents and a servant. He entered Rugby School in September 1907 as a Town Foundationer, leaving in 1912 to go up to Balliol College, Oxford as a Williams Exhibitioner. He did not formally take his BA until 1917, having left Oxford in July 1915 when he joined the Midland Brigade of the Royal Field Artillery as a 2nd Lieutenant. He served with them in France in 1915 and 1916. The *Herald* reported on 5 May 1916 that he had been dangerously wounded and his father went to visit him shortly afterwards: Kenneth was later reported to be out of danger and making good progress. He was promoted Lieutenant on 1 July 1917 and was attached to the Ministry of Munitions.

He married in 1918 and had two sons. He was an Analytical Chemist and went to Hong Kong in 1920 as Assistant Analyst with the government. Kenneth later went into teaching and was Physics Master at the Imperial Service College, Windsor in 1926, Science Master at Clayesmore School in 1927 and Assistant Master at Weymouth College in 1930, becoming Senior Science Master there in 1933. He published two novels, writing under the name of Keith West: *Bamboo* in 1931 and *Hanging Waters* in 1933. He later lived at Winderton, Brailes and died in 1954.

1915 Star, British War Medal and Victory Medal.

1901 & 1911 Census; MIC; Higginbotham, pp 303, 545; Elliott, p 333; *Herald* (5, 12 & 19 May 1916).

† Long, Frederick Ernest (1882-1914)

Private 6922, 1st Battalion Royal Warwickshire Regiment.

He was born in Henley in 1882, the son of Thomas and Polly Long. No Census record has been traced, but he was living in Birmingham when he enlisted in Warwick. CWGC records that his parents were living in Pretoria Road, Bordesley Green, Birmingham and his widow Beatrice Mary Mottram Long was living at

Prowse Point Military Cemetery

1, Third Avenue, Bordesley Green. He went to France on 22 October 1914 and was killed in action on 3 December 1914, aged 32. He is buried in Prowse Point Military Cemetery (some 7 miles south of Ypres), grave II A 3.

1914 Star with clasp, British War Medal and Victory Medal.

MIC; CWGC, SDGW.

Lowe, Arthur (1881-fl 1919)

There are many hundreds of MICs in the name of Arthur Lowe, but the two most likely are Private 15301, Arthur Lowe, Royal Warwickshire Regiment and Private 10638, Arthur Lowe, Royal Warwickshire Regiment. The former was awarded the British War Medal and Victory Medal. The latter had enlisted on 16 January 1915, landed in France on 19 August 1915 and was discharged on 19 August 1916, having been wounded: he was awarded the British War Medal, Victory Medal and Silver War Badge (118434).

Arthur was baptised in St John's on 4 December 1881, the son of John and Harriet Lowe of Henley, on the same day as his sister Annie. His father was a Carpenter. In 1901 he was 19 and living in the High Street with his parents, his brothers George (31) and Harry (12) and his sister Annie (25). He was a House Painter.

Arthur married Emily Arthur of Henley in St John's on 8 October 1910. In 1911 they were living at 151 Henley in Arden and had a boarder. Arthur was still working as a House Painter. In 1916 they were living in Droitwich House in the High Street. Arthur Lowe was a member of the Fire Brigade in 1919.

> Children: Arthur Harry, baptised St John's Church 17 September 1911
> James Sidney, baptised 29 November 1914
> Frank, baptised 6 February 1916
> Mona Kathleen Edith, baptised 26 October 1919

Henley PR; 1901 and 1911 Census; MICs.

†Lowe, Frederick Ernest (1881-1918)

Private T/306108, Mechanical Transport Company, 35th Motor Ambulance Convoy, Royal Army Service Corps.

He was born in Henley in 1881 and the 1891 Census shows him living on the west side of the High Street with his parents Thomas and Lucy and three elder brothers, Thomas (18), William (16) and Joseph (13). His father was a General Labourer. By 1901 Frederick had moved to Nuneaton, was working as a General Labourer and was one of three boarders at 18-19 Upper Abbey Street. He was living at 2 Windsor Street, Chilvers Coton, Nuneaton in 1911, by which time he had been married for six years to his wife Kate and had a son Reginald Jesse (6), a daughter Agnes Annie (3) and another son Bertram Ernest (3 months). Frederick was working as a Fireman. He was still living in Nuneaton when he enlisted there.

Jerusalem War Cemetery

He was serving with the RASC when he died in Egypt on 12 July 1918 and is buried in the Jerusalem War Cemetery, grave V 4.

CWGC records his next of kin as Mrs S Smith (formerly Lowe) of 51 Princess Street, Nuneaton.

British War Medal and Victory Medal.

1891, 1901 & 1911 Census; MIC; CWGC; SDGW.

Lowe, Harry (1888-fl 1919)

Private 1743, Royal Warwickshire Regiment.

He was baptised in St John's on 12 August 1888, the son of John and Harriet Lowe of Henley. His father was a carpenter. In 1901 he was 12 and living with his family in the High Street (see Lowe, Arthur for details of his family). He was still living with his parents at 56 Henley in Arden in 1911, together with his elder brother George and his sister Annie. His father and George were butchers and Annie was also assisting in the business. His mother was a Laundress and Harry was working as a House Painter.

He joined the RWR and went overseas in 1916. The *Birmingham Post* of 4 September and 17 October 1916 reported that he was suffering from shell shock and that of 29 October 1917 that he had been wounded. Early in 1918 much concern was caused on his account as he was reported missing after the heavy fighting resulting from the German Spring Offensive. News was then received at the end of April that, after several perilous experiences, he was safe and well and had rejoined his unit. He later took advantage of a period of rest to play various games: he captained a hockey team, the other members being American, and succeeded in winning a cup.

He was a member of the Fire Brigade in 1919. In August 1919 he was chosen as captain of the Forest of Arden football team.

British War Medal and Victory Medal.

1901 & 1911 Census; St John's PR; MIC; *Herald* (3 May & 20 September 1918, 15 August 1919).

Maine, Frederick George (1885-1961)

Private 5110, 2/7th Durham Light Infantry.

He was known as Fred and was born in Stratford upon Avon on 24 February 1885, the son of John Maine and his wife Hannah (*nee* Bennett). In 1901 he was living at 27 Meer Street, Stratford upon Avon with his parents, his younger brother Francis and his younger sisters Daisy and Violet. He was employed as an Errand Boy. He started sweeping chimneys as a boy of 11 and frequently had to climb the chimney; on one occasion he became stuck in a chimney at Coldicott House and it was necessary to make a hole in the chimney to get him out. In 1908, when his first son was baptised, he was living at 1 Beaudesert Lane. His principal occupation was as a chimney sweep, but he sold vegetables and newspapers as a side-line. He earned 15/- a week as a chimney sweep and in 1907 bought a barrow and sold greengrocery around the streets of Henley to supplement his income. He later bought a horse and cart to help him in his greengrocery business.[196] On 7 August

Fred Maine and family in Beaudesert Street c 1913

---

196 Welham, pp 98-102

1905 he married Ellen Jane Holt, the daughter of Richard and Ellen Holt, at St Mary's Church, Wythall.

In 1911 he was living in a three-roomed house in Beaudesert Street with his wife, his son Frederick William (3) and his daughters Ellen Louisa (4) and Katherine Margaret (1). They also had a boarder, James Harris (*qv*).

They had six children in all; Ellen Louise Charlotte born 12 May 1906; Frederick William baptised on 8 March 1908; Katherine Margaret baptised 20 March 1910 (died 18 May 1911); George Edward baptised 9 March 1913; Violet Maude baptised 15 March 1914 and Mary Alexandra baptised 28 February 1915; they later adopted a daughter, Christina Mary, who was born on 26 December 1931.

Fred kept a diary covering the years of the war, its principal contents being the price of vegetables. He was a member of the Beaudesert Parish Meeting in March 1916. When he was called up he applied to the Stratford Rural District Tribunal. At its meeting on 16 June 1916 he claimed that he was the only sweep in the district and that, if its chimneys were not swept, Henley would present a good target for Zeppelins; he was also secretary of the State Insurance Society with 130 members and 60 on the voluntary side. He was granted one month's exemption. The State Insurance Society appealed against the Tribunal's decision to refuse him an extended exemption and the case was heard at an Appeals Tribunal in Warwick on 29 June 1916, with Lord Ilkeston in the chair. Fred stated that he was a married man with 4 children and had previously served four years in the Yeomanry: he was the only sweep within an 8-mile radius of the town. His point about Zeppelins created more amusement than sympathy and his appeal was refused.

Fred Maine enlisted in the Public Hall at Worcester on 10 July 1916 and joined the 2/7th Durham Light Infantry (Territorial Force). His age was 31 years 5 months and his trade was Chimbley Sweep (*sic*). His medical report shows that he was 5'8" tall, weighed 149 pounds and had a chest of 37½". His physical development was good, but he had an inguinal hernia and stiffness of the toes. He was graded B1 and stated to be fit for garrison service abroad. However, Captain J B MacLean RAMC examined him at Catterick on 23 August 1916 and completed Army Form B 204 (Application for Discharge of a Recruit as not likely to become an efficient Soldier). He stated that Private Maine was suffering from epilepsy and that he had seen him in a true epileptic fit. Fred was discharged on 19 September 1916, having served 68 days.

In 1936 Maine & Sons were chimney sweeps at 237 High Street and his wife Ellen Jane had a shop at the same address. They celebrated their golden wedding at a large party in the Memorial Hall, Henley in August 1955. Fred Maine died in Leamington Spa on 1 July 1961 aged 76. He was cremated at Robin Hood, Shirley and his ashes scattered in the churchyard of St Nicholas'.

1901 & 1911 Census; WW1 Pension Records; Welham; Kelly's Directory; *Herald* (23 June & 7 July 1916); Owen Maine (his grandson).

Malins, Edward John (1894-1962)

Probably Lance Corporal 130399, Royal Engineers; formerly Private, 16167 Royal Warwickshire Regiment (John Malins).

He was known as Jack. His birth in 1894 was registered as Edward John Malins and in 1901 he was six and living in Henley High Street with his parents Edward John and Harriet Malins, his elder brother William (11) and elder sister Florence Ellen (9). His father was a Bricklayer's Labourer and his mother the Caretaker of Henley School.

Jack Malins lived at 283 High Street. He died on 1 May 1962 and is buried in St Nicholas' churchyard.

British War Medal and the Victory Medal.

1901 Census; MIC; W G Haytree.

Mannox, Frank Cecil (1898/9-fl 1923)

2nd Lieutenant, 5th Battalion Royal Munster Fusiliers; formerly Lance Corporal, Northumberland Fusiliers.

He was the only son of Frank Henry Mannox and his wife Helena of Whitley House, Henley. In 1901 they were living at 282 Rotton Park Road, Edgbaston, Birmingham; his father was a Commercial Traveller in the jewellery business. The family was living at Westland, Walsall Road, Four Oaks, Sutton Coldfield in 1911 and had a resident domestic servant. His father was then a Wholesale Jewellery Dealer. His parents had been married 12 years and also had a daughter Gladys (9). Frank went to King Edward's School Birmingham in 1911 and left in 1916. He enlisted as a Private in the Northumberland Fusiliers in November of that year and was promoted Lance Corporal in February 1917. In November 1917 he went as a cadet to 7th Officer Cadet Battalion in Fermoy, Ireland. He was commissioned as a temporary 2nd Lieutenant in the Regular Army with the 5th Battalion Royal Munster Fusiliers in April 1918 (*London Gazette* 29 April 1918). He went to France on 31 July 1918 and was wounded at Cambrai on 7 October, going into hospital. His MIC with a note dated 21 July 1921 gives the address to which his medals were to be sent as Whitley House, Henley in Arden, Warwickshire. Frank married a Miss Ivens in 1923.

British War Medal and Victory Medal.

1901 & 1911 Census; Heath, p 99; MIC; *Herald* (18 October 1918).

Marsh, George (1875/6-1951)

The details of his service cannot be identified.

He was known as 'Bluey' Marsh (Florence Beard). His wife was Eliza Jane and they had five children:

Margaret Ellen, baptised St John's 27 December 1908 (George was then a Labourer of Handsworth)

Elsie, baptised 26 July 1910 (Labourer of Henley)

Harry, baptised 24 June 1917 (Soldier of Henley)

Irene, baptised 24 June 1917 (Soldier of Henley)

Dorothy, baptised 12 October 1919 (Labourer of Henley)

Florence Beard recalled that he drove for Eveson's after the war. George Marsh died on 18 February 1951, aged 75, and is buried in St Nicholas' churchyard.

St John's PR; Florence Beard.

Mason, Joseph (1874-1948)

He is likely to be either Private 305401, Royal Warwickshire Regiment or Private 170157, Machine Gun Corps; formerly Private 2843, Warwickshire Yeomanry.

Joseph Mason was born at Radford in Warwickshire. He was 26 in 1901 and living in Beaudesert Lane with his widowed mother Alice (who had been born in Mickleton, Gloucestershire), his younger brother Walter (*qv*) and two younger sisters, Joyce (14) and Jessie (12). Joseph was employed as a Carter. In 1911 he was living in a three-roomed house at 229 Henley in Arden with his wife Ellen Elizabeth: they had been married seven years and had no children. Joseph was a member of the Henley Fire Brigade in 1919. He died on 18 August 1948 aged 75 and is buried in St Nicholas' churchyard.

Joseph Mason of the RWR was entitled to the British War Medal and Victory Medal. Joseph Mason of the Warwickshire Yeomanry was also entitled to the 1914-15 Star, having gone overseas on 6 November 1915.

1901 & 1911 Census; MICs.

Mason, Walter Clifton (1884/5-fl 1919)

Probably Private 247344, Labour Corps.

Walter was born at Oak Farm, Aston Cantlow and was the younger brother of Joseph Mason (*qv*). In 1901 he was 16, employed as a Cowman on a farm and living with his family in Beaudesert. In 1911 he was the only one still living with his mother in Beaudesert Street; he was then employed as a Mason's Labourer.

He enlisted on 10 October 1916 and was discharged due to sickness on 11 September 1919. He was issued with a Silver War Badge (B305658) on 6 October 1919. There is no evidence that he served overseas, so it is not known whether he was entitled to the British War Medal and Victory Medal.

He was a member of the Fire Brigade in 1919.

Silver War Badge.

1901 & 1911 Census.

Midwinter, Charles Thomas Joseph (1900-fl 1945)

Private 43884, Dorsetshire Regiment.

He was known as Charlie and was baptised in St John's Church on 25 July 1900, the son of Thomas and Elizabeth M Midwinter. At the time of the Census in 1901 he was 10 months old and living in Henley with his parents: his father was a Journeyman Tailor. The 1911 Census shows that the same family was living at 190 Henley in Arden. His father was still a Journeyman Tailor, but his mother was described as an Army Pensioner: they had been married for 13 years.

His Attestation shows that he enlisted in Coventry on 12 July 1918 and was posted to the Dorsetshire Regiment on 13 July at the age of 18 years and 1 month. His height was 5'6", his chest 35" and he was put in medical category A1. His trade was given as Motor Mechanic and his Military History Sheet shows that he was awarded the 3rd Class Certificate of Education. On 1 March 1919 he was made a paid Acting Lance Corporal and posted to the 3rd Battalion on 22 March. He was promoted to Lance Corporal on 28 June and posted to the 1st Battalion on 26 July. On 25 August 1919 he reverted to the rank of Private at his own request. He was given 28 days paid leave on 24 November 1919 from Prees Heath, near Whitchurch. His Certificate of Identity shows that he was a 1st Class shot and also that he had been serving in Ireland. He transferred to Class Z Reserve on his demobilization on 23 December 1919, his address being 190 Chingley Bank, Henley in Arden.

He worked for Newcombe's transport when he first came out of the army and was subsequently an insurance agent for Liverpool Victoria. Charlie Midwinter lived at 1 Barley Close when it was first built in about 1930, having previously lived at Chingley Bank in the High Street.

1901 & 1911 Census; Service Record; W G Haytree.

Mitchell

He has not been positively identified. Robert Glasson Clifton Mitchell, born in Truro in 1872, was living at Crocketts Farm in Beaudesert at the time of the 1891 census, as was his younger brother Preston, also born in Truro some two years later. They were the sons of Robert and Mary Mitchell and were still living there in 1901, Robert being a Farmer and Clifton's occupation being given as Farmer's Son. In 1911 Clifton was living at Crocketts Farm as the Farmer, together with his wife Mary, born in Henley, to whom he had been married for 10 years. No military records have been found for either Clifton or Preston Mitchell. As a Farmer, Clifton could have claimed exemption from military service.

Another possibility is Frederick J Mitchell, born in Claverdon in 1898, the son of Arthur and Alice Mitchell. In 1911 the family was living Preston Bagot, Arthur Mitchell being a Farmer and Frederick Mitchell being 13 years old: he was probably at school, though this is not recorded on the Census Return. There are too many MICs in the name of Frederick J Mitchell to be able to make a reasonable attribution.

Moore, Frank (1870/1-fl 1921)

614354 Wheeler Staff Sergeant, 1/1st Warwickshire Royal Horse Artillery.

Frank Moore was born in Rowington on 14 July 1876. He married Rose Goddard at St Andrew's, Bordesley on 21 November 1909. In 1911 he was a cycle manufacturer, working on his own account, and living at 147 High Street with his wife Rose and his mother Anne.

Frank joined the Warwickshire Battery of the RHA on 15 July 1908, when living at Claverdon. He was promoted to Wheeler Staff Sergeant on 7 May .

He served in France from 30 October 1914 to 25 April 1919 and was living in the High Street when he was demobilized on 30 May 1919. He was a member of the Fire Brigade in 1919.

1914 Star, British War Medal, Victory Medal and Territorial Force Efficiency Medal.

1911 Census; MIC; Service Record.

Morris, C W

There are 23 MICs in the name of Charles W Morris.

He was possibly the son of Joseph and Sarah Morris, who were living in Erdington in 1891. Charles was the fifth of their seven sons and had one sister. His father was a Milkman. In 1901 Charles W Morris was living as a boarder in Highbridge Road, Sutton Coldfield and working as a Stable Boy in the household of Samuel and Eliza Woodward, the former being a Coachman.

1891 & 1901 Census.

Newcombe, Peter Thomas (1883-1945)

Warrant Officer, Royal Navy.

He was born in Wootton Wawen on 26 June 1883, the second son of Robert Newcombe, a Watch Maker and Jeweller, and his wife Mary. In 1891 the family was living at 60 High Street, the other three children being Kathleen (15), Robert (11) and Winifred (4). In 1911 he was visiting Mr & Mrs Salter and their family at 62 Boswell Street, Toxteth Park, Liverpool: his occupation was Vulcaniser in a Motor Works. One of his claims to fame was that at a time of serious flooding in Henley he swam the length of the High Street from the Black Swan to Back Lane.

He first enlisted in the Royal Navy on 26 June 1901 (his 18th birthday) for a 12 year term, when his occupation was given as a Labourer. He rose through the ranks of Ordinary Seaman, Able Seaman and Leading Seaman to Petty Officer, a rank he attained on 8 November 1912 but for which he had qualified educationally on 1 March 1910. His first term of service ended on 25 June 1913.

On the outbreak of war he was recalled to the navy and served throughout the war. When he re-enlisted on 18 August 1914 he was 5'6¾" tall with dark hair, brown eyes and a fresh complexion: he had a tattoo of an anchor on his left forearm. He joined HMS *Kent* on 3 October 1914, an armoured cruiser of 9,800 tons launched in 1901. Her heaviest gun was a 6-inch quick-firer. She served on the China Station from 1906 to 1913. *Kent* sailed to the Falkland Islands, where she took part in the

HMS Blenheim

Battle of the Falkland Islands on 8 December 1914, in which a British force under Rear-Admiral Sturdee defeated a German force commanded by Admiral Graf von Spee. The German heavy cruisers *Gneisenau* and *Scharnhorst* were sunk and the *Kent* was responsible for sinking the German light cruiser *Nurnberg*. *Kent* returned to Britain in May 1915. Peter served on *Kent* from 3 October 1914 to 16 September 1915. He was home on leave in March and in May 1916 awaiting a posting. On 9 May 1916 he joined HMS *Blenheim*.

Blenheim was a Blake-Class Cruiser, launched on 26 May 1894. Her displacement was 9,150 tons with a length of 375 feet, beam of 65 feet, a maximum draught of 25'9" and a speed of 22 knots. She carried a crew of 570, her principal armaments being two 9.2 inch guns, 10 six inch guns and 18 three-pounders. She had gone to Mudros in April 1915 to take part in the Dardanelles campaign. Peter Newcombe served on *Blenheim* until 17 June 1919 and it was on this ship that he was confirmed in the rank of Boatswain on 6 October 1916.

Peter Newcombe married Gladys Warwick after the war, the banns being called in St John's in May 1921. He remained in the navy until 10 October 1925, when he was placed on the Retired List at his own request. He served in the navy again during the Second World War, reaching the rank of acting Lieutenant. He was returned to the Retired List as medically unfit on 12 July 1944 and died of a cerebral haemorrhage on 8 February 1945 at the age of 61.

British War Medal and Victory Medal.

1891 & 1911 Census; RN Service Record; *Herald* (4 February, 17 March & 19 May 1916).

Noon, Joseph (1877-fl 1919)

Driver 93726, Royal Field Artillery.

Joseph was born in 1875 and married Margaret Hanson of Salter Street, Earlswood on 23 November 1903. They had two daughters, Ellen and Margaret Alice, both born in Solihull. Joseph was living at Blackford Hill, Henley when he enlisted at Stratford upon Avon on 5 February 1915. He was then 37 and working as a Labourer: his height was 5'3" and his medical category A1.

He went to the RFA Depot in Glasgow on 8 February 1915, being posted to the 3rd Reserve Brigade on 12 May and the 4th Reserve Brigade on 23 June. He joined the BEF in France on 31 August 1915 and was a Driver at the Base Depot on 25 September. He was on leave from 3 February to 18 February 1918. On 10

April 1918 he was sentenced to 7 days Field Punishment Number 2 for failing to comply with an order and using obscene language to an NCO in the presence of an officer. He was wounded on 28 May 1918. While with 106 Brigade RFA he demonstrated his skill in making horseshoes and shoeing horses to qualify as a Shoeing Smith on 22 February 1919.

Joseph returned to Henley on his demobilization on 12 April 1919 after 3 years and 169 days service with the BEF.

British War Medal and Victory Medal.

MIC; Service Record.

O'Donnell, Arthur (1874/5-fl 1919)

Private 294649, Labour Corps; formerly Pioneer 117947, Royal Engineers.

Arthur was the son of Thomas and Harriet O'Donnell. His father was an Agricultural Labourer, born in County Mayo in Ireland, his mother a Laundress born in King's Norton. The family was living in the High Street, Henley in 1881, at which time Arthur was 7 and had been born in Henley: with him were his father Thomas (47), his mother Harriet (48), his brothers Thomas (22) and Edward (3) and his sisters Agnes (18) and Ada (7). In 1901 he was 26 and living in Henley with his widowed mother Harriet (68) and his sister Maggie (33). He was a carpenter and said to have been born in King's Norton.

Arthur enlisted in London at the age of 40 on 28 August 1915 at which time he was living at 23 Masshouse Lane, Dale End, Birmingham. He was 5'4" tall, with a 36" chest, unmarried and gave his next of kin as his nephew Thomas O'Donnell of Tan Yard Terrace, Henley. He became a Pioneer in the Labour Section of the Royal Engineers at a rate of 3s 0d per day. His initial posting was to 6th Labour Battalion of the Royal Engineers. Between 4 and 15 September 1915 he was in Number 9 Stationary Hospital. He landed in France on 1 October 1915. On 1 April 1916 he was transferred to 9th Labour Battalion and was again in hospital from 22 to 25 June 1916. From 27 November to 7 December 1916 he was on leave in England. Arthur was transferred to the Labour Corps on 1 August 1917, joining 708 Company. He went to England on leave on 4 December 1917 and was admitted to 2/1st Southern General Hospital in Dudley Road, Birmingham suffering from acute bronchitis and pulmonary oedema.

He was still a patient there on 19 January 1918. Arthur was discharged on 15 March 1918 as being permanently unfit for war service. He was diagnosed as suffering from arterio sclerosis with cardio vascular degeneration. It was thought impossible to give the date of origin of his disability, but it was said to have been aggravated by active service. He was given a good character and his address on demobilisation was 25 Fagley Street, Birmingham.

1914-15 Star, British War Medal and Victory Medal.

1881 and 1901 Census; Pension Records; MIC.

O'Donnell, Thomas Edgar (1893-1974)

Private 242987, 5th Battalion Royal Warwickshire Regiment.

Known as Tom, he was the son of Thomas O'Donnell, a blacksmith, and his wife Mary (both born in Henley). In 1901 Tom was 8, had been born in Henley and was living in the Tanyard with his parents and four sisters Nellie (14), May (10), Lillian (4) and Trisa (1). He married Emily Lily Edginton of Henley on 3 August 1913 in St John's Church. Tom was a member of the Warwick Number 11 VAD and scored 60% in the examinations held in the autumn of 1914.

He enlisted on 9 November 1915 and joined the 5th Battalion of the Royal Warwicks. His son Arthur stated that his father walked to Budbrook Barracks to enlist. At a medical examination in Warwick on 20 September 1916 he was described as being 22 years and 330 days old: his occupation was a Blacksmith. His height was then 5'1", his weight 118 pounds, his chest measurement 35" and his complexion was fair: he had very good eyesight, but his teeth were defective.

His right knee gave him trouble from 21 July 1917, when he was stated to have a 30% degree of disablement: his problem was attributed to active service. From 24 August to 29 October 1917 he was in the 2nd Southern General Hospital, Bristol suffering from synovitis of the right knee. From 30 October to 4 December 1917 he was in the Military Hospital, Horfield, Bristol before being returned to 2nd Southern General. The date of his final discharge from hospital is not known. He was discharged from the army on 14 October 1919, his medical grade then being 3.

He continued to suffer from problems with his right knee: an examination at Coventry on 19 February 1920 found he had a floating patella, with a very definite history of "locking". An operation was recommended and accepted. On 1 February 1921 he was again examined at Coventry. It was noted that he had a healed operation scar on his right knee and that there was free movement with his right knee joint. His other organs were healthy and he was advised to cycle. A final examination at Coventry on 16 February 1922 stated that his right knee gave way at times and that he limped slightly, his right leg being a little shorter than his left.

He had three children:

Harold Edgar, baptised St John's Church 24 June 1917 (when Tom was described as a Soldier of 228 High St)
Thomas Henry, baptised 31 August 1919
Arthur Ernest, born 27 August 1923

Tom died on 27 February 1974 aged 81 and is buried in St Nicholas' churchyard. British War Medal and Victory Medal.

1901 Census; MIC; Pension Records; Arthur O'Donnell (his son).

Ollier, Harold (1897-fl 1919)

Private 455722, Labour Corps; formerly Private 1929, Royal Warwickshire Regiment.

Harold was born in Church Lawton, Cheshire the son of Orlando and Katherine Ollier. In 1901 he was aged 4 and living in Holly Villas, Church Lawton with his parents and a servant: his father was a railway clerk and his mother a school mistress. Some time after 1911 they moved to Henley and ran the Golden Cross. Their son Cecil Rupert was baptised in St John's on 2 February 1913. Harold joined the RWR and was wounded in January 1916, subsequently becoming a Private in the Labour Corps.

British War Medal and Victory Medal.

1901 Census; MIC; *Birmingham Post* (31 January 1916).

Parkes, Frederick Charles (1879-fl 1921)

Quarter Master Sergeant 668, Warwickshire Yeomanry.

Frederick was born in Beaudesert, the elder son of George and Mary Parkes of Buckley Green Farm. He entered the Junior School in Henley from the Infant Department on 12 May 1890 and left on 8 March 1897 for farm work. The family living at Buckley Green Farm in 1901 comprised his father George (57), his mother Mary (52), his brother Francis (17) and his sisters Beatrice (21) and Mildred (9). Frederick's occupation was recorded as Farmer's Son and his age as 22. He acted as Enumerator for the parishes of Beaudesert and Preston Bagot in the 1911 Census. At that time he had taken over Buckley Green Farm and was living there with his wife Mary Holland Parkes (31) and his daughter Eva (4): his parents had moved to Mobbs Farm in Beaudesert.

At the Beaudesert Parish Meeting on 23 March 1914, Frederick was appointed Assistant Overseer for the parish at an annual salary of £8.10s.0d. At the next meeting on 8 September 1914 it was noted that he had resigned, having been called up for war service with the Warwickshire Yeomanry.[197]

Sergeant Parkes was at the head of the Henley troop of D Squadron of the Warwickshire Yeomanry when they left for their annual camp at Warwick Park in May 1914. He was called up on the outbreak of war and marched with his squadron to Warwick on 10 August. His name is not recorded in Adderley, so that he was left behind in Egypt when the regiment sailed for Gallipoli. The *Herald* reported that Sergeant Frank Parkes, son of Mr George Parkes, was expected in Henley for a day or two in February 1918. In 1921 he applied for the position of Clerk to the Parish Council. He was one of three candidates to be interviewed, but failed to secure any votes (Minutes 11 and 18 April 1921). He was a farmer in Buckley Green in 1924.

The Guild Hall contains a silver cup presented to the Court Leet in his memory by his daughter Eva. It is inscribed as follows:

---

197 Warwickshire County Record Office, CR1098/1

1910
Warwickshire Yeomanry
D Squadron
Major R Arthur Richardson
Prize Shooting
1st Prize
Presented by Mrs Arthur Richardson
Won by
Sergeant F C Parkes

1914-15 Star, British War Medal, Victory Medal and Territorial Force Efficiency Medal (awarded on 1 April 1912).

1901 & 1911 Census; Warwickshire Record Office, CR1098/1; MIC; Kelly 1924; *Herald* (29 May & 25 September 1914, 15 February 1918).

Partington, J

No information has been found.

Payne

H Payne was a member of Warwick Number 11 VAD in August 1914. Private Payne was married to one of the sisters of Maurice Horsnett and was present at his funeral on 15 April 1917.

Pearce, Thomas Albert

He and his wife (Annie Alice Paine) had a daughter Jean Caroline baptised at St Nicholas' on 8 September 1918. He was then described as a soldier and their address was given as High Hurst Cottages.

†Perkins, Herbert Henry (1894-1916)

Sergeant 305396, 8th Battalion Royal Warwickshire Regiment.

He was born in Henley, the son of Edward Henry and Elizabeth Millie Perkins. In 1901 he was living at 266 Wellington Road, Handsworth with his parents and a younger sister, Janet (4): his father was a Domestic Coachman. By 1911 the family had moved to 60 Wellhead Lane, Perry Barr, Handsworth and had been increased by a daughter Ursula Winifred (9) and a son Edward William (6). Herbert's occupation was given as Dairy Work on a Farm. He was still living in Handsworth when he enlisted at Warwick.

The 8th Battalion was a Territorial Force battalion and mobilised at Aston Manor, Birmingham on 4 August 1914. It served in the Chelmsford area until it landed at Le Havre on 22 March 1915. On 14 May it became part of 143rd Brigade, 48th Division. As his MIC does not give the date he went overseas or show any entitlement to the 1914-15 Star, Herbert must have joined his battalion at some time early in 1916. He was killed in action on 1 July 1916, one of the 584 men of the 8th Battalion who were casualties on the first day of the Somme. He is buried in Serre Road Cemetery No. 2, grave I G 9.

British War Medal and Victory Medal.

1901 & 1911 Census; CWGC; SDGW; MIC.

Perks, James DCM (1870-fl 1919)

Staff Sergeant Major T/9149, Army Service Corps.

James Perks was born in Ullenhall in 1870, the seventh son of John Perks, an agricultural labourer, and his wife Ann. By the time of the census of 1881, the family had been increased by three girls. James Perks joined the Royal Artillery on 30 April 1889 as a Gunner (73104) at the age of 18 years and 6 months. He was still living in Ullenhall, where he worked as a labourer, and enlisted in Worcester. His attestation shows him to have been 5'5¾" tall, weighing 133 pounds and with a chest measurement of 35". He was a member of the Church of England, with a fresh complexion, blue eyes and brown hair. He served for over 30 years in the army, the first 10 years of which were spent on the home front. On 25 November 1889 he transferred to the Army Service Corps as a Driver (9149). During his time in England he passed his 3rd class Certificate of Education on 22 March 1892 and his 2nd class on 27 June 1894. He also qualified as a Rough Rider on 28 August 1894. On 13 February 1898 he married Nellie Burton in Farnborough Parish Church. Before he left England he was promoted to Lance Corporal on 19 June 1894, to Corporal on 21 November 1895 and to Sergeant on 6 May 1899. On 5 October 1899 he re-engaged at Woolwich for such time as would complete 21 years service with the colours.

The following day he sailed for South Africa, where he served until 23 November 1900, being awarded the Queen's Medal. In 1902 he was given a South African War Gratuity of £12.10s.0d. In 1901 he was a Company Sergeant Major in the Army Service Corps, living with his wife Nellie (30) and his three sons Frederick James (6), Herbert George (2) and Arthur John Robert (10 months) at Farnham in Surrey. In 1911 the family was living at 66 Strathmills Road, Southfields, Surrey: he and his wife had been married for 18 years. Their eldest son Frederick was not with them, but they now had a daughter Jessie (9). James was still a Sergeant Major in the ASC, having served for 22 years and was working as an Instructor with the T & S Column of 2nd London Division.

He was mentioned in Sir Douglas Haig's dispatch of 13 November 1916 (*LG* 4 January 1917). It was later reported that Staff Sergeant J Perks, ASC, Henley in Arden, had been awarded the DCM "For conspicuous gallantry and devotion to duty. On several occasions he displayed great courage while in charge of convoys under heavy fire, and his personal example and untiring energy largely assisted in preventing casualties" (*LG* 17 April 1918, at which time he was a Temporary 1st

Class Staff Sergeant Major). He was discharged on the termination of his second period of engagement on 17 November 1919.

Distinguished Conduct Medal, Mentioned in Dispatches, Queen's South African Medal with 3 clasps (Transvaal, Orange Free State and Cape Colony), Long Service & Good Conduct Medal, 1914-15 Star, British War Medal and Victory Medal.

1871, 1881, 1901 & 1911 Census; Pension Records 1914-1920; MIC; *Herald* (19 April 1918).

Petty, Frederick William (1882-fl 1921)

Private 33338, Oxford & Buckinghamshire Light Infantry.

Born in Ettington in 1882, he was 32 and living at 198 Wootton Road, Henley when he enlisted on 17 November 1915. He was working as a Gardener. In 1901 he was working as a resident Footman at a house in Chelsea and in 1911 was living with his wife and four children in Main Road, Ettington, working as a Farm Labourer. Frederick had married Caroline Elizabeth Drew in Ettington on 28 April 1904 and they had a total of six children. During the war his wife and family moved back to Ettington.

He served in the UK from 5 June to 12 December 1916 and joined the 2nd Battalion of the Oxford & Buckinghamshire Light Infantry with the BEF in France on 13 December. He continued to serve with them until 28 February 1919, with the exception of leave in the UK from 8 to 24 January 1919.

British War Medal and Victory Medal.

1901 and 1911 Census; MIC; Service Record.

Plowman

Probably Henry Plowman, Driver 35178, Royal Field Artillery.

Only the surname is given in the Henley Peace Celebrations Booklet, but it is likely to have been Henry Plowman, who was born in Rowington in 1879, the son of Paul and Jane Plowman. He had a younger sister, Ellen and a younger brother Frederick. The family was living in Rowington in 1891 and 1901: in the latter year Henry was employed as a Carter on a farm. In 1911 the family was living at Bushwood, Henley in Arden. Paul Plowman was a Farmer, Henry's occupation being given as Wagoner on a Farm. The occupation of his brother Frederick was "Farmer's Son Working on Farm", which is likely to have kept him from being conscripted.

Henry served with 9th Brigade RFA and went overseas on 14 October 1914.

Norman Welch remembered him being a farmer at Lowsonford.

1914 Star with clasp, British War Medal, Victory Medal.

1891, 1901 and 1911 Census; MIC; H N Welch.

Preedy, Thomas (1888/9-fl 1919)

Private T/40969, ASC formerly Private 662, Royal Warwickshire Regiment (this is the most likely of five MICs in the name of Thomas Preedy).

He was known as Tom and was living with his parents, Thomas and Margaret, three brothers and three sisters at Shelley Green in Solihull in 1891, when he was 2. His father was a Farm Labourer who had been born in North Aston, Oxfordshire, while his mother had been born in Henley. His father was evidently an itinerant labourer, as his seven children were born in six different locations; Thomas was recorded as being born in Wootton Wawen. In 1901 he was living with his parents and two elder brothers George and William in Forest Road, Hay Mill, Yardley (then part of Worcestershire). Tom was then recorded as having been born in Henley. He married Jane Trinder of Henley in 1911.

The *Birmingham Post* of 12 October 1916 reported that he had been wounded. He was described as a widower when he married Florence Amy Elvins, also of Henley, in 1919. He was a member of the Fire Brigade in 1919.

He lived in a cottage in the High Street next to the Nag's Head (now part of it) and became a Sergeant in the RWR.

British War Medal and Victory Medal.

1891 & 1901 Census; *Birmingham Post* (12 Oct 1916); MIC; W G Haytree.

Price, William (1884-fl 1936)

Private 1734, Warwickshire Yeomanry.

William was born in Preston Bagot, the son of William and Elizabeth Jane Price. The 1891 Census records that he was 7 and was living with his parents at Whitley Farm, Wootton Wawen together with four brothers and an elder sister. His father was a Farm Bailiff. In 1901 he was 17, still living in Wootton Wawen with his parents, a younger brother and sister, and working as a painter and glazier. By 1911 he was assisting in his father's business as a farmer at Whitley: his sister Lucy Daisy was also living there and working as a Dressmaker. A grandson, Frederick Lawrence Price was also resident with them on the day of the census.

William joined the Warwickshire Yeomanry in about 1910. He arrived in Egypt with them on 24 April 1915 and sailed for Gallipoli on 14 August, returning to Egypt in December. He was discharged on 22 April 1916, but was called up again almost immediately, as on 28 July 1916 he appeared before the Stratford Rural District Tribunal seeking exemption from further service. He was then aged 32, of Whitley Farm, Henley in Arden and wished to help his father on his farm of 90 acres. He stated that had put in over 5 years with the Yeomanry, going out to Egypt and the Dardanelles and thought that he was entitled to recuperate: he was a time-expired man. He was granted exemption to 1 January 1917. On 23 March 1917 the Tribunal agreed to his conditional exemption, which appears to have lasted to the end of the war.

1915 Star, British War Medal and Victory Medal.

In 1936 William Price was farming at Pinks Farm in Beaudesert.

1891 & 1901 Census; Adderley, p 25; MIC; Herald (10 December 1915, 4 August 1916, 30 March 1917).

Rathbone, Frank (1895-fl 1919)

Private 47108, Royal Inniskilling Fusiliers; formerly Private 40703, Royal Warwickshire Regiment.

Frank Rathbone was born in Rowington, the son of Charles and Eliza. His father was a domestic coachman. In 1901 Frank was 5 and living in Rowington with his parents, four brothers and a sister (all aged 7 and under). By 1911 he was living in the household of Harry Harper, a butcher of Hampton in Arden and working as a Journeyman Slaughterman.

He was 21 and single when he appeared before the Stratford District Tribunal on 20 October 1916. He was then working as a slaughterman for Harry Hawkes, butcher and farmer of Henley: Rathbone was said to be the only man Hawkes had left, apart from a man of 74. Both Hawkes' sons were in the Colours and he would have to sell his stock if the appellant went. Rathbone had been examined and passed fit for general service to Hawkes' surprise, as "he is more or less a cripple". He said his son who did the slaughtering (Percy Hawkes) was out in Egypt; his son's time had expired a little while back and, thinking he could retain Rathbone's services, Hawkes had told his son he could continue for the duration of the war. Rathbone was given exemption until 1 January and the Tribunal recommended that the medical board should be asked to re-examine him or send him to London for examination. On 26 January 1917, Hawkes asked for a further period of exemption, but the military representative pointed out that one man was enough to do all the slaughtering in Henley. Rathbone's exemption was extended to 31 March 1917, but this would be final. It is likely that he was called up very soon afterwards.

British War Medal and Victory Medal.

1901 & 1911 Census; MIC; *Herald* (27 October 1916 & 2 February 1917).

Rhodes, Benjamin (1869-1938)

142510, Labour Corps, formerly Colour Sergeant 3481, Royal Dublin Fusiliers and Lance Corporal 4211, King's Royal Rifle Corps.

Benjamin Rhodes was the son of Joseph Rhodes and was born in Bradford in 1869. He joined the King's Royal Rifle Corps in Winchester on 2 November 1887, having enlisted in Bradford on 26 October at the age of 18 years and 1 month. He had worked as an Iron Turner and had previously served in the 3rd West Yorkshire Rifle Volunteers. His medical examination was in Halifax on 31 October, when his height was 5'4½", his weight 123 lbs and his chest 33". His physical development was fair. His next of kin was his father Joseph of 1 Oakroyd Terrace, Manningham, Bradford.

Benjamin was promoted to Lance Corporal in the 2nd Battalion KRRC on 8 April 1889 and was transferred in that rank to the Royal Dublin Fusiliers on 1 December 1889. He served for some time in the Depot, during which he was promoted Corporal on 1 September 1890, unpaid Lance Sergeant on 17 December 1891 and paid Lance Sergeant on 1 August 1892. He was posted to the 1st Battalion on 11 April 1894, and was promoted to Sergeant on 27 August 1894. Benjamin was posted to the 3rd Battalion in that rank on 1 March 1898. His final promotion was to Colour Sergeant on 23 August 1898. He had extended his service to 18 years with the colours at Naas on 7 April 1894 and to 21 years at Naas on 10 November 1898.[198] He served in the UK until he was discharged after 21 years service on 25 October 1908.

He married Jane Lily Agnes about 1895. In 1911 they were living in a five roomed house in Beaudesert with their three sons and three daughters: Evelyn Elizabeth was 14, Louis 12, Edward 5, Norah 4, Walter Valintine (*sic*) 2 and Ruth was 1. The eldest daughter was born in Portsmouth, the next three children at Naas, Walter in Birmingham and Ruth in Henley. Benjamin then understated his age as 40: his occupation was School Drill Instructor at a Preparatory College (Arden House). His youngest daughter Ruth was baptised at St John's Church on 31 July 1910, when Benjamin was described as an Instructor of Henley. In 1911 he was the Superintendent of the Rifle Range at the Public Hall, being described as "late Colour Sergeant, Royal Dublin Fusiliers"; his wife was the Caretaker of the Public Hall.

Benjamin rejoined the army as a Sergeant in the 6th Battalion Royal Dublin Fusiliers on 12 September 1914 and was demobilized on 13 May 1919 from the Labour Corps. It is likely that he served in the UK throughout this period, as there is no MIC in his name.

Benjamin Rhodes died of carcinoma of the oesophagus on 28 January 1938 at 269 Longmore Road, Shirley, Birmingham. At the time of his death he was in receipt of an army pension of 5s 1½d per day.

1911 Census; Service Record; *Herald* (25 September 1914).

Rhodes, Louis (1898-*fl* 1919)

Able Seaman J28210, Royal Navy.

Louis was born at Naas on 17 June 1898, the son of Benjamin and Jane Rhodes. In 1911 he was living with his parents in Beaudesert (see Benjamin Rhodes above). He joined the Royal Navy as a boy on 23 October 1913, making him the youngest man from Henley to join the armed forces. His previous occupation was a Cycle Fitter.

His first posting was a brief one to HMS *Impregnable* (a training establishment at Devonport) between 23 and 29 October 1913, followed by a posting to HMS *Powerful* (a training ship) between 30 October 1913 and 24 June 1914. On 25 June he joined *Edgar* (a cruiser), on 5 December *Victory I* (an accounting base at Portsmouth) and on 9 June 1915 he joined *Temeraire* on which he served until 27 May 1917. *Temeraire* was an 18,600 ton battleship of the Dreadnought class, launched at Devonport in 1907 and with a principal armament of ten 12" guns.

---

198 Naas is in County Kildare, Ireland and had a large barracks

It took part in the Battle of Jutland on 31 May and 1 June 1916, during which it fired 54 of its 12" shells and scored 2 or 3 hits on the German cruiser *Wiesbaden*. *Temeraire* was not itself damaged, though a few shots were close. Louis was promoted to Able Seaman on 1 November 1916.

HMS Temeraire

Subsequent ships on which he served during the war were *Victory I*, *Excellent* (the naval school of gunnery), *Egremont* (a base ship) and *Duke*.

On 17 June 1916, his eighteenth birthday, Louis signed on for 12 years in the Royal Navy. His height at that time was 5'2¾", his chest 34", his hair red, his eyes grey and his complexion fresh. He served his 12 years in the navy and joined the Royal Naval Reserve on his demobilization on 17 June 1928. His conduct throughout his service was Very Good.

British War Medal and Victory Medal.

1911 Census; RN Record of Service.

Richards, William Henry (1893-1976)

Lance Corporal 36470, Royal Army Medical Corps.

William was the only child of William Henry and Mary Elizabeth Richards. In 1911 William was 17, living with his parents in a five-roomed house at 178 High Street and working as an Apprentice Plumber and Painter. His father was a Plumber and Painter, his mother a Grocer. William served his indentures before the war with E T Kennard (a builder of 54 Rother St, Stratford upon Avon).

He joined the RAMC on 10 September 1914 and went to Gallipoli on 15 September 1915. While on the peninsula he acted as a medical dispatch rider and had a number of exciting experiences and several narrow escapes. He was promoted to Lance Corporal before suffering an attack of enteric fever and returning to hospital in Brighton in November 1915. By March 1916 he had been in 5 hospitals abroad and at home, with a good constitution helping his recovery from a very serious illness. He went to France as a Corporal in January 1918 and returned home for Christmas leave on 10 December. On 12 December he was taken to 1st Southern General Hospital (on the campus of the University of Birmingham) and had an immediate operation for appendicitis. The following day he needed another operation for a different condition and his parents were sent for. He was later reported as making satisfactory progress. His sickness resulted in his discharge from the army on 15 April 1919 and he was issued with a Silver War Badge (B213300) on 17 June 1919.

William married Margaret Dumper of Twyford, Hampshire in 1921, the banns having been called in St John's Church in July of that year. He lived in Gorse Lane, Wootton Wawen after the war and subsequently emigrated to the USA.

1914-15 Star, British War Medal and Victory Medal.

1901 & 1911 Census; MIC; SWB; *Herald* (17 March 1916, 11 January, 17 May and 20 December 1918, 10 January 1919); W G Haytree.

Ritchings, R George (1885-1969)

Sergeant 11460, 3rd Battalion Grenadier Guards.

George Ritchings was born in Winchcombe, Gloucestershire in 1885. He was the son of William and Esther Ritchings and had two brothers and five sisters. In 1901 he was living at Stone Pits, Inkberrow in Worcestershire with his parents and four sisters. He was working as an Agricultural Labourer, as he was when he enlisted into the 3rd Battalion of the Grenadier Guards at the age of 18 on 20 April 1904. At that time he was 5'7¼" tall, weighed 132 lbs and had a chest of 36": after six months service his height had not changed but he had put on 12 lbs in weight and an extra inch on his chest.

He was described as having a fresh complexion, blue eyes and fair hair and entered his religious denomination as Church of England. He was awarded a 3rd Class Certificate of Education in September 1905.

On 16 October 1905 he was promoted to Lance Corporal and given an additional 6d a day. He was also granted a Good Conduct badge on 19 April 1906. He blotted his copybook the following year, as he was reduced to the rank of Private on 10 September 1906 and forfeited his additional pay. This did not seem to dent his enthusiasm, as on 3 December 1906 he extended his period of service with the colours from three years to seven and was given 6d a day proficiency pay. He was promoted to Lance Corporal again on 24 December 1906, only to forfeit his Good Conduct badge on 9 March 1907 and to revert to the rank of Private on 20 July, when his proficiency pay was reduced to 3d a day. Promoted to Lance Corporal for the third time on 19 October 1908, he was reduced to the rank of Private yet again on 23 December 1908 and was still in that rank when he transferred to the Reserve on 19 April 1911.

In 1911 George was living with his parents in Gloster Street, Winchcombe: he was 24 but did not have any occupation. On 7 April 1912 he married Annie Eliza Forrest, a widow, in St John's Church, Henley. The witnesses were William Thomas Robbins (*qv*) and Mary Ann Robbins. He was a Railway Platelayer when his eldest son William George was baptised at St Nicholas' Church on 11 May 1913. A daughter Florence Gertrude was baptised on 13 September 1914. He had four other children, Winifred May (baptised on 6 May 1917 at St Nicholas'); Albert Thomas (baptised on 21 November 1920 when George was living in Beaudesert Lane and working on the railway); Margaret (baptised 6 February 1922); Beatrice Rose (baptised on 5 October 1919) and Christopher.

George was called from the reserve back into the army on 5 August 1914 and mobilised at Wellington Barracks in London. The 3rd Battalion did not leave London until 26 July 1915 and landed in Le Havre on the following day, as part

of the 2nd Guards Brigade in the Guards Division. George had been promoted Corporal some two weeks before on 15 July and to Lance Sergeant on 17 July. George's stay in the front line was a short one, as he received gunshot wounds to the arm and head and returned to England on 4 October 1915. His wounds were sufficiently serious to ensure that he did not return to active service, but served the rest of his time in England probably in a training capacity. He was promoted to Acting Sergeant on 26 August 1916 and confirmed in that rank on 14 November 1916. George Ritchings was demobilised on 14 February 1919.

George & Annie Ritchings, c 1955

He returned to his family in Beaudesert Lane and to his job on the railway. He later lived at Freeman House in the High Street. His second son, Albert Thomas, served with the Royal Artillery in Hong Kong during World War 2 and died while a prisoner of the Japanese. His wife Annie died on 8 February 1956 aged 67 and George died in Stratford Hospital on 6 November 1969 aged 84. They are buried in St Nicholas' churchyard.

1914-15 Star, British War Medal and Victory Medal.

1901 & 1911 Census; Grenadier Guards archives; MIC; W G Haytree.

Robbins, Arthur (1897-1970)

Gunner 94103, Royal Field Artillery.

Arthur was born in Solihull on 7 October 1897, the youngest of the three sons of Mr & Mrs Thomas Robbins (for details of the family see Harry Robbins below). He was baptised in St Alphege's Church on 14 November 1897, when the family was living in Warwick Road, Solihull and his father was a Foreman Platelayer. He went to school in Henley following their move to 82 High Street, Henley. Arthur had left school by 1911, when he was still living with his family and working as a Saddler's Assistant.

In July 1915 he was serving with 16th Battery Royal Field Artillery, stationed at Topsham Barracks, Exeter. He was promoted to Bombardier, the *Herald* commenting that he had got on well in the service, and had a promising career before him, being not yet eighteen. He landed in France on 29 October 1915, moving to Salonika in January 1916 and elsewhere in Greece soon afterwards.

His MIC records his rank only as Gunner.

He married Jane McCulloch of Irvine, Ayrshire, the banns being called in St John's Church in February and March 1920.

1914-15 Star, British War Medal and Victory Medal.

1901 & 1911 Census; MIC; *Herald* (23 July, 24 September, 5 November 1915 & 24 March 1916).

Robbins, Harry (1891-fl 1919)

Able Seaman Z/9053, Royal Naval Reserve Bristol Division.

Harry was born in Solihull on 26 April 1891, the second son of Thomas and Ellen Robbins, and baptised in St Alphege's Church on 7 June 1891. In 1901 he was living with his parents, an elder sister Alice (13) and two younger brothers, Frank (6) and Arthur (3) in the High Street, Henley. All four children had been born in Solihull.

Harry's father served about twenty years with the GWR and was a Gauger on the line to Lapworth: he had also served as a Lance Corporal with 6th Battalion Royal Warwickshire Regiment in India. He died in August 1917, after ailing for some time. Harry went to school in Henley. In 1911 he was living with his parents in a three-roomed house at 34 High Street, Henley, was single and was employed as a Platform Attendant by the GWR: his parents had been married for 27 years and now also had a daughter, Beatrice Edna (7), who had been born in Henley.

Harry was still employed by the GWR when he joined the Royal Naval Reserve on 24 November 1915, his occupation being given as Ticket Collector. His height was 5'9½", his chest 35½", his hair light brown, his eyes blue and his complexion fair. He served in HMS *Victory VI*, *Pembroke I* and *President III*, all of which were shore bases. He was demobilised on 21 February 1917, when he left *Pembroke I* but remobilised the following day when he joined *President III*. He was finally demobilised on 6 February 1919. His conduct throughout his service was Very Good.

1901 & 1911 Census; RNVR Service Record; *Herald* (23 July 1915).

Robbins, William Thomas (1885-fl 1920)

Private R39511, 12th Battalion King's Royal Rifle Corps.

The son of Thomas and Mary Robbins, he was baptised in St Alphege's Church, Solihull on 19 July 1885. In 1891 he was 5 and living with his parents in Warwick Road, Solihull, together with his elder sister Mary (8) and his younger sister Alice (3). His father was a Platelayer. William went to school in Henley. In 1901 he was working as an Engine Cleaner and boarding with Oliver Douglas and his family in Aston. He married Mary Ann Knight on 20 August 1905 at St Peter's, Wootton Wawen. In 1911 they were living in Wootton Wawen with her widowed father Henry Knight and three children – Doris (6), William Henry (4) and Arthur (2): William was working as a Labourer with the GWR. They had three more children: Bernard Cyril Ernest, baptised in St John's on 11 May 1913 (when William was described as a Platelayer of Henley); Edna Mary Ethel, baptised 2 May 1915

(Platelayer, 182 High St, now serving in HM's Forces, King's Royal Rifle Corps) and Annie Lily Ellen, baptised 8 February 1920 (Platelayer of Henley).

The *Herald* reported that in July 1915 he was serving in 6th Platoon, B Company, 1st Battalion, King's Royal Rifle Corps, attached to the BEF in France. It went on to report regularly on his progress, being informed of events by his wife and parents. After rendering good service for some time in the trenches, he was shot in the stomach at Loos on 27 September 1915. He was moved to a hospital in Leicester at the beginning of October, where he had regular visits from his relatives. He had narrowly escaped death, a bullet ripping through his tobacco tin, piercing a half-franc piece and smashing up some cigarettes in his pocket. He was discharged from hospital on 30 October and was on leave in the UK until 8 November. His wound continued to give trouble and in March 1916 he was in one of the large hospitals in Brighton, having had an operation.

When he returned to the front he was transferred to the 12th Battalion. His wife was notified by the regimental Record Office in Winchester that he had been posted missing. On 20 September 1917 she received a postcard from him stating that he was wounded and a POW in Germany and was going on very well.

The MIC for Private William T Robbins R39511 King's Royal Rifle Corps, does not give a date when he began service overseas. It is evident from the above that he was serving in France in July 1915: the 1st Battalion had been in France with 6th Brigade, 2nd Division since 13 August 1914. He therefore seems to have been entitled to either the 1914 or 1914-1915 Star, in addition to the medals below, which are the only ones shown on his MIC.

British War Medal and Victory Medal.

1891, 1901 and 1911 Census; MIC; *Herald* (23 July, 24 September, 22 October, 5 November 1915, 24 March 1916, 21 September 1917).

Roy, R

Possibly John R Roy, Private 112046, RAMC.

The only information relating to him which has been found is that he was on the clerical staff of the GWR at Henley station before the war and during the war served in the Dardanelles with the RAMC, as reported in the *Herald*. There is an MIC in the name of John R Roy, Private 112046 in the RAMC. This may not be his as it does not mention any entitlement to the 1914-15 Star, but as in the case of William Robbins above this may have been a clerical error.

British War Medal and Victory Medal.

MIC; *Herald* (3 September 1915).

Sadler, C

No information on his military service has been found.

He is probably Charles Sadler, who was born in Snitterfield in 1886. If so, he was the elder brother of Thomas Sadler (*qv*). In 1901 he was 14 and living with his grandmother Mary in Snitterfield and was working on a farm. In 1911 he was boarding with Charles Willis at Oldberrow Cottages, near Henley in Arden and working as a Farm Labourer.

He lived in the Alms Houses.

1901 & 1911 Census; W G Haytree.

†Sadler, Tom (1890/1-1918)

Private 12165, 1st Battalion Royal Warwickshire Regiment.

Tom Sadler was born in Snitterfield, the son of William and Alice Sadler. In 1901 he was 10 and living at 1 High Street, Henley in Arden with his parents and six sisters. By 1911 he had moved to Birmingham and in that year was boarding with Mr and Mrs John Douglas at 3 Spring Hill Avenue, Spring Hill, Birmingham: he was working as a Carman on the Great Western Railway.

Tom was recorded as living in Henley in Arden when he enlisted in Birmingham. The 1st was one of the regular battalions of the Royal Warwickshire Regiment and he is unlikely to have joined it immediately. Tom Sadler first went to France in the first half of 1916. It is possible that he was one of the 250 other ranks who joined the battalion from the 11th (Service) Battalion on 8 February 1918, when the latter battalion was disbanded. In 1918 the 1st Battalion was serving with 10th Brigade, 4th Division. On 28 March the Germans mounted a massive attack on Arras as part of their Spring Offensive. The 1st Battalion arrived in the frontline on 30 March and was immediately involved in heavy fighting. By the following night the Battalion had lost one officer killed, two wounded and 25 other ranks either killed or wounded. Tom Sadler was wounded on 2 April 1918 and died of his wounds two days later. His parents were informed by telegram on 9 April.

He is buried in the Duisans British Cemetery at Etrun, about 9 kilometres west of Arras, grave VI F 36. It was selected as the site for the cemetery of 8th Casualty Clearing Station (CCS) in February 1917. It built up quickly with those who died from that CCS (until April 1918), 19th CCS (until March 1918) and 41st CCS (until July 1918). It is likely therefore that Tom Sadler was being treated in 41st CCS when he died. A memorial service was held in the Baptist Church in Henley on Sunday, 14 April 1918 and his name is recorded on the War Memorial there.

British War Medal and Victory Medal.

1901 & 1911 Census; CWGC; SDGW; MIC; *Herald* (12 April 1918).

†Sammons, Albert Alfred (1899-1918)

Private 90052, 2/4th Battalion London Regiment (Royal Fusiliers); formerly Private 40350, 4th Battalion Somerset Light Infantry.

Albert Sammons was born in Small Heath, near Birmingham, the son of Alfred and Laura Agnes Sammons. In 1901 his father was a cowman, living at Avenue Cottage, North Bromsgrove and Albert was 1. By 1911 the family was living in Henley, where his father was now a Fruiterer. Albert's mother had died and his father had married again in about 1909. Albert, aged 11, now had a younger brother Frank Edward (8). His father was conscripted in 1916, and was described as a Greengrocer of Henley in Arden when he made a successful application for exemption before the War Tribunal on 2 June 1916.

Albert enlisted in Stratford upon Avon, when his next of kin was given as his father, Alfred Sammons of Little Alne, Wootton Wawen. Albert was home on leave in January 1918.

He was killed in action at Villers Bretonneux on 25 April 1918, aged 18, but his parents cannot have been informed until some weeks later as the *Herald* of 31 May reported that he had been posted missing on 25 April. His name appears on the Pozieres Memorial on the Somme. The Memorial commemorates over 14,000 men who have no known grave and were killed during the retreat of 5th Army from 21 March to 7 August 1918.

British War Medal and Victory Medal.

1901 & 1911 Census; CWGC; SDGW; MIC; *Herald* (1 February & 31 May 1918).

Shelton, Mark (1876-fl 1919)

Sergeant 24005, 5th Battalion Royal West Surrey Regiment.

Mark was born in Henley in 1876, the son of Henry and Ann Shelton. In 1881 they were living in Applethwaite, Westmorland where his father was working as a Domestic Gardener. Living with them were his younger brother and sister. At the time of the 1901 Census he was in a Military Hospital in the City of Westminster serving as a Private in the 2nd Battalion of the Scots Guards: he was later invalided out of the Battalion. In 1911 he was living at his father in law's house in Holmwood, Surrey: Mark was now a widower, had a son Henry Edward (7) and was working as a Fly Driver.

He had enlisted in the 5th Battalion of the Royal West Surrey Regiment (Territorial Force) on 7 January 1909, by which time his wife had already died. At his medical examination on 14 January his height was 6'2", his vision good and his physical development excellent. He went on a training camp each year and was promoted to Lance Corporal in 1910. His regiment served in India from 29 October 1914 until 1 December 1915 during which time he was promoted to Sergeant. His next of kin was a friend, Revd Canon Palmes of The Vicarage, Holmwood, Surrey. He moved with his regiment to France on 2 December 1915. In 1918 he was awarded the DCM, the citation appearing in the *London Gazette* of 12 June: "For conspicuous gallantry and devotion to duty. As Transport Sergeant he brought up ammunition and water under heavy fire. His conduct in action has at all times been of a high order."

Mark was discharged on 26 May 1919 as "surplus to requirements, having suffered impairment since entry into the service".

DCM, British War Medal, Victory Medal, Territorial Efficiency Medal.

1881, 1901 and 1911 Census; *London Gazette* (12 June 1918); MIC; Service Record.

Shilton, Frederick Walton OBE (1883/4-fl 1921)

Major, Army Dental Corps; formerly Lieutenant, Royal Army Medical Corps.

He was born in Handsworth, the eldest son of Edward and Isabella Shilton (see Shilton, Roy O for details of his family in 1891 and 1901). He studied at the University of Birmingham. Married to Mary Elizabeth, at the time of the 1911 Census he was a Dental Surgeon and was staying in Llandudno with her and their newly born daughter, Dorothy Margaret Walton Shilton (aged 1 month), his sister Nellie Kathleen and a nurse. He was a Dental Surgeon living at The Elms in the High Street when his son Vincent Walton was baptised in St John's on 13 December 1913. (WGH's mother was his cook/housekeeper).

He went to France on 1 July 1916.

He stayed in the forces for some years after the war, as his MIC gives his rank in the Army Dental Corps, which was not formed until 1921. The Supplement to the *London Gazette* of 7 April 1920 noted that temporary Captain Frederick W. Shilton OBE was to be temporary Major (without increased emoluments) whilst specially employed, with effect from 2 June 1919.

OBE, British War Medal and Victory Medal.

1901 & 1911 Census; MIC.

Shilton, Roy O (1889/90-fl 1921)

Lieutenant, Somerset Light Infantry; formerly Corporal 113064, Royal Engineers and Lance Corporal 11154, Coldstream Guards.

He was born in Handsworth, the third son of Edward Shilton, a Surgeon Dentist, and his wife Isabella. In 1891 he was one and living at 190 Soho Hill, Handsworth with his parents and his brothers Frederick Walton (7) and Arthur Victor (2). In 1901 the family was living at 61 Soho Road, Handsworth and Roy now had a younger sister Nellie (2). In 1911 Roy was a Dental Student, visiting Mr & Mrs William Innes in the borough of Poplar in London.

Roy had gone up to the University of Birmingham in 1908 to read Medicine. He could have been commissioned into the RAMC, but joined the Coldstream Guards as a Private on the outbreak of war and went to France on 27 November 1914. He was a Lance Corporal when he was wounded in France in March 1915 and incapacitated for three months. On his return to active service he was transferred to the Royal Engineers because of his knowledge of chemistry. He was promoted to Corporal and subsequently commissioned into the Somerset Light Infantry on 19 February 1916. The Supplement to the *London Gazette* of 22 December 1919 reported the temporary appointment of Lieutenant R O Shilton to the Service Battalion, Somerset Light Infantry with effect from 19 November 1919. He applied for his 1914-15 Star on 23 January 1920, at which time his address was 97 Hagley Road, Edgbaston, Birmingham.

His two brothers also attended Birmingham University and also enlisted. Frederick (*qv*) was a Lieutenant in the RAMC. Arthur joined the Inns of Court

Officer Training Corps on 11 October 1915, number 6746; he was commissioned into the Oxford & Bucks Light Infantry on 7 May 1916 and subsequently attached to the Royal Inniskilling Fusiliers where he reached the rank of Lieutenant (*Inns of Court*, p 316).

1914-15 Star, British War Medal and Victory Medal.

1901 & 1911 Census; MIC; *LG* (22 December 1919).

Sladen, Gerald Carew CB, CMG, DSO & Bar, MC (1881-1930)

Brigadier-General, Rifle Brigade.

Gerald was born on 1 January 1881, the son of Colonel Sir Edward Bose Sladen and his second wife, Katherine Jane Carew. He was educated at Eton, leaving in 1897. He married Mabel Ursula, daughter of Sir Archibald Ernest Orr-Ewing, 3rd Bart, in 1913 and had one son (Edward Carew) and two daughters (Geraldine and Ruth Violet). He was commissioned as a 2nd Lieutenant in the Rifle Brigade on 19 October 1901; Lieutenant, 8 March 1905; Captain, 3 October 1911; Major, 18 May 1916; Brevet Lieutenant-Colonel 1 January 1917 and promoted to temporary Brigadier-General during the years 1916-1919.

Gerald had served in the South African War from 1899-1902; he was slightly wounded at Standerton on 27 April 1902 when serving as a 2nd Lieutenant with the 4th Battalion of the Rifle Brigade; he was mentioned in dispatches and was awarded the Queen's Medal with 3 clasps and the King's Medal with 2 clasps. He served in Somaliland 1908-1910 (medal & clasp). In 1911 he was serving as a Lieutenant with the 4th Battalion, stationed at the Citadel in Cairo.

He began the war as a Captain in the Rifle Brigade, but was one of the regular soldiers who were transferred to stiffen up the Territorial Army and was Adjutant of 8th Battalion, Royal Warwickshire Regiment when he went to France in March

Lt-Col Sladen and 5th Battalion HQ. Near Ovillers 1916

1915. On 12 July 1915 he took over command of 5th Battalion with the temporary rank of Lieutenant-Colonel.

He commanded the Battalion for over a year until he took over command of 143rd Infantry Brigade on 4 September 1916 with the temporary rank of Brigadier-General. He was mentioned 8 times in dispatches. During his service with the 5th Battalion he was awarded the DSO in January 1916, an MC on 28 June 1916 and a bar to his DSO for gallantry near Ovillers in the Somme on 16 July 1916. The *Herald* reported that the bar to his DSO and the Russian Order of St Stanislaus had been awarded "for taking a whole system of enemy trenches". In December 1917 he was mentioned in Sir Douglas Haig's dispatches for distinguished and gallant service and devotion to duty while serving in Italy. He was awarded the CMG on 1 January 1919 and the CB later in the year. He was also awarded the Italian *Croce di Guerra* and the Order of St Maurice and St Lazarus.

Gerald and his wife lived at Hillfield, Liveridge Hill, Beaudesert during the war years. He retired from the army in 1919 with the honorary rank of Brigadier-General and moved to Fintry, Rongai, Kenya. He died on 21 April 1930 at Nakuru in Kenya, leaving an estate in England of £3,735.

CB, CMG, DSO & Bar, MC, Order of St Stanislaus with Swords, *Croce di Guerra* & Order of St Maurice & St Lazarus, Mentioned in Dispatches on numerous occasions.

Queen's South African Medal with 3 clasps, King's South African Medal with 2 clasps, 1914-15 Star, British War Medal & Victory Medal.

1911 Census; MIC; *Who Was Who*; Distinguished Service Order Part II p 342; LG (14 January & 26 October 1916); *Herald* (29 September & 10 November 1916, 21 December 1917).

Smallwood, George Edward (1898-1967)

Private 16592, Labour Corps; formerly Private 69091, Nottinghamshire & Derbyshire Regiment.

There are four MICs in the names of George E Smallwood, of which the above is the most likely.

He was baptised in St John's on 14 August 1898, the son of George Smallwood, a carpenter of Henley, and his wife Sarah Anne. In 1901 he was living in Henley with his parents, his sisters Fanny Gertrude (10), Alice Lilian (7) and Daisy(5) and his brother Thomas Harry (4 months). His father had died by 1911 and he was living with his mother, younger brother Henry Thomas (10) and younger sister Mary Elizabeth (7) in a three-roomed house at 269 Henley. All of the children were at school.

The *Herald* reported in February 1918 that Private H Smallwood (*sic*) had recently been home on leave.

He married Emma (maiden name not known). He died on 27 April 1967 and is buried in St Nicholas' churchyard.

1901 & 1911 Census; *Herald* (15 February 1918).

† Spears, George Amos (1898-1918)

Private 30729, 5th (Service) Battalion Dorsetshire Regiment.

He was the only child of George and Florrie Spears (*nee* Harbridge) of 220 Warwick Road, Henley in Arden. Amos was born in Birmingham in 1898 and in 1901 was living with his parents at 36 Lingard Street, Aston. His father was a warehouseman in a screw works. By 1911 his father was a Screw Works Manager and the family was living in a five-roomed house at 10 Asquith Road, Ward End, Birmingham. Amos was at school.

He enlisted in July 1917, at which time he was working in Birmingham. His battalion was serving with 34th Brigade, 11th Division when he was killed instantly by a shell on 12 April 1918, at the age of 19. He had been in France for just over three weeks. His commanding officer wrote that "he was buried at a small village behind the line and I have had a white wooden cross put up with his name, regiment and date on it". He was subsequently buried in Philosophe British Cemetery, Mazingarbe, Pas de Calais, grave III C 33.

Philosophe British Cemetery

His name was added to the Members of His Majesty's Forces by F C Parkes in the latter's copy of the Henley Peace Celebrations Booklet.

British War Medal and Victory Medal.

1901 & 1911 Census; CWGC; MIC; *Herald* (3 May 1918).

Stanton, Leonard Thomas (1896-fl 1973)

Leonard was born on 3 November 1896, the elder son of Thomas and Ellen Stanton.

In 1901 he was living with his parents in the High Street, together with his elder sisters Lilian (9) and Dorothy (8). His father was a Postman. In 1911 he was living with his parents, his elder sister Lilian and younger brother Clarence (9) in a six-roomed house at 52 Henley in Arden and was employed as an Errand Boy. He was a member of the Warwick Number 11 VAD and took part in their annual inspection and field display on 6 August 1914. He was reported as having joined the colours in the *Herald* of 28 January 1916. In the absence of an MIC, it is unlikely that he served overseas. In the photograph, Leonard is standing on the right.

After the war he emigrated to the United States. His US passport issued in 1959 states that he was a Painter Contractor and was living on Long Island, New York: he was 5'4" tall, with brown eyes and grey hair. He married Lucy Hargreaves and had a son (Leonard T Stanton Jnr).

1901 & 1911 Census; *Herald* (28 January 1916).

Steele, Joseph Harold (1894-1975)

Sergeant 144954, Machine Gun Corps; formerly Sergeant 1972, Warwickshire Yeomanry.

Joseph was born in Swynnerton, Staffordshire on 21 February 1894 the eighth of the 11 children of Joseph and Sarah Steele (*nee* Richardson). In 1901 the family

was living at Mays Hill Farm and was still living there in 1911. At the latter date, Joseph was 17 and was described as a Farmer's Son working on the farm. He was an elder brother of Wallace Harold Steele (*qv*).

Joseph was called up as a member of D Squadron with the Yeomanry on 5 August 1915. He sailed with them on the *Saturnia* from Avonmouth on 11 April 1915, reaching Alexandria on 24 April. He embarked for Gallipoli with the Yeomanry as infantry on the *Ascania* on 14 August 1915 (Adderley, p 25). Joseph survived the Gallipoli campaign and returned with the regiment to Alexandria on the *Themistocles* on 28 November. By the time he was mentioned in Lieutenant-Colonel Cheapes' dispatches on 17 June 1917 for "exceptionally good work" during the period 1 to 31 May 1917, he had been promoted to Corporal

(Adderley, p 104). He took part in Allenby's advance through Sinai, Palestine and Syria and left Alexandria on 23 May 1918, sailing for France on the *Leasowe Castle*. He survived its sinking on 27 May. He then served in France, transferred with the rest of the Warwickshire Yeomanry to the Machine Gun Corps.

1914-15 Star, British War Medal and Victory Medal.

1901 & 1911 Census; Adderley; MIC; *Herald* (10 December 1915).

Steele, Wallace Herbert (1898-1987)

Flight Cadet 175608, Royal Air Force.

Wallace was a younger brother of Joseph Harold Steele (*qv*) and was born in Wootton Wawen on 5 February 1898. In 1901 he was three and living with his parents Joseph and Sarah Steele at Mays Hill Farm, the youngest of their 10 children, the others being John (20), Charlotte (18), Richard (16), Fanny (15), William Otho (13), Rose (11), Beatrice (8), Joseph (7) and Daisy (4). In 1911 he was still living there with his parents (who had been married for 30 years) and now had a younger sister Doris Hilda (9). Wallace was 13 and at school. He was 19 and a farm bailiff working for his mother on Mays Hill Farm, a farm of 370 acres, when he appeared before the Stratford District Tribunal on 30 March 1917. One of his elder brothers attended (probably William Otho) and said that as he had  now taken on another farm, the management of this one practically devolved upon Wallace. Wallace was given exemption for two months. At the meeting of the Tribunal on 22 June, his case was further adjourned for one month to enable instructions from the War Office to be clarified. At the meeting held on 27 July, he was given conditional exemption until 1 January 1918. At the meeting on 15 March 1918, the National Service representative agreed to his exemption.

Despite this, Wallace joined the Royal Air Force at Hampstead in June 1918. He was on leave in early January 1919, when it was reported that he had done much flying during the last two months.

1901 & 1911 Census; RAF record; *Herald* (6 April & 27 July 1917, 22 March 1918 & 10 January 1919).

Stinson, Frederic (*sic*) (1884-fl 1927)

Private M/338376, Army Service Corps.

Known as Fred, he was born in Whitwick, Leicestershire in 1884 the second son of John and Emma Stinson. He was living with them in North Street, Whitwick in 1901 together with his elder brother John (24) and younger brothers Oscar (12) and Arnold (3). His father was a butcher and Fred was working as a Joiner's Apprentice. In 1911 he was 26 and living in a five-roomed house at 185 High Street with his housekeeper Louisa Langford (55). His occupation was given as Master Builder.

He married May Kathleen Southgate at Melton Mowbray in 1912 and their daughter Mary was baptised at St John's Church on 27 June 1916, when Fred was described as a Builder of Henley. Mary lived only a few days, dying on 1 July.

Fred applied for exemption from military service to the Stratford Rural District Tribunal on 25 August 1916. A builder and plumber of Henley in Arden, he said he was the largest employer of labour in the locality. Before the war he had employed 31 men but this number was now down to 14. If he was called up it would mean financial ruin for him. He had been to Budbrook for a medical and passed for garrison duty abroad. Fred devoted a portion of his time to Red Cross work, being a member of Warwick Number 11 VAD (he scored 70% in the examinations held in the autumn of 1914). He was granted exemption until 1 January 1917. At the tribunal held on 26 January 1917 Frank claimed to be exempt as he was a machinist and this was a certified trade: the military representative did not accept this. He was given a final exemption to 31 March. He took his case to the Warwickshire Appeal Tribunal, where he presented a petition signed by over 40 local residents on the importance of his business to the town. The Tribunal removed the condition of finality attached to his exemption. However, Frank made no further appearance before the District Tribunal and he enlisted at some time after 31 March 1917. On 19 October 1917, the *Herald* reported that "Mr Fred Stinson of Henley, who entered the army some little time ago, has sent word that he has arrived safely at Basra on the Persian Gulf". He was later reported as being "in the neighbourhood of the Garden of Eden". He was in hospital in January 1918. Fred was demobilised in May 1919 and re-opened his Mile Stone Works in the High Street after a brief holiday.

He was working as a builder at 183 High Street in 1924 and appears on a photograph of the Court Leet in 1921, wearing his medals.

British War Medal and Victory Medal.

1901 & 1911 Census; MIC; Kelly 1924; *Herald* (1 September 1916, 2 & 16 February, 19 October & 30 November 1917, 1 February 1918 & 16 May 1919).

Stockley, William (1888-fl 1921)

Lance Corporal 201968, Royal Warwickshire Regiment.

He was living in New Road, Henley when he enlisted at Stratford upon Avon on 15 November 1915: his height was 5'7", his weight was 145 lbs and he was working on a farm.

William was mobilized on 15 May 1916 and was posted to the 5th Battalion on 2 September 1916. He was wounded on 17 November 1916 and left the BEF on 10 September 1917, being in Hospital in Honiton, Devon from 13 September to 20 October suffering from a gunshot wound to the left hand and having the index finger amputated: he joined the 7th Reserve Battalion in the UK on 30 October 1917. William returned to the BEF on 15 December 1917 and was posted to the 2/8th Battalion on 23 December. He remained with the BEF until 12 October 1918. He was in Hospital in Bury St Edmunds from 12 to 21 October with a gunshot wound in the abdomen, caused by a machine gun bullet. He was posted to 2/7th Battalion on 14 December 1918 and became a paid Lance Corporal. He married Annie Page at St Nicholas' Church, Pershore on 30 December 1918.

William was awarded the MM on a date which does not appear in his Service Record and was awarded the DCM while serving with the 10th Battalion, his citation appearing in the *London Gazette* of 5 December 1918 "For conspicuous gallantry and endurance. He took part in the capture of three strong posts, including one machine gun post. Although badly wounded three times, he continued to lead his men until a fourth serious wound rendered him helpless. His conduct was magnificent". William was discharged from the 10th Battalion on 18 January 1919 and was awarded the Silver War Badge (B90345) on 13 February 1919.

DCM, MM, British War Medal, Victory Medal and Silver War Badge; Belgian Decoration Militaire.

MIC; Service Record.

Stokes, Francis Edward (1892/3-fl 1919)

Sapper 4011, Canadian Overseas Expeditionary Force.

Known as Frank, his Attestation records his date of birth as 28 January 1892 and his place of birth as Birmingham, England. However, the 1901 Census states that he was 8 years old and had been born in Henley in Arden. He was then living in the High Street in Henley with his mother, Hannah Sutton Stokes, his grandmother, Mary Hannah Stokes, his half sister, Mary Hannah Sutton Findon (19), his half-brother William Sutton Findon (*qv*) (18) and his younger brother Roland (7). His mother was head of the household, married (rather than widowed) and employed as a Baker. He was working as a Butcher in 1911, living in what is now the Guild Hall (see Findon, William Sutton for details of the household at that time).

When Frank enlisted in Montreal on 12 February 1915 his address was 1275 Wellington Street, Verdun, Montreal and he gave his brother Roland as his next of kin. He was employed as a Butcher. Frank had passed his medical two days earlier, when he was 5'10½" tall with a 37" chest: his complexion was pale, his eyes blue, his hair brown and he had vaccination marks on his left arm. In April 1915 the *Herald* reported that he had emigrated to Canada some time ago and had joined the forces. In June 1916 he was serving with the Canadian forces at home or in France and had recently visited Henley.

1901 & 1911 Census; Canadian Attestation Paper; *Herald* (23 April 1915 & 23 June 1916).

Taylor, Ernest Frank (1886-1963)

The nature of his military service cannot be established. In the absence of an MIC he is unlikely to have gone overseas.

Ernest was baptised in St John's Church on 11 April 1886, the son of William and Emma Taylor of Henley: his father was then a Labourer. In 1891 he was living in the High Street with his parents, three elder brothers William (14), John (12) and

James (9) and his younger brother Herbert (*qv*) (2): his father was now a Bricklayer and his eldest brother William was working as a Plough Boy. In 1901 he was living in the High Street, Henley with his parents, and three brothers Harry John (23), James Charles (19) and Herbert Alfred (12). Ernest was now working as an Errand Boy. He had become a Butcher by 1911, when he was living in an eight-roomed house at 271 South End, Henley in Arden with his parents (who had been married for 35 years), elder brother John Henry and younger brother Herbert.

He was still living in Henley when he married Elizabeth Thompson Craddock of Walsall Wood in 1915. He died in 1963.

St John's PR; 1891, 1901 and 1911 Census.

Taylor, Herbert Alfred (1889-1968)

The nature of his military service cannot be established.

Herbert was baptised in St John's Church on 21 April 1889, the son of William and Emma Taylor of Henley and the younger brother of Ernest Frank Taylor (*qv*): his father was a Bricklayer. In 1891 and 1901 he was living in Henley with his parents (see Taylor, Ernest Frank for details of his family), as he was in 1911. In that year was employed as a Domestic Groom.

He married Alice Jane and had two children baptised in St John's: Alice Emma in December 1915 (when he was a Carter of 159 High Street) and William Herbert in December 1920 (when he was a Labourer and still at 159 High Street).

At the Military Tribunal on 12 May 1916 Herbert Taylor (27) of 159 High Street was employed by Thomas Hood Truelove, coal merchant, as his bag wagoner. Truelove had already had 7 of his men go to the front and claimed hardship if Taylor were to go. Taylor was granted exemption for a month. He was later granted a further exemption until 29 September. When the case came before the tribunal again on 20 October Taylor was referred for medical examination at Budbrook. At a third appeal, Truelove stated that he couldn't find anyone to take Taylor's place. Taylor was given exemption until 25 March 1917 and the military representative stated his intention to appeal against this decision. The case came before the tribunal again on 1 December 1916 and Truelove now pleaded Taylor's honesty as the chief reason for Taylor's exemption. He was given exemption until 31 January 1917, but there was to be no further appeal without leave.

Herbert is likely to have enlisted shortly after this date, as he did not appear again before the Tribunal. There are no service records in his name.

He died in 1968 at the age of 79.

St John's PR; 1891, 1901 and 1911 Census; *Herald* (19 May, 23 June, 2 October, 17 November & 1 December 1916).

Tippett, George Charles (1862-1943)

WO II 203569, Suffolk Regiment; formerly Regimental Quartermaster Sergeant 464, Warwickshire Yeomanry.

George Tippett was born in Helston, Cornwall. In 1911 he was living in the seven-roomed Red House in Henley with his wife Mary, his two daughters Mary Catherine (15) and Alice Margaret (13) and his son Edward George (9). He was then described as an Army Pensioner and a Clerk in a Tax Office. His son was at King Edward's School in Stratford in 1915. George was a member of the Forest of Arden Bowling Club.

He was a professional soldier, who joined the 18th Hussars in 1879. He spent some years in Ireland, his wife Mary (whom he married in about 1894) being born in Tipperary and his elder daughter Mary in Dublin. His younger daughter Alice was born in Aldershot and his son Edward in Snitterfield: another child is recorded in the 1911 Census as having died. George remained with the 18th Hussars for about 8 years, until he joined the Warwickshire Yeomanry in 1897.

The permanent staff of the Warwickshire Yeomanry (c 1910) with RQMS Tippett seated front left

During the annual camp in May 1910 he was presented with a gold watch and a purse of gold by the commanding officer, Colonel Beech, in appreciation of his long and valuable service with the regiment. He was one of the HQ staff, who paraded at Warwick Common when the 1st line of the Warwickshire Yeomanry was mobilized on 10 August 1914 (Adderley, p 6.). The *Herald* reported in September 1915 that he had a long and good record, had already done much useful organisational work in the present campaign and was on full active service, being then in Alexandria. He did not go to Gallipoli with the regiment. In March 1916 he was home on leave: he had responded at the outbreak of war as an old campaigner and was "certainly now entitled to a share of less exacting duties". It was probably at this stage of his career that he was transferred to the Suffolk Regiment.

He was discharged on 26 March 1919 at the age of 55 on medical grounds, as he had developed a hernia. A Silver War Badge (B165011) was issued to him on 9 May 1919.

He died in 1943, aged 81.

1914-15 Star, British War Medal, Victory Medal and Silver War Badge.

1911 Census; Adderley; MIC; SWB; *Herald* (3 September 1915 & 10 March1916).

Topham, Cecil William (1892-1969)

Lance Corporal.

He was born in Wolverhampton on 18 October 1892, the son of Joseph and Clara Topham. In 1901 he was 8 and living with his parents and his elder brother Alfred (10) at 22 Arthur Street, Wolverhampton. His father was a Telegraph Clerk. He had left the family home by 1911, when he was lodging at 61 North Street, Wednesfield and working as a Postman.

Cecil married Lilian Elisabeth Victoria Huggard of Henley in St John's Church on 3 August 1913. She was an elder sister of three Huggard brothers who served in the war (see Cyril Godfrey, Gordon Cuthbert and Leslie Sydney Huggard). In 1901 she had been 14 and in domestic service. They had three children baptised in Henley: Cecil Gordon on 8 August 1915, Eileen Lilian on 19 October 1919 (both in St John's) and Rita Ann on 12 May 1921 in St Nicholas'. In each of these entries Cecil Topham is recorded as being a Postman and living at 247 High Street.

He served in the UK, as no MIC has been found. In November 1917 the *Herald* reported that Lance Corporal Topham was home on leave for a short period.

He died in Wolverhampton in 1969, aged 76.

St John's & St Nicholas' PR; 1901 & 1911 Census; *Herald* (30 November 1917).

Wain, William George (1888-fl 1919)

Private 20194, Royal Warwickshire Regiment.

William was born in Wootton Wawen, the son of George and Elizabeth Wain, and was baptised in St Peter's Church on 14 February 1888. In 1891 he was 3 and living with his parents, his brother Harry (8) and his sisters Margaret (7) and Mary (5) in Wootton Wawen. His father was a Wagoner. He was still living with his parents in 1901, when his father was described as a Miller's Wagoner; also living with them were his sister Elizabeth (9) and his brother George (7). By 1911 his father had died and he was living with his mother and brother George, in a four-roomed house in Wootton Wawen. William was then a Jobbing Gardener. The 1911 Census shows that he was one of six children.

He served abroad from 1916 or later. The *Birmingham Post* of 28 May 1917 reported that he had been wounded.

William married Louisa Thorneycroft in 1915 and was described as a Soldier of Henley when their daughter Margaret was baptised in St John's on 19 May 1918.

British War Medal and Victory Medal.

St John's PR; 1891, 1901 & 1911 Census; MIC.

Wall, Frank (1884/5-fl 1919)

Possibly Frank Samuel Wall, Sergeant 614081, Royal Horse Artillery (Territorial Force). Other possibilities are F Wall, Private 2082, RWR wounded (*Birmingham Post* 30 September 1915) for whom no MIC has been found and Frank Wall, Private 77142 Royal Defence Corps, formerly Private 7879, 10th Battalion RWR. The last named had enlisted on 22 September 1914 and went to France on 19 July 1915: he was discharged having been wounded on 15 October 1918 and was issued with a Silver War Badge (B28668) on 7 November 1918. No connection of any of them with Henley has been found, other that the fact that Frank Samuel Wall was the elder brother of Thomas Wall (*qv*), who lived in Henley.

Frank Samuel Wall was the second son of Thomas and Elizabeth Wall of Studley. In 1891 he was living in Studley with his mother, two brothers (including his younger brother Thomas (*qv*)) and three sisters. His mother was then a Charwoman. In 1901 Frank S Wall was living in Station Road, Studley with his brother in law's family (John & Harriet Stanford and their three children) and Frank's grandmother Caroline Wall: Frank was then working as a Farm Labourer. By 1911 he was married, working as a Cab Driver and living with his wife Edith Mary Ada (26) and his sister Emily Edith (20) in a five-roomed house at Ferndale, Station Road, Studley.

Frank joined the Territorial Force at Redditch on 22 June 1908 at the age of 22 years and ten months. He was then a Groom, living at The Nook, Station Road, Studley. At his medical inspection at Redditch on 6 July 1908 his height was 5'8"and his physical development was good. He was appointed to 2nd South Midland Brigade, Royal Field Artillery, but transferred to the Warwickshire Royal Horse Artillery on 23 July 1909. Frank attended camp for two weeks in each of the years 1908, 1910, 1911 and 1912.

He was a Gunner in the Warwickshire Royal Horse Artillery (Reserve) when he signed at Leamington for service overseas on 14 November 1914. He was promoted Corporal on 5 February 1915 and was in 2/1st Warwickshire Royal Horse Artillery at Diss when he agreed to extend his service on 28 April 1915. Frank was a Sergeant and still in Norfolk when he signed for a further four years on 13 March 1916. He had a gunshot wound in his left forearm on 15 August 1917. Frank was given special leave for a week in March 1920 and was in the Royal Victoria Hospital when he was again given leave from 19 June to September 1920, his address while on leave being Park Cottage, Hewell, Redditch. He served with the colours from 5 August 1914 until his discharge as physically unfit on 21 September 1920 having served a total of 12 years and 95 days since 1908: his character was given as "very good". He was still living there in May 1922 when he applied for the Territorial Force Medal.

He had four sons, Gordon (born 7 April 1911), Sidney (21 November 1913), Percival (15 January 1917) and Douglas (2 February 1919). In November 1936 he applied to join the Post Office in Redditch and gave his consent for details of his army service to be supplied.

British War Medal, Victory Medal and Territorial Force Medal.

1891, 1901 & 1911 Census; Service Record; MIC.

Wall, Thomas (1889-1936)

Private Ply/2433/S, 1st Royal Marine Battalion.

Known as Tom, he was 12 in 1901 and living in Averys Yard, Alcester Road, Studley with his parents. His father was also Thomas Wall, then aged 43 and a Needle Stamper: his mother Elizabeth was 40 and employed as a Laundress. They had five daughters and two other sons. The family was living at Allendale, Station Road, Studley in 1911: it then comprised his parents (who had been married for 30 years), Thomas, his younger sisters Harriet Elizabeth (15) and Gladys Mary (10) together with his parents' granddaughter Edith Mary Elsie Briney (2). Thomas was working as a Needle Hardener.

Tom married Elizabeth (surname not known) and had the following children:

Leslie Robert, baptised St John's Church 18 October 1915. (He is likely to have died in infancy, as his brother Bernard has no knowledge of him.)
A daughter, born 1920 (Dorothy?)
Bernard, born 1929.

At the time of his son's baptism in 1915, Tom Wall was 28, living at 6 High Street and was employed as a carter by Hawkes and Sinclair-Brown, millers of Henley. He had been passed for general service when he appeared before the Stratford Rural District Tribunal on 20 July 1917 with two of his colleagues. Both of his colleagues, Dobbs and Haines (*qv*) were given conditional exemption, but the Tribunal considered Wall ought to go for military service.

The *Herald* of 31 May 1918 reported that Private T Wall, 1st R M Battalion, was a POW at Limburg. He had been captured on 26 March and a letter from him posted early April only arrived on 25 May. Although nothing had been heard of him for 2 months, his wife had never given up hope. He returned to Henley in January 1919.

He died in 1936 at the age of 47.

British War Medal & Victory Medal

1891, 1901 & 1911 Census; Royal Marine Medal Roll 1914-1920; *Herald* (27 July 1917, 31 May 1918 & 24 January 1919); Bernard Wall (his son).

Watkins, Frank Kelsey (1894-fl 1919)

Private 72763, Royal Army Medical Corps.

He was born in Northampton, the son of William and Annie Watkins. In 1901 Frank was seven and living in the parish of St James', Northampton with his parents, three brothers, three sisters and his paternal grandparents. His father worked in a shoe factory. Frank was living with his family in a six-roomed house at 5 Althorp Road, Northampton in 1911, his age then being given as 16. He was employed as a Boot Clicker: six other members of his family were also working in the boot industry, two of them as Boot Clickers, three as Boot Closers and one as a Boot Laster.

Frank moved to Henley and took part in the annual inspection and field display of the Warwick Number 11 VAD on 6 August 1914. He had a mark of 55% in the examinations on Hygiene and Sanitation in the autumn of that year.

Frank enlisted in Northampton on 28 October 1915 and at his Attestation gave his address as 5 Althorp Road and his next of kin as his father (though this was changed to his mother later in his service, presumably on the death of his father). He was 5'10" tall with a chest of 34". Frank was posted to the RAMC on 2 November 1915 and went overseas as part of the BEF on 24 September 1916. He was reported missing on 29 May 1918 and was subsequently found to be a Prisoner of War, remaining such until 17 December 1918. Army Form 804 gives the dates of 6 letters and postcards from Frank to his mother. His camp address was Number 3106, 3P Company, Kriegsgefangenen-Lager, Langensalza, Germany. Langensalza was a small spa town in Saxony.

Frank was repatriated to England from Germany on the SS *Prince George*, landing in Hull on 10 January 1919. He was then sent to Ripon POW Camp, from which he was given leave on 12 January. Frank was demobilized in medical category B1 on 18 April 1919 from Number 1 Dispersal Unit, Purfleet. His military history sheet shows that he spent 3 years and 174 days in the Army, made up as follows:

Home Service	28 October 1915 to 23 September 1916	331 days
BEF	24 September 1916 to 26 May 1918	1 year 245 days
POW	27 May 1918 to 17 December 1918	205 days
Home	18 December 1918 to 18 April 1918	122 days

On 16 June 1919 the Ministry of Pensions awarded him a pension of 8s 3d per week in respect of a 30% disability, the precise nature of which cannot be determined from the records, but which was regarded as having been aggravated by his military service. It was awarded from 25 April 1919 and was to be reviewed in six weeks.

British War Medal and Victory Medal.

1901 & 1911 Census; Service Record; MIC; *Herald* (14 August 1914 & 28 January 1916).

Watkins, J

This is insufficient information to identify his military service.

He was a casual helper with the Fire Brigade in 1919.

Watkins, John Valentine (1884-1965)

Private M/402985, Royal Army Service Corps.

Known in his childhood as Valentine, he was later known as Jack. He was born in Alcester, the son of John and Emma Watkins. In 1891 he was seven and living in Broadway with his parents, his sisters Violet (9) and Daisy (4) and his brother James (2). He was a groom in 1901, being one of six servants employed by the Revd George Arbuthnot, Vicar of Stratford upon Avon. In 1911 he was 27 and employed as a Domestic Coachman. He had been married for four years and was living at Greengates, 88 Henley in Arden with his wife Florence (27), his daughters Lillian Evelyn (3) and Alice Florence (3 months) and his son John Edward (2). He was still living there in 1914: his wife Florence (*nee* Bartlett) was housekeeper and he was chauffeur to Dr Nelson. They had 9 children:

Lilian Evelyn, baptised at St John's on 8 March 1908;
John Edward, baptised 18 July 1909;
Alice Florence, baptised 5 February 1911;
Margaret Annie, baptised 24 November 1912;
Frederick Frank, baptised 15 August 1915;
Constance May, baptised 9 June 1918;
Dorothy Agnes, baptised 3 June 1920;
Monica;
Fred.

Jack was a member of Warwick Number 11 VAD and scored 70% in the examinations held in the autumn of 1914.

He was called up in October 1916 and on 20 October Dr Ernest Nelson applied for exemption for him at the Stratford Tribunal on the grounds that Watkins took charge of his surgery and acted as his chauffeur and confidential servant. If Watkins were taken, he (Nelson) wouldn't have time to devote to Red Cross work. Watkins was 32 and married with 5 children. The chairman of the tribunal, Charles Couchman, thought that in view of the voluntary work done by Nelson, he might be allowed to retain Watkins' services. Watkins was given conditional exemption while he remained in his occupation.

Nelson again applied for exemption for Watkins in February 1918. Watkins' family responsibilities were now increased by helping to keep an invalid mother and sister. Nelson thought that Watkins was entitled to some consideration, especially as there were thousands of young men working in munitions and on the land who had never been called. He (Nelson) would not be able to maintain his work as the

Medical Director of the Red Cross Society for the county, which had 39 auxiliary hospitals, if Watkins were taken. The Army representative said that he appreciated Nelson's work, but felt bound to bring the case forward as Watkins was a class A man. The tribunal (Couchman in the chair) felt that Watkins had a strong domestic case, so postponed the decision to enable him to put in a personal appeal[199]. At a meeting of the Tribunal in March, Watkins put in a personal appearance. He stated that he was quite willing to do his bit if called upon, but did not think he should be called up while so many strong young people were available with no responsibilities. He had a wife and five children and an invalid mother and sister who were more or less dependent on him. The chairman (Couchman) said this was a very difficult case and he personally sympathized with Watkins. He did not know if anything could be done to comb out some of those men who were hiding under an umbrella in the Henley district and earning plenty of money at munitions. But Watkins was an 'A' man and they could not grant him a long period of grace. He was exempted until 1 June 1918 and probably enlisted in that month.

Jack Watkins (on the right) somewhere in France

Jack served in France and returned home with a dent in his helmet where it had been hit by shrapnel.

In 1936 he was a grocer at 263 High Street. He died in 1965, aged 81.

British War Medal and Victory Medal.

1891, 1901 & 1911 Census; MIC; *Herald* (27 October 1916, 15 February and 22 March 1918); Mrs Rita Redfern (his granddaughter).

---

199 *Herald* 15 February 1918

Webster, Fisher (1897-fl 1919)

Lance Bombardier 89535, Royal Field Artillery.

Fisher was baptised in St John's on 7 March 1897, the son of James and Mary Ann Webster. There is some doubt about Fisher's date of birth. His Attestation gives his age as 19 years and 4 months on 24 August 1914, making his year of birth 1893, while his Certificate of Identity (Army Form Z 11) issued when he left the Army in 1919 gives his year of birth as 1895. It is likely that he over-stated his age when he enlisted. The 1901 Census gave his age as 4 (see Webster, James W for details of his family). In 1911, when his age was given as 14, he was working as a Farmer's Boy. Fisher left Henley in Arden on 24 August 1914, to join the RA at Portsmouth with his elder brother James. At his Attestation in the Town Hall, Birmingham on that day he gave his occupation as Labourer and his religion as C of E. His height was 5'8", his weight 123 lbs and his chest 33": his complexion was fresh, his eyes blue and his hair light brown. He joined the RFA at Hilsea on 25 August 1914.

He was posted to Number 3 Depot RFA as a Driver. On 26 April 1915 he was charged with overstaying special leave by 19 hours and forfeited one day's pay. He went to France on 20 May 1915. On 23 October he was admitted to hospital. He went to hospital again on 30 October, but was discharged the same day. He was then serving in C Battery, 49th Brigade RFA and was serving with D Battery, 46th Brigade RFA when he went on leave to the UK on 27 December 1917, returning on 6 January 1918. He was promoted to Lance Bombardier on 22 April 1918 and on 24 August 1918 his War Pay was increased to 15s.4d on completing four years service. On 22 November 1918 he was given 14 days leave in the UK.

On 27 January 1919 he signed Army Form Z22 confirming that he was not suffering from any disability due to his military service. His permanent address was then given as 5 Bungalow, Redbourne Hill, Scunthorpe, Lincolnshire. Fisher finally left France on 31 January 1919. On 1 March 1919 he went to Number 1 Dispersal Unit, Harrowby Camp, Grantham and was transferred to the Army Reserve the following day. In the same month he wrote asking for Civilian Clothes (he was entitled to a suit or cash in lieu), but the outcome is not recorded. He had spent 258 days of his service in the UK and 3 years 258 days in France. On his Military History Sheet his next of kin was given as his mother Mary Webster, 28 High Street, Henley in Arden.

1914-15 Star, British War Medal and Victory Medal.

St John's PR; 1901 & 1911 Census; Service Record; MIC; *Herald* (28 August 1914).

Webster, James William (1888-fl 1919)

Bombardier 89079, Royal Field Artillery.

James was baptised in St John's on 22 August 1888, the son of James and Mary Ann Webster of Henley. His father was a labourer. In 1901 he was living in the High Street with his parents, his younger sister Mary (9) and his younger brother Fisher (4). His father was then described as a Bricklayer's Labourer. In 1911 the family was living at 28 Henley in Arden and also had a daughter Naomi (7): his parents had been married for 22 years, his father now being 64 and his mother 44. James was 22 and worked as a Timber Feller.

James enlisted in the Royal Warwickshire Horse Artillery, Territorial Force on 16 April 1908 at the age of 19 years and 10 months. His trade was Farm Labourer, but he was then "out of employment". His medical examination in Warwick on the following day showed him to be 5'10" tall with a chest of 35½". He attended the annual training camp from 19 May to 2 June but was discharged from the service on 11 March 1910 in consequence of being "not likely to become an Efficient Soldier".

He enlisted again in Birmingham on 20 August 1914. His Attestation shows that he failed to disclose his previous service with the Territorial Force. By this time he had apparently lost height and put on weight, as his height was 5'8½" and his chest was 38": his weight was 156 lbs, his complexion florid, his eyes and hair brown and he gave his religion as C of E. His next of kin was his mother Mary, of 28 High Street, Henley in Arden.

James left Henley with his younger brother Fisher on 24 August 1914, to join the RA at Portsmouth. It will be noted that their service numbers are very close. He was posted as a Gunner to 3 Depot RFA on 20 April 1915.

He arrived in France on 20 May 1915 and was serving with A Battery, 49th Brigade RFA on 3 September when it was redesignated 130th Brigade. He embarked from Marseilles on 3 November, reaching Alexandria on 11 November and leaving there again on 27 November. He disembarked in Salonika on 10 December 1915. James was in 80th Field Ambulance there on 19 August 1917 suffering from malaria. He rejoined his unit, then in 31st Brigade, on 10 October 1917. He was in 86th Field Ambulance from 25 May to 1 June 1918. On 2 November 1918 he was promoted Lance Bombardier and on 14 November embarked for 21 days leave in the UK, being also granted 21 days ration allowance. On 7 January 1919 he was further promoted to Acting Bombardier and on 9 April embarked for the UK for demobilization. On 23 April 1919 he was at Number 1 Dispersal Unit in Fovant where he was granted 28 days furlough. His rank when his Protection Certificate and Certificate of Identity was issued (Army Form Z 11) was Lance Bombardier and his Medical Category was A. He was transferred to Class Z Army Reserve on 21 May 1919 on his demobilization in Woolwich. His home address was given as 164 Weston Lane, Greet, Birmingham.

1914-15 Star, British War Medal and Victory Medal.
St John's PR; 1901 & 1911 Census; Service Record; MIC; *Herald* (28 August 1914).

Webster, Philip (1885/6-fl 1919)

No information on his service record has been found.

The 1901 Census shows that he was born in Henley and was working as a Blacksmith's Striker at Abbey Farm, Wroxall at the age of 15.
1901 Census.

Welch, Sidney James (1893-1966)

439917, Canadian Overseas Expeditionary Force.

Sidney was born in Birmingham in 1893, the son of James and Annie Welch. In 1901 he was living with his parents in Birmingham at 24 Cannon Hill Grove, Hallam Street, Balsall Heath. By 1911 the family had moved to a seven-roomed house at 91 High Street, Henley where his father was working as a Baker and Confectioner. His father had married again five years earlier and he now had twin half-brothers, Frank J and Harry Norman (2). Sidney was working as a Baker and his father also had two resident employees Alfred Payne and Thomas Donald.

Sidney emigrated to Canada at some time between 1911 and 1915. He told his daughter Jean that he took various jobs there, one as a steward on the trans-Canada railroad and another as a lumberjack, living mostly in Saskatchewan. In the latter occupation he made money not only from logging but by shooting and trapping, selling the animal pelts to the Hudsons Bay Company.

Sidney joined the Canadian forces on 22 October 1915 in Port Arthur, Ontario giving his father, James Welch of Henley in Arden, as his next of kin. Sidney was then unmarried and working as a sign painter. His height was 5'8" and his chest 36"; his complexion was medium, his eyes blue and his hair brown. He stated that he had served three years with the Warwickshire Imperial Yeomanry. He gave his religious denomination as Church of England and was passed fit at his medical examination. His Attestation included at least two false entries: he stated that he had been born in Sydney, New South Wales; he also gave his date of birth as 3 August 1889 when he was in fact born in 1893 (the day of the month may have been accurate).

Sidney went to France with the Machine Gun Corps in 1915 and served at Passchendaele and at Vimy Ridge. He was seriously wounded with a jagged piece of shrapnel in the brain and was immediately returned to hospital in England. A decision had to be taken on whether to let him die or to try a radical new surgical operation. The latter option was taken and he was operated on by the surgeon to King George V. Part of his skull was removed and the shrapnel was eventually taken out by a magnet. He was left with a metal plate in his head for the rest of his life and his future prospects were uncertain, with the possibility of a vegetative existence. After months in hospital he didn't return to Canada, but came back to Henley. In 1920 he married Dorothy Mary Hawkes, a sister of Percy and Jack Hawkes (qv). They lived in St Leonard's, Chestnut Walk and she helped to nurse him back to health. Their daughter, Audrey Jean, was born in 1922. He was a keen member of the White Swan Bowling Club. He was employed as a commercial traveller by Chance Brothers of Birmingham, a glass manufacturer specialising in prisms for lighthouses. During World War II he was area manager for British Fondants Limited, a Surrey-based company that made cake decorations and also supplied ingredients for the cake industry. He enrolled with the Henley Observer Corps, based in a wooden hut on the Mount. The observers worked 4-hour shifts day and night, plotting German aircraft on their way across the Midlands. Sidney retired in his sixties and died in 1966.

1901 & 1911 Census; Canadian Attestation Paper; Mrs Jean Palmer (his daughter); H N Welch (his half-brother).

White, Frank Reginald

No details of his military service have been found.

He was married to Kathleen Jessie (surname not known) and was described as a Soldier of Henley when their son Francis John was baptised in St John's Church on 8 April 1917.

St John's PR.

White, William Daniel

Private C/12081, King's Royal Rifle Corps.

He left Henley on 24 August 1914, to join the KRRC. No further information on him has been found.

British War Medal and Victory Medal.

MIC; *Herald* (28 August 1914).

Williams, Frederick William (1897-fl 1919)

No information on his military service has been found.

He was the second son of Mary Ann Williams, who was living as Housekeeper with Daniel White in 1911 (see Thomas Daniel Williams for details of the White and Williams families).

1911 Census.

Williams, Percy Henry (1900-1976)

In view of his age, he would not have been called up until 1918 and in the absence of a MIC for him he is unlikely to have served overseas.

His birth on 2 February 1900 in Henley is recorded under this name, but he appears in the 1901 census as Percy Henry Daniels, aged 1. In the 1911 Census he is recorded as Percy Williams, aged 11 (see Thomas Daniel Williams for details of the White and Williams families).

He married Elizabeth Mole of Henley in 1921, the banns being read in St John's in July of that year. He died in 1976.

1901 & 1911 Census.

Williams, Thomas Daniel (1895-fl 1919)

Rifleman 1421, 10th (Service) Battalion, King's Royal Rifle Corps.

He was baptised in St Nicholas' on 19 May 1895, the son of Daniel and Mary Ann White. In 1901 Daniel White was living in the Tanyard with his wife, also named Mary Ann (27) and their children Gertrude (11), Frances (8), Thomas Daniel (6) Frederick Henry (3) and Percy Henry (1). The situation then becomes confusing, as the 1911 census shows him as the eldest son of Mary Ann Williams, who was single, aged 50 and living as a Housekeeper with Daniel a widower aged 60 and an Agricultural Labourer. The other children living with Daniel White and Mary Ann Williams in 1911 all had the surname Williams and were Frederick (13), Percy (11) George (9) and Gladys (6). They were living in a four-roomed house at 222 Tanyard, Henley.

Thomas enlisted in Birmingham on 20 August 1914. He was then working as a Labourer. His medical report states that he was 5'10½" tall, weighed 138 lbs and had a chest of 37". His complexion was fresh, eyes and hair brown and he was a member of the Church of England. He had been born in Beaudesert and was 19 years, 6 months and 5 days old, indicating that he had been born in February 1895. He joined his regiment at Winchester on 28 August, but was discharged on 6 October 1914 as medically unfit. The causes of his discharge were recorded as shortness of breath and irregularity of the heart.

St Nicholas' PR; 1901 & 1911 Census; Service Record.

Wilsdon, Albert Edward (1889-fl 1919)

Private 48990, Lancashire Fusiliers; formerly 22452, Royal Warwickshire Regiment.

He was born in Henley 1889 and was known as Edward. In 1891 he was 1 and living with his grandfather Joseph (a widower, 60), his father Thomas (single, 32) uncle James (29), aunt Jane (24) and Joseph's grand-daughter Jane Elizabeth (3) on the west side of the High Street. In 1901 he was living in the Tanyard on the west side of the High Street with his grandfather Joseph, his father Thomas and his aunt Jane. His father and grandfather were Shoemakers. In 1911 he, his father and his aunt Jane (44) were living at 75 High Street, a house with two bedrooms, Edward then being a Farm Labourer.

He first went overseas in 1916 or later. His name was added to the Members of His Majesty's Forces by F C Parkes in his copy of the Peace Celebrations booklet.

British War Medal and Victory Medal.

1891, 1901 & 1911 Census; MIC.

†Woodward, Francis Harry (1897-1917)

Private 21199, 10th (Service) Battalion Royal Warwickshire Regiment.

Known as Frank, he was born in Henley in 1897, the third son of Walter Charles and Lucy Anne Woodward. As well as his brothers Allen and Harold, he had three sisters (Constance, Rachel and Mary). In 1901 the family was living in Beaudesert Lane, Beaudesert. His father had been born in Henley in Arden and worked as a Hay Trusser: his mother was born in Alcester. In 1911 the family (parents, three sons and two daughters) were living in a four-roomed house in Beaudesert. His parents Walter and Lucy had been married for 27 years and had nine children in total, all of whom were surviving. Frank was then at school. Their address was later 163 High Street, Henley. Frank was a chorister at both St Nicholas' and St John's churches.

Frank enlisted in Stratford upon Avon. The 10th Battalion had been formed at Warwick in September 1914. It landed in France on 17 July 1915 as part of 57th Brigade, 19th Division. It saw its first fighting at the Battle of Loos on 25 September 1915. During 1916 it was involved in the Battle of the Somme, fighting at La Boisselle, High Wood and Pozieres Ridge. It seems likely that Francis was sent with a draft of reinforcements during or after the Battle of the Somme. The battalion ended the year with severe fighting around the River Ancre.

Frank Woodward was killed in action on 11 January 1917, aged 19. A Memorial Service was held for him in St John's Church on the evening of Sunday, 4 February. He is buried in the cemetery of Sailly au Boisse (a village between Arras and Amiens), grave II G 19.

Sailly au Boisse Cemetery

British War Medal and Victory Medal.
1901 & 1911 Census; MIC; CWGC; SDGW; James, p 48; *Herald* (9 February 1917).

Wright, Howard (1899-fl 1920)

Corporal 94124, King's Liverpool Regiment; formerly Private 38638, Royal Warwickshire Regiment.

Howard Wright was the third son of George and Clara Wright and was born in Aston Manor in 1899. In 1901 he was a year old and living at Police Station Yard in New Town, Aston where his father was a Sergeant of Police. Howard's elder brothers were Alfred Thomas (13) and Charles (9). In 1911 the family (other than Alfred) was living at the Police Station, Lozells Road, Aston Manor. His father was now a Police Inspector and his parents had been married for 24 years: Howard was at school. Subsequently the family moved to Henley.

Howard enlisted at Birmingham in the 17th (Local Reserve) Battalion of the Royal Warwickshire Regiment on 9 February 1916, giving his age as 19 although he was actually only 16. He was passed fit for general service. He was employed as a Clerk, living at the Police Station in Henley, was 5'7½" tall, had a 35½" chest and weighed 132 pounds.

It is likely that he was suspected of being under age, as he did not go overseas for two years. He had two periods in Basildon Military Hospital in 1916, the first being for 13 days in April suffering from Rubella and the second for 26 days in July and August with Impetigo. He joined the 92nd Training Reserve Battalion at Chiseldon on 1 September 1916, where he was promoted to Lance Corporal on 27 January 1917, acting Corporal on 19 March and acting Sergeant on 7 July. He embarked from Southampton on 14 March 1918 and landed in Le Havre on 15 March. He was posted to the 10th Battalion RWR as a Private at Rouen on 16 March 1918.

On 20 March he was transferred to the 1st Battalion King's Liverpool Regiment and given the rank of paid acting Corporal on 9 April. The battalion had been fighting in France since August 1914 and was part of 6th Brigade, 2nd Division. On 12 April the *Herald* reported that Inspector Wright's son was well after a trying period in the trenches. However, he was in 3rd Canadian CCS on 27 April suffering from diarrhoea and did not rejoin his unit until 25 May. On 27 September he was wounded in the abdomen by a bullet and moved to 56th Casualty Clearing Station in Varennes.

He was then moved to 59th CCS and 22nd General Hospital before being sent to England on 30 September. His wound was reported in the *Herald* of 4 October, which stated that he was in hospital in Lincoln. "Only 19, he joined the colours about 2½ years ago and has seen about 7 months hard fighting."

He was discharged from the army on 31 January 1919. On 9 February 1920 he appeared before a medical board in Coventry in an attempt to obtain a pension relating to his wound, claiming that he was suffering pain in the left side of his abdomen. The board found that he had been discharged from the army with the grade of A1; that his general physical condition was good; he had no anaemia; his heart and lungs were good and although he had a small scar 1" x ¼" in the left iliac region, it was soundly healed and he had no abdominal tenderness. He was found to have no disability and there were no grounds for an award.

British War Medal and Victory Medal.

1901 & 1911 Census; WW1 Pension Records; MIC; *Herald* (12 April & 4 October 1918).

Wright, Walter William (1894-1966)

Rifleman 1418, King's Royal Rifle Corps.

Known as William, he was born in Chessetts Wood, Knowle, Warwickshire in 1894, the son of Michael Henry and Elizabeth Wright. In 1901 he was 6 and living with his parents and his sister Emma in Nortons Green, Knowle: his father (39) was a Platelayer, born in Rowington, his mother (32) and his sister (9) were both born in Snitterfield. When he joined the King's Royal Rifle Corps in Birmingham for a term of three years on 20 August 1914 William was working as a Baker and living at 4 High Street, Henley. He declared himself a member of the Church of England, was 5'4" tall, weighed 130 lbs and had a chest of 37½". His complexion was fair, his eyes blue and his hair dark brown. His next of kin was his mother Elizabeth Wright, then of 286 Oldknow Road, Small Heath, Birmingham.

The *Herald* reported that he was one of the men who left Henley in Arden on 24 August 1914, to join the KRRC. He joined the 7th Battalion of the regiment at Winchester on 27 August. His service was brief, as he was discharged on 25 February 1915 as "not likely to become an efficient soldier" on medical grounds (unspecified).

Walter died in Birmingham in 1966.

Knowle PR; 1901 Census; Service Record; *Herald* (28 August 1914).

Yarwood, Albert (1877- fl 1919)

Private 476152, Labour Corps; formerly Private 35845, Worcestershire Regiment.

He was born in Birmingham on 19 October 1877, the son of Joseph and Emma Yarwood. In 1881 he was 3 and living with his parents, his elder brother Joseph and elder sisters Emma and Ann in the High Street: his father was a Publican and had been born in Castle Donington, Leicestershire; his mother was born in Bath. Albert attended the Council School from 12 January 1885 to 13 June 1890. In 1891 his father was an Agricultural Labourer. At the time of the 1901 Census, Albert was a domestic gardener, aged 23 and living with his mother Emma on the western side of the

High Street. The two were living in a three-roomed house at 8 High Street in 1911, probably the same house the family had been living in for 30 years, Albert describing himself as a Jobbing Gardener. He was the uncle of Percy Yarwood (*qv*) and did not marry. The photograph was taken by W H Wakefield of Devonport and shows him wearing the badge of the Worcestershire Regiment.

His move to the Labour Corps may have been because he was wounded, or it may have been other factors that made him unfit for service in the line.

In July 1919 he was secretary of the Henley branch of the Discharged Soldiers and Sailors Federation, a predecessor of the British Legion.

British War Medal and Victory Medal.

1881, 1891, 1901 and 1911 Census; MIC; *Herald* (11 July 1919).

Yarwood, Joseph Percy (1899-1944)

Rifleman 474541, 2/16th Battalion London Regiment (Queen's Westminster Rifles); formerly Private 474541, 12th London Regiment (The Rangers) and Private 50166, 51st Battalion Devonshire Regiment.

Known as Percy, he was born in Henley in 1899, the son of Joseph and Laura Ann Yarwood: his father had been born in Castle Donington, Leicestershire and his mother in Ettington, Warwickshire. In 1901 he was living in the High Street

with his father (a Rural Postman), mother and his sisters Laura May (3) and Dorothy Emily (5 months). In 1911 they were still living in Henley with a brother Frederick (7) now the youngest member of the family. Percy was the nephew of Albert Yarwood (*qv*).

Percy enlisted at Stratford upon Avon on 4 October 1917 and was accepted at Warwick the following day. He was 18 years and 30 days old and working as a Gardener. His height was 5'8¼" and his chest 37". He was living at Kyte Green, Preston Bagot, his next of kin being his father Joseph Yarwood of the same address. His medical showed a slight physical defect (the nature of which is illegible), but he was noted as "suitable for artillery". He was posted as Private 50166 to 35th Battalion, Training Reserve in Salisbury.

On 16 January 1918 he was posted to 51st (Graduated) Battalion of the

Devonshire Regiment in Norwich as Private 474541. During his service with them he was charged on 12 March 1918 with not complying with an order and with insolence to a NCO, for which he was given 168 hours detention. He arrived in France on 1 May 1918 and from the depot at Etaples he was posted to 12th Battalion London Regiment (The Rangers) on 13 May. He was at an LTM School from 3 September 1918, rejoining his battalion on 22 December. On 10 February 1919 he joined the 2/16th Battalion of the London Regiment (The Queen's Westminster Rifles). He had 14 days leave in the UK in March 1919, a further 14 days from 30 August to 13 September and again from 14 to 28 October 1919. He was transferred to the UK for demobilisation on 6 November 1919 and transferred to Class Z reserve on 5 December 1919. His service record shows that he had 209 days service at home from 4 October 1917 to 30 April 1918, 1 year and 190 days with the BEF in France from 1 May to 6 November 1919 and a final 29 days of home service from 7 November to 5 December 1919. Percy's companion in the photograph is wearing three wound stripes.

Percy Yarwood attempted to join the police service in Birmingham in November 1921. Correspondence included in his service record shows that the London Infantry Record Office wrote a reference, in response to a request from the Chief Constable of Birmingham, stating that 474541 Rifleman Yarwood's character during his service was "Good". The Chief Constable's office responded by asking for a copy of Rifleman Yarwood's Army Conduct Sheet, "as it is observed that his character is only assessed as 'Good' after 2 years and 2 months service". Infantry Records regretted that they could not comply with this request, as "Conduct Sheets of ex-Soldiers are privileged documents". The Chief Constable seems to have reacted by not taking Percy Yarwood on, as Percy went on to work as a platelayer with the Great Western Railway.

He married Emily Rose Corbett of King's Heath Birmingham in January 1929. Their only child Emily (the late Mrs John Ambler) was born in November of that year, her mother dying 9 days later. Percy lived at Kyte Green until his death in 1944.

His name did not appear in the Peace Celebrations booklet, but his name was added to the Members of His Majesty's Forces by F C Parkes in his copy.

British War Medal and Victory Medal.

1901 & 1911 Census; MIC: Service Record.

Roll of Honour
Old Boys of Arden House School Died 1914-1918

†Barker, Allen Noel Birkett (1893/4-1918)
Sergeant 50675, 66th Brigade HQ, Royal Garrison Artillery.

He was known as Noel and was the son of Tom Birkett Barker JP and his wife Marianne of The Croft, Lapworth. He subsequently went to Warwick School and later lived at West Bridgeford, Nottinghamshire.

He arrived in France on 1 October 1915. He died of wounds on 12 September 1918, aged 24 and is buried in Aubigny Communal Cemetery. His elder brother Holroyd was also killed, while his younger brothers Fred and Greville served and survived. Noel left an estate of £3,094 and probate was granted to his father on 21 May 1919. Noel is also commemorated in Lapworth and in Warwick School Chapel.

1914-15 Star, British War Medal, Victory Medal.

†Barlow, Henry Loftus (18??-1918)
Lieutenant, Royal Flying Corps; formerly Corporal 28236, Motor Cycle Battalion, Royal Engineers.

Henry Barlow first served in the Royal Engineers and went to France on 12 September 1914. He was commissioned into the Royal Flying Corps on 23 May 1916. He died on 18 March 1918 and is buried in Stourbridge Cemetery.

1914 Star, British War Medal, Victory Medal.

†Beard, Frederic Gerald Vesey (1889-1916)
Lieutenant, Worcestershire Regiment; formerly Corporal 2300, Royal Fusiliers.

He was born in 1889, the son of Frederick Beard MB and his wife Geraldine of The Old Smithy, Sanderstead, Surrey. Known as Gerald, he was a Boarder at Arden House in 1901, the Census recording that he was born in Croydon. Gerald attended Epsom College from 1903 to 1908 (Prefect, XV, XI and hockey XI). He obtained a BA at Dublin University and went on to become a Schoolmaster. After serving in the Royal Fusiliers he was commissioned into the Worcestershire Regiment on 23 November 1914 and joined his unit in France on 2 December 1915. He was killed in action in the Battle of the Somme on 4 July 1916, aged 27. His name appears on the Thiepval Memorial.

1914-15 Star, British War Medal, Victory Medal.

†Beaver, John Denistoun Campbell (1893-1918)

2nd Lieutenant, 13th Battalion King's Royal Rifle Corps; formerly Corporal 22507, Oxford & Bucks Light Infantry.

John was born in Ireland on 2 January 1893. He was a Boarder at Arden House in 1901 and attended Bradfield College from 1906 to 1910 (Prefect, Cricket XI). He enlisted in 1914 and was commissioned into the KRRC on 18 December 1916. He died of wounds on 17 May 1918, aged 25 and is buried in Holy Trinity Churchyard, Penn, Buckinghamshire. He left an estate of £681 and probate was granted to his widow Cerise Campbell Beaver on 11 July 1918.

British War Medal, Victory Medal.

†Brand, Geoffrey Jermyn (1893-1916)

2nd Lieutenant, Royal Scots; formerly Private, Royal Fusiliers.

He was born on 3 August 1893, the son of Charles and Annie Brand. In 1901 he was living with his parents and his elder sister Maud in Woodside, Dorridge. He attended Rossall School from 1908 to 1910 and left to take up an occupation in shipping. He served as a Private in the Royal Fusiliers and was then commissioned in the General List. He went to France in 1915 and was serving with the Royal Scots when he was killed in action on 1 July 1916, the first day of the Battle of the Somme, aged 22. He is commemorated on the Thiepval Memorial.

1914-15 Star, British War Medal, Victory Medal.

†Brooke, George Townshend (1878-1915)

Captain, 1st North Midland Field Company, Royal Engineers.

He was born on 9 May 1878, the son of John Townshend and Lady Wilhelmina Brooke of Shifnal. His wife was Ida May Brooke of Elmleigh, Queens Road, Cheltenham. George went to Haileybury from 1892 to 1896 and on leaving there joined the Public Works Department in Egypt. A member of the Territorial Force, he was killed in action near Ypres on 5 May 1915, aged 36. He is buried in White House Cemetery, St Jean les Ypres, grave IV A 13.

1914-15 Star, British War Medal, Victory Medal.

†Brooks, Walter Leslie (1892-1915)

Lieutenant, 4th Battalion Prince of Wales' Own (West Yorkshire) Regiment, attached 2nd Battalion Lincolnshire Regiment.

He was born in 1892, the son of John and Alice Brooks of Finstall Park, Bromsgrove. Although his names were recorded as Walter Leslie at his birth, they appear as Leslie Walter in the 1901 Census and on his MIC (he was generally known as Leslie). He moved to Uppingham in September 1907, where he played for the Rugby XV in 1909 and 1910. In 1911 he went up to Clare College, Cambridge. He married Blanche Ann Birley, the elder daughter of Mr A J Birley of Throstle Nest, Thornton-in-Craven in November 1914, when he was a 2nd Lieutenant in the West Yorkshire Regiment. The wedding took place at All Saints' Church, Falmouth, his regiment then being stationed in Falmouth.

He embarked for France in May 1915 and was attached to the 2nd Battalion of the Lincolnshire Regiment serving with 25th Brigade, 2nd Division. He was killed on 25 September 1915, the first day of the Battle of Loos. Probate was granted to his widow on 17 January 1916, his estate amounting to £2,350. Mrs Blanche Ann Brooks of Throstle Nest, Thornton-in-Craven, Nr Shipton, Yorkshire applied for her husband's medals on 27 October 1920. His name is one of over 11,000 commemorated on the Ploegsteert Memorial.

1914-15 Star, British War Medal, Victory Medal.

†Clive, Reginald Dennis (1898-1917)

Flight Sub Lieutenant, Royal Naval Air Service.

He was born in Leamington on 6 June 1898, the son of Herbert and Lydia Clive. He was living with his parents at Fieldgate Lawn, Kenilworth when he was awarded his Royal Aero Club Aviator's Certificate (number 4788) on 9 May 1917. He had taken his test on a Maurice Farman Biplane. He presumably crashed in a flight in the UK, as he died of injuries on 10 November 1917 and is buried in St Nicholas' Churchyard, Kenilworth.

†Dickinson, Colin James Henry (1896/7-1916)

2nd Lieutenant, 15th Battalion Cheshire Regiment.

Born in Dacca, India, he was a Boarder aged 14 at Arden House in 1911. He went to France on 31 January 1916 and was killed in action on the Somme on 28 July. He is buried in Flatiron Copse Cemetery, Mametz, grave I I 9.

British War Medal, Victory Medal.

†Hayley, Cyril William Seaforth Burrell (1892-1915)

Captain, 10th Battalion Highland Light Infantry.

He was born in 1892, the son of John Newton and Alice Hayley of 2 Ryder Street, St James' Square, London and the elder brother of John Hayley (qv). Cyril was at Radley from 1907 to 1910, leaving for the Royal Military College, Sandhurst. He was commissioned into the Highland Light Infantry in 1911. He went to France on 12 May 1915 and died of wounds on 18 September 1915, aged 23. He is buried in Chocques Military Cemetery (4 km NW of Bethune), grave I B 26.

1914-15 Star, British War Medal, Victory Medal.

†Hayley, John Rudolf Burrell (1895-1917)

Rifleman 553700, 16th Battalion London Regiment (Queen's Westminster Rifles), formerly Sergeant, 50th Battalion Canadian Infantry.

He was born in 1895, the son of J N and Alice Hayley and the younger brother of Cyril Hayley (*qv*). He went on to Radley from 1910 to 1912, where he was a member of the Officer Training Corps for over two years. He joined the Dominion Express Company, Calgary, Canada. He enlisted into the Canadian Expeditionary Force in Calgary on 30 December 1914 when he was working as a Clerk, but was a member of the Active Militia. At that time he was 5'5½" tall, with a fair complexion, grey eyes and light brown hair. He became a Sergeant in the 50th Battalion Canadian Infantry and later served in the ranks of the Queen's Westminster Rifles.

He died of wounds received near Arras on 30 April 1917, aged 21 and is buried in Etaples Military Cemetery, grave 18 D 1A.

British War Medal, Victory Medal.

†Inchbald, John Chantrey Elliot (1894/5-1917)

Captain, 9th Battalion Devonshire Regiment.

He was the second son of Charles Chantrey Inchbald of The Grey House, Thurlestone, Devon and his wife Mary Katherine (*nee* Elliot). A Scholar of both Winchester College and New College, Oxford, he went to Winchester in 1907 and to Oxford in 1913. He left Oxford to enlist in September 1914. He went to France on 28 July 1915 and was quickly promoted Captain. He was serving with the 9th Battalion of the Devonshire Regiment when was killed in action near Bapaume on 2 April 1917, aged 22 and is buried in HAC Cemetery, Ecoust St Mein (Mory-Ecoust Road, Cemetery No 1, Memorial 1).

He left an estate of £490. His younger brother also served in the war as a Lieutenant in the Berkshire Yeomanry.

1914-15 Star, British War Medal, Victory Medal.

†Jaffray, Sir John Henry, Bart (1893-1916)

Lieutenant, 1/1st Queen's Own Worcestershire Hussars.

Known as Jock, he was the 3rd Baronet, son of Sir William Jaffray, 2nd Baronet, of Skilts, Studley, Warwickshire and his wife Alice (*nee* Galloway). He went on to Eton (leaving in 1912) and Trinity Hall, Cambridge (matriculated 1913). He joined the Yeomanry before the war and was with his regiment when it assembled on 4 August 1914. He embarked with the regiment at Avonmouth on 9 April 1915 as a 2nd Lieutenant, disembarking in Alexandria on 24 April. After service in Gallipoli, he was killed in action at Oghratina in Sinai on 23 April 1916 at the age of 22. He is commemorated on the Jerusalem Memorial.

1914-15 Star, British War Medal, Victory Medal.

†Lindner, Philip Edward (1899-1918)

Lieutenant, 224 Squadron Royal Air Force, formerly 2nd Lieutenant, 3rd Battalion Royal Warwickshire Regiment.

He was born in 1899 and baptised in St Alphege's Church, Solihull on 10 May 1889, the son of Frederick William and Lucy Jane Lindner. Philip was a Boarder at Arden House in 1901. He married Jane Baldwin in 1915. He was killed in action in Salonika on 21 July 1918 in an Airco DH4 (Number B9500) when flying as an Observer. The pilot Lieutenant E L Bragg was also killed. He is buried in Salonika Military Cemetery, grave 1627.

British War Medal, Victory Medal, Bronze Medal for Military Valour (Italy).

†Milward, Philip Henry (1873-1915)

Captain, 7th Battalion, Rifle Brigade.

Philip was the son of John and Frances Milward of Southmead, Redditch. He went on to Uppingham from 1897 to 1890. He served in the ranks in South Africa in 1901 and was a Sergeant in the Rifle Brigade in 1914. His wife Marguerite filed for divorce on 20 December 1911. He was promoted to Captain and transferred to the 7th Battalion on 7 May 1915. He died of wounds in 10th Casualty Clearing Station on 7 December 1915 and is buried in Grave II A 8 in Lijssenthoek Military Cemetery, near Ypres. He left £7,192 when probate was granted on 15 February 1916, at which time he was said to be of Southmead, Redditch and San Sebastian Mills, Colombo, Ceylon.

1914-15 Star, British War Medal, Victory Medal.

†Morris, Henry Gage (1897-1915)

2nd Lieutenant, 2nd Battalion Duke of Cornwall's Light Infantry.

He was born in Bodmin in Cornwall on 14 August 1897, and was the only surviving child of Colonel Henry Gage Morris and his wife Maude. After Arden House, Henry went to Marlborough College in September 1911, leaving in July 1914 and going on to the Royal Military College, Sandhurst. He was gazetted 2nd Lieutenant to the 2nd Battalion of the Duke of Cornwall's Light Infantry, a battalion which his father had previously commanded, on 12 January 1915. He went to France with them on 15 February 1915 and was killed in action leading his platoon at the 2nd Battle of Ypres on 23 April 1915, being buried where he fell.

His age was 17 years and 8 months and his name is engraved on the Menin Gate in Ypres.

1914-15 Star, British War Medal, Victory Medal.

†Newton, Horace Gerard Townsend (1885-1917)

Captain, 13th Hussars.

He was born on 7 July 1885, the only son of Rev Canon Horace Newton, Holmwood, Redditch and his wife Frances Jane (*nee* Storrs). His father was Rural

Dean of Bromsgrove and formerly Vicar of Redditch. He attended Rugby School from 1899-1904 and matriculated at St John's College, Cambridge in 1904.

He did not complete his degree course, as he was commissioned into the 13th Hussars in 1906 and joined his Regiment in India in the spring of that year. In 1911 he married Margaretta Violet Powell and had a daughter. He served in India until December 1914 when he went to France. He served with the force which re-captured Kut el Amara on 24 February 1917 and played an important part in a cavalry charge against the Turks on 5 March 1917 during which all his senior officers were killed or wounded. Due to a breakdown in health he was sent to India on sick leave. He had begun to walk in his sleep and fell overboard from a barge on the River Tigris on the night of 25 April 1917: every effort to save him failed and he was drowned. His widow applied for his medals and they were sent to her at Woodhill Farm, Tilford, Farnham, Surrey. He is buried in Basra War Cemetery, grave V L 2.

1914-15 Star, British War Medal, Victory Medal.

†Pearson, Bertram Walter Mockley (1887-1918)

Captain, Army Service Corps.

He was born in Knowle in 1887, the son of Edwin and Laura Pearson of Norton Grange and later of Edstone Hall, Wootton Wawen. He was a Boarder at Arden House in 1901 and was at Harrow from 1901 to 1905 (his death is not recorded in their Register or in the Harrow Memorials). He died on 25 October 1918 and is buried in Vadencourt British Cemetery, Maisseny, grave II B22.

British War Medal, Victory Medal.

†Richardson, Robert Scovill MC (1893-1916)

Lieutenant, 91st Company, Machine Gun Corps.

He was born on 8 May 1893, the eldest son of Robert Lyman Richardson of Rosary Gardens, London and his wife Mary Winifred. On leaving Arden House, he went on to Rugby School which he left in 1910. He entered Pembroke College, Cambridge in 1911 and played golf for the University in 1913 and 1914.

Robert enlisted as a Private in the Public Schools Battalion of the Middlesex Regiment. He was commissioned as a 2nd Lieutenant with the Cameronians (Scottish Rifles) and served with them as Machine Gun Officer. Robert transferred to the Machine Gun Corps in December 1915, serving with 91st Company and went to the front in France in March, 1916. He was awarded the Military Cross for his service on the first day of the Somme, 1 July 1916, "for conspicuous gallantry.

Though twice buried by shell fire he succeeded in rescuing five of his men and bringing his guns into action in a captured enemy position. He was under heavy shell fire the whole time. Later he did fine work, clearing up the position". Robert was wounded in action at Ginchy on 31 August while helping to bandage a wounded man outside the trenches. He died of his wounds the next day, 1 September 1916, aged 23. His promotion to Lieutenant appeared posthumously in the *London Gazette* of 16 September 1916. He is buried in La Neuville British Cemetery, Corbie, grave II B 31.

Military Cross, British War Medal, Victory Medal.

†Rickards, Hew Wardrop Brooke (1896-1917)

Lieutenant, Royal Field Artillery, attached 57 Squadron Royal Flying Corps.

Hew Rickards was born on 21 May 1896 in Stocksfield on Tyne, the son of the Revd Walter Brooke and Mrs Mary Christini Rickards. On leaving Arden House he went to Uppingham in September 1910, leaving in December 1913. His parents were then living in Filgrove Rectory, Newport Pagnell. Early in 1914 he went to a tutor in France to learn the language. When war broke out in August he couldn't wait to get back to England, so joined the French Army and saw almost six months active service with the Foreign Legion. He returned to England in February 1915 and was commissioned into the Royal Field Artillery, with which he served in France until August 1916. At his own request he was transferred to the Royal Flying Corps. He was wounded when flying near the trenches in November and was invalided home. On coming out of hospital he trained at a number of flying schools in England, was given his wings in May 1917 and returned to France the following month.

At this time 57th Squadron began to convert to Rolls-Royce Eagle-engined DH4s and in June moved up into the Ypres sector. There it was engaged in long-distance reconnaissance, bombing and photography. The Squadron met with strong opposition from enemy fighters and suffered many casualties. Hew was seen in combat with a German squadron near Courtrai on 28 July 1917, after which he was reported missing, presumed killed. His body was subsequently recovered and he is buried in Wielsbeke Communal Cemetery, Flanders, grave 2 on the north side of the church.

1914-15 Star, British War Medal and Victory Medal.

†Ross-Taylor, Ian Henry Munro (1894/5-1916)

2nd Lieutenant, 7th Battalion Bedfordshire Regiment.

He was born in Madras, the son of James Walter Ross-Taylor. On leaving Arden House in 1908 he went to Radley, which he left in 1911. He was commissioned into the 8th Battalion of the Bedfordshire Regiment in 1915 and went to France on 8 February 1916. He was wounded and recovered, but was killed in action on 27 June 1916 when serving with the 7th Battalion, attached to 54th Brigade, 18th Division. His name appears on the Thiepval Memorial.

British War Medal and Victory Medal.

†Smith, John Basil (1894-1917)

2nd Lieutenant, 'A' Company 14th Battalion Royal Warwickshire Regiment.

He was born on 30 March 1894, son of Albert Edward Smith of The Quarry, Cliffe Hill, Warwick. He was at Cheltenham from 1908 to 1910. His battalion was serving with 13th Brigade, 5th Division. He died of wounds at Arleux, France on 19 August 1917 and is buried in Duisans British Cemetery, Etrun (NW of Arras), grave VI C 12.

British War Medal and Victory Medal.

†Steer, Gordon Pemberton (1884/5-1915)

Captain, 3rd Battalion Somerset Light Infantry, attached 2nd Battalion Wiltshire Regiment.

He was the son of Edward and Augusta Louisa Steer of Malpas, near Newport, Monmouthshire. He went on to Shrewsbury School, then Magdalen College Oxford (1904-07). He was a professional soldier and was serving in India at the outbreak of war with 2nd Battalion. He transferred to the 3rd Battalion in June 1915 and went with them to France on 15 October 1915. He was wounded at Wimereux on 25 November 1915 when attached to the 2nd Battalion of the Wiltshire Regiment, 21st Brigade, 13th Division. He died of his wounds on 26 December 1915, aged 31 and is buried in Wimereux Communal Cemetery, grave III M 3.

1914-15 Star, British War Medal and Victory Medal.

†Williams, Thomas Clifford (1891-1918)

Rifleman 393057, 9th Battalion London Regiment (Queen Victoria's Rifles).

He was the son of Thomas Joseph Edward and Minnie Williams of Solihull. He went to France in 1916 or later and died of wounds on 28 April 1918, aged 27. His battalion was then part of 169th Brigade, 56th Division. He is buried in Crouy British Cemetery, Crouy sur Somme, grave II A 26.

British War Medal and Victory Medal.

†Wilson, Gordon Ivor (1896/7-1917)

2nd Lieutenant, Royal Flying Corps, formerly of the Yorkshire Dragoons Yeomanry.

He was the son of Alexander Mills and Amy Evelyn Wilson of The Moor, Presteign, Radnorshire. He was accidentally killed in the UK on 12 February 1917, probably in a flying accident. He is buried in Upavon Cemetery, Wiltshire. It is unlikely that he served overseas.

†Woods, Frank Cecil (1887-1917)

Lieutenant, 3rd Battalion, attached 2nd Battalion, Queen's (Royal West Surrey) Regiment.

He was born in 1887, the son of Surgeon Major David Woods and his wife Constance of Camberley. He was at Epsom College from 1901 to 1902. He was killed in action on 2 April 1917 when his battalion was serving with 91st Brigade, 7th Division. He is buried in Croisilles British Cemetery (SE of Arras), grave I A 3.

1914-15 Star, British War Medal and Victory Medal.

Roll of Honour
Beaudesert Park School
Old Boys Who Served 1914-1918

Beddington, Horace Geoffrey (1899-1962)

London Regiment.

He was born in London on 14 June 1899, the son of Frank and Helena Beddington. In 1901 he was living in Portsmouth with his parents and his elder sister. He was a Boarder at Beaudesert Park in 1911, aged 11.

No military records have been found relating to him. In view of age it is unlikely that he served overseas.

†Behrens, Walter Louis (1897-1917)

2nd Lieutenant, 'C' Battery, 127th Brigade, Royal Field Artillery.

He was born on 7 February 1897, the son of Walter Louis & Evelyn Behrens (*nee* Beddington). He joined the Inns of Court OTC on 17 May 1915 and was commissioned into the Royal Field Artillery on 15 September 1915. He served in France and Flanders from January 1916 and died on 10 July 1917, aged 20. He is buried in Bard Cottage Cemetery, Ypres, grave II M 1.

He left an estate of £103, probate being granted to Charles Lindsay Beddington on 19 December 1917. He had a twin brother Edward, who went to Charterhouse in 1910.

British War Medal and Victory Medal.

Beville, Charles (1902-?)

RN, HMS *Dreadnought*.

Born in India, c 1892. He was 9 and a Boarder at Beaudesert Park in 1911. He won a Cadetship to the Royal Naval College, Osborne.

Beville, Edward Launcelot Granville (1896-1977)

Captain, 2nd Battalion North Staffordshire Regiment.

He was born on 18 August 1896, the son of Major Francis Granville Beville CIE, Indian Army. He won a scholarship to Cheltenham in 1910, leaving in 1914. He went to serve in India in December 1915. After the war he was attached to the Sierra Leone Battalion of the West African Frontier Force.

British War Medal and Indian General Service Medal (Afghanistan).

Borrett, Giles (1901-1998)

Midshipman, HMS *Indomitable.*

He was born in Marylebone on 17 January 1901, the son of Claude and Isabelle Borrett. In 1911 he was a Boarder in Beaudesert Park and went on to win a Cadetship with distinction to the Royal Naval College, Osborne. He became a Midshipman on 15 August 1917. He continued to serve in the Navy after the war, becoming a Lieutenant on 15 February 1922. He also served throughout World War 2, when he was a Commander.

†Burn, Arthur Sidney Pelham (1895-1915)

Lieutenant, 6th Battalion Gordon Highlanders.

He was born in Norwich in 1895, the younger son of William Pelham Burn (then Archdeacon of Norfolk) and his wife Margaret. Arthur went on to Lancing College. He matriculated for New College, Oxford (1915 entry) and was intended for Holy Orders, but did not take up his place at Oxford, as he enlisted on 5 November 1914. He served in France and Belgium from November 1914 and was killed in action near Festubert on 2 May 1915, aged 19. His battalion was then serving with 20th Brigade, 7th Division. By this time his father had died and his mother was living in Limpsfield, Surrey. Arthur is buried in Estaires Cemetery, grave II A 1.

Mentioned in Dispatches, 1914 Star, British War Medal and Victory Medal.

His elder brother Maurice Edward Pelham Burn was also killed in the war. He had entered Hertford College, Oxford in 1912 and enlisted on 26 August 1914. He served as a Lieutenant in the 8th Battalion of the Black Watch and was killed at Vimy Ridge on 9 April 1917.

Byrne, Raymond Rice (1897-1972)

Lieutenant, Royal Flying Corps.

He was born in Eton on 28 June 1897. He went on to Eton, rowed in the Eton eight and was a member of Pop. He left Eton in 1916. Served in France, Egypt and Palestine.

Mentioned in dispatches, British War Medal and Victory Medal.

†Egerton, Brian Raleigh (1897-1918)

Lieutenant, 87th Field Company, Royal Engineers.

He was born in 1897, the son of Colonel C P Egerton (Indian Army) and his wife Lilian. In 1911 he was a Boarder at Beaudesert Park (as was his younger brother Robert Charles). He won a scholarship to Sherborne that year, leaving it for Woolwich in 1914. He served in France from 6 February 1916. He was killed at Lacelle on 23 October 1918, aged 20 and is buried in Villers-Pol Communal Cemetery Extension, grave K 1.

Mentioned in Dispatches, British War Medal and Victory Medal.

Hill, Charles J H

Private 37690, Royal Welch Fusiliers.

He was born in Hyderabad, India and in 1911 was a Boarder at Beaudesert Park, aged 12.

Ingpen, James Percy

RN, HMS *Indomitable*.

He was born in Worthing, Sussex. In 1911 he was a Boarder (aged 9) at Beaudesert Park, as was his elder brother Robert Lyall. He won a Cadetship to the Royal Naval College, Osborne and pursued a career in the Navy. He became a Lieutenant Commander on 15 June 1931 and went on to serve in the Royal Naval Volunteer Reserve in World War II.

Jellicoe, John Andrew (1897-1976)

2nd Lieutenant, 19th Battalion Northumberland Fusiliers.

John was born in Chelsea on 14 October 1897, the son of George and Florence Jellicoe. His father was a Director of a publishing company. In 1901 John was living in Kensington with his parents, his younger brother Geoffrey and three domestic servants. In 1911 he was a Boarder at Beaudesert Park (as was Geoffrey) and left in 1912. He was in Germany when war was declared, but returned to England shortly before the commencement of hostilities. He died in Hampshire in 1976.

British War Medal and Victory Medal.

Jope-Slade, Robert (1896/7-fl 1919)

Observer Lieutenant, Royal Naval Air Service.

Born in London he was living at Burnham, Buckinghamshire in 1911 with his mother and step-father. He was awarded his Flying Certificate on 9 April 1916. His award of the DSC appeared in the *London Gazette* on 14 September 1917.

DSC, British War Medal, Victory Medal.

Matthews, G

Royal Flying Corps.

Plowden, James Miles Bindon Chicheley (1898-fl 1919)

Captain, 2nd/39th Garwhali Rifles.

Born 10 September 1898, son of Lieutenant-Colonel Walter Francis Courtenay Chicheley Plowden, Indian Army. He went with a Scholarship to Cheltenham from 1912 to 1916 and on leaving went to the RMC Sandhurst. Served in India.

British War Medal.

Richardson, Maurice Bradshaw (1899-1993)

Army of Occupation.

He was born in September 1899, the son of Frank and Emily Richardson. He was at Uppingham from September 1914 to April 1918 and went up to Emmanuel College Cambridge later that year, being awarded a BA in History in 1921. No records of military service during the war years have been found.

Seligman, Vincent Julian

Army Service Corps.

He was born on 4 March 1896, the son of David Seligman. He won a Junior Scholarship to Charterhouse in 1909. He was serving in France in 1916.

Templar, James

RN, HMS *Ajax*.

Cadetship to Royal Naval College, Osborne.

Vanderbyl, L

Royal Flying Corps.

†Ward, Eric Seth (1898-1917)

Lieutenant, Royal Flying Corps.

He was born in Pinner, Middlesex in 1898, the son of Captain Melville Seth Ward (RFC). He was commissioned as a 2nd Lieutenant in the Oxford & Bucks Light Infantry and was subsequently attached to 32 Squadron RFC. He was sent to Flanders in July 1917 and died on 10 August 1917, aged 19. His name appears on the Arras Flying Services Memorial, having no known grave.

British War Medal and Victory Medal.

†Williamson, Hugh Henshall Clifford (1895-1916)

Lieutenant, 1st Battalion Coldstream Guards.

He was born in London in January 1895, the son of Hugh and Emily Williamson: his father was a colliery owner, who had been born in Newcastle, Staffordshire. He went on to Eton, which he left in 1911 and entered Christ Church College, Oxford in 1912. He joined the Inns of Court OTC as a Private on 14 September 1914 and subsequently served as a Lieutenant in the Coldstream Guards, going to France on 2 November 1915 with 2nd Guards Brigade, Guards Division. He was killed in action at the Battle of the Ancre on 16 September 1916 and his name is recorded on the Thiepval Memorial. He was 21.

1914-15 Star, British War Medal and Victory Medal.

12. War Memorials
Beaudesert & Henley in Arden

UNLIKE many of the surrounding villages, Henley does not have a cross in a prominent position to commemorate those who died in the Great War, possibly because its ancient Market Cross was in the obvious position in the town to place such a memorial.

The first recorded mention of a war memorial was during the Court Leet Service held in St John's Church on 2 December 1917. The Rector appealed for a generous offering in aid of a fund to be raised for a permanent war memorial to the men on the Roll of Honour of the parish: the collection amounted to £4.5s.9d.[200] Over a year elapsed before a meeting was held in the parish room on Friday, 31 January 1919 to discuss the question of a memorial. It was presided over by Dr Nelson and it was decided that there should be a brass memorial containing the names of fallen parishioners of various denominations erected in the parish church: it was hoped to have a simple memorial in the Baptist Church also. Contributions were requested, to be paid to a committee consisting of the High Bailiff (Dr Nelson), Revd F D Lane and Messrs A C Coldicott, F Bayliss, W T Taylor and H Hawkes (A C Coldicott and H Hawkes had each lost a son in the war).[201] A town meeting was called on Thursday of the following week, presided over by the High Bailiff and held in the Guild Hall. Mr W T Taylor thought that the scheme for an additional memorial should be put aside until peace was declared, the industrial strife in the country settled and the brass memorial scheme completed. This proposal was supported by Mr G F Lodder and it was agreed that the matter be deferred to a time to be decided by the High Bailiff. The meeting also considered the question of peace celebrations.[202]

The first list of war dead appeared in the Henley Peace Celebrations booklet in July 1919 and included the following sixteen names:

George William Andrews
Frederick Charles Atkins
Arden Cotterell Coldicott MC
Stephen Hastings
Laurence John Arden Hodges
Owen Holt

Harry Richard Arnold
Sidney Bickley
William Sutton Findon
John Aubrey Hawkes
Harry Hugh Holt
Edward Hopkins

---

200 *Herald*, 7 December 1917
201 *Herald*, 7 February 1919
202 *Herald*, 14 February 1919

Maurice Horsnett	Thomas Sadler
Albert Alfred Sammons	Francis Henry Woodward

The first memorial unveiled in the town was on 9 October 1920 and was that of that of the Ancient Order of Foresters. It took the form of a framed illuminated scroll and was unveiled in the Assembly Room of the White Swan by the High Bailiff (Dr Nelson). Unfortunately it is now lost and may have contained more names than the following, which are known to have been on it:

George William Andrews	Harry Hugh Holt
Owen Holt	Edward Hopkins

The official Henley and Beaudesert War Memorial on the north wall in St John's Church was unveiled by the High Bailiff on the following day, 10 October. The brass plate included the following names in addition to those in the Peace Celebrations booklet:

William Louis Clare	William Collins
George Amos Spears	

It was dedicated by the Revd F H Lawson of St Nicholas' Church, Warwick and above the names of the dead is inscribed:

1914-1918
The names of those who in these years
went forth from this place for God and the Right
and came not back again are here inscribed
to be honoured for evermore

The Baptist Church War Memorial was unveiled on 30 January 1921 by Mr J Herbert Anson of Beaudesert Park. The stone memorial tablet on the north wall of the Baptist Church contains the names of seven members of its congregation who died.

The name of Howard Hobbins does not appear on the memorial in St John's Church, nor does that of William Dawes: the latter did not serve in the armed forces, but was Quartermaster of Warwick Number 11 Voluntary Aid Detachment.

The question of a memorial for the Wesleyan Methodist church did not arise, as it was reported in March 1919 that the young men of the Wesleyan congregation who joined the army "have all come safely through and have all been demobilised".

For some years consideration continued to be given to providing a memorial in addition to the brass plate. At the annual meeting of the Court Leet on 10 November 1920, the High Bailiff reported on the result of negotiations of a two-

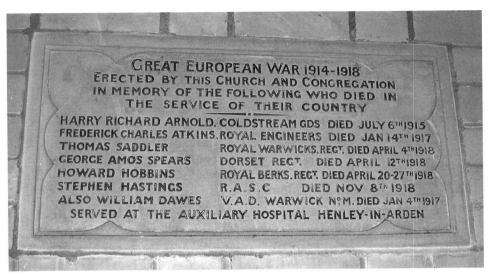

The Baptist Church War Memorial

man sub Committee (himself and Mr Lodder) to purchase land for a playing field or athletic ground. They had not been able to obtain a suitable field. He was unable to report any progress the following year, "but the matter was not being lost sight of". At the same meeting in 1921, Dr Agar suggested that the names of those who had fallen in the Great War should be recorded. The Lord of the Manor, William Fieldhouse, agreed that this should be done and said that the record would be placed in an air-tight case, which should stand in the Guild Hall and become the property of the High Bailiff and Burgesses. This does not seem to have been done. There is no further report on an additional memorial until the matter was raised by Edwin Stephens (Mace Bearer) on 10 November 1925. He urged that some effort should be made to complete arrangements for the War Memorial. The Lord of the Manor offered £100 towards the cost if suitable ground could be acquired. Nothing happened and Edwin Stephens raised the matter again at the 1926 meeting of the Court. Dr Nelson said "he desired to correct a report which appeared in the newspapers after the last meeting from which it appeared that nothing had been done. This was a mistake because when he was High Bailiff a sum of over £100 was subscribed for the purpose and a very beautiful plate was provided and erected in the Church". On 9 November 1927 the then High Bailiff reported that "attempts had been made to procure a suitable field for the War Memorial but it had been impossible to find one". There seem to have been no further attempt to find a field and no alternative memorial was suggested.

There is no mention of a War Memorial in the minutes of the Parish Council or of the Beaudesert Parish Meeting. The town was offered a War Trophy, but at the Parish Council meeting on 10 December 1919 it was proposed by the Chairman, Howard Sinclair Brown, that "the offer of War Trophies for the Parish be respectfully declined" and the resolution was duly carried. A trophy did arrive in the town in the course of the next few years despite this decision, as at the meeting on 9 January 1928 it was agreed that "the old German gun now standing in the White Swan Croft should be scrapped". The proposal was made by Councillor A C Coldicott. It was agreed that the fate of the gun should be considered at the next annual Parish Council meeting, which was held on 28 March 1928. It was there decided that the gun should be scrapped and the proceeds given to the Nursing Association: it was further agreed that the sale should be left in the hands of the Parish Council. By 28 September 1928 the gun had been sold, as at the meeting held on that day the Clerk was instructed to write to Mr W T Taylor, who had paid the cost of the gun's delivery by rail and of hauling it to its site when it arrived. Mr Taylor was to be asked if would accept the cheque for the gun or whether the Council should hand the cheque over to the Nursing Association or to the Stratford upon Avon Hospital. No record of his decision appears in subsequent Minutes.

In October 2009 a memorial for those Henley men who served in the Great War but were not included on the original memorial brass plate was placed alongside it in St John's Church. The men were identified by the author and the manufacture of the additional brass plate was arranged by Leslie Goodman, Secretary of the Henley Branch of the British Legion, who also made the arrangements for the parade and memorial service which accompanied its unveiling. The men named on this memorial are:

Albert Charles Adkins
William Oliver Burden
Percival Thomas Evans
Howard Hobbins
Frederick Ernest Long
Herbert Henry Perkins

William Beard
George Valentine Crompton
William Eardley Hayward
Harold Ingram MM
Frederick Ernest Lowe

Leslie Goodman and Douglas Bridgewater
at the unveiling of the memorial in October 2009
(copyright of the Herald *and published with their permission)*

War Memorial
Arden House School

THE Arden House War Memorial containing the names of old boys of the school who died in the Great War was unveiled on 5 June 1924 during an impressive and well-attended ceremony, with music provided by the bands of the 5th and 6th Battalions of the Royal Warwickshire Regiment. The Memorial was dedicated by the Archdeacon of Warwick (Revd H C A Back, Rector of Hampton Lucy) and unveiled by Lieutenant-Colonel J C Brinton CVO, DSO of 2nd Life Guards: both of these men were old boys of the school.[203] The Memorial stood in a Garden of Rest, the oak gates of which opened onto a garden with lawns and stone-flagged paths and pergolas of brick and oak, with seats and herbaceous borders at intervals. The garden sloped down to a Swimming Pool, the whole having been built as a memorial by Dr Ernest and Mr Oswald Nelson. The Memorial itself was given by:

Parents, Old Boys and Friends of the School
in memory of those Arden House Boys who
gave their lives in the Great War
1914-1919
This inscription appears on the north side of the base of the Memorial.

The Swimming Pool had been opened in 1923. Built into its wall was a Memorial Plaque which read:

In Memoriam illorum qui olim in hoc campo ludebant. Idem super pro rege, pro patris, pro nobis ante diem mortem milites obierunt.

W.E.N.   MDCCCCXXIII   O.T.P.N.

This may be translated as:

In memory of those who once as boys played on this field, who recently for King, country and for us suffered death as soldiers before their time.

W.E.N.   1923   O.T.P.N.

---

203 John Chaytor Brinton was born in 1867 and joined the 2nd Life Guards in 1891. He was at the Battle of Khartoum in 1898 where he was severely wounded and was mentioned in despatches. He served throughout the Boer War and was awarded the DSO in 1901. He retired in 1911 but rejoined on the outbreak of war in 1914: he was twice mentioned in despatches and was made a Chevalier of the Legion of Honour

The initials are those of William Ernest Nelson and Oswald Thomas Pemberton Nelson.

The Arden House Memorial was much more elaborate than the Henley Memorial. Its 26 names also exceeded the 19 names on the brass plate in St John's Church, though the addition of another brass plate in 2009 with a further 11 names has changed that. The old boys had a high casualty rate, resulting from the fact that a large proportion of them were junior officers. Of the 26 who died, all but three had been commissioned.

The Unveiling of the Arden House Memorial by Lt-Col J C Brinton (above) and its Dedication by the Revd H C A Back (below)

The Swimming Pool and the Garden of Rest have now disappeared. The Memorial itself has been rescued and re-positioned in the grounds of Warwickshire College, which now owns the site. It is no longer in its original form, as the four-sided sundial set on top of the stone shaft and the stone steps on which it was raised have also disappeared.

War Memorial
Beaudesert Park School

The oak-panel memorial in the entrance hall of Beaudesert Park School, Minchinhampton, lists the names of all its old boys who served. The casualty rate is higher than that of Henley, but lower than that of Arden House: this results in part from the fact that although the great majority were commissioned, five men served in the Royal Navy, which had a much lower casualty rate than the army.

Abbreviations

AB	Able Seaman
AFC	Air Force Cross
ARRC	Associate of the Royal Red Cross
AVC	Army Veterinary Corps
Bart	Baronet
BEF	British Expeditionary Force
Bdr	Bombardier
Capt	Captain
Col	Colonel
Coy	Company
Cpl	Corporal
CB	Companion of the Order of the Bath
CMG	Companion of the Order of St Michael and St George
CWGC	Commonwealth War Graves Commission
CVO	Companion of the Victorian Order
DL	Deputy Lieutenant
DFC	Distinguished Flying Cross
DSO	Distinguished Service Order
EEF	Egyptian Expeditionary Force
FC	Flight Cadet
FO	Flying Officer
FQMS	Farrier Quartermaster Sergeant
Gen	General
Gnr	Gunner
HAC	Honourable Artillery Company
Herald	*The Stratford upon Avon Herald and South Warwickshire Advertiser*
IAR	Indian Army Reserve
JP	Justice of the Peace
LG	*London Gazette*
LRCP	Licentiate of the Royal College of Physicians
Lt	Lieutenant
Lt-Col	Lieutenant-Colonel
Maj	Major
Maj-Gen	Major-General
MC	Military Cross
MG	Machine gun
Mid	Midshipman
MP	Member of Parliament

MRCS	Member of the Royal College of Surgeons
OTC	Officers' Training Corps
PR	Parish Register
Pte	Private
QMS	Quarter Master Sergeant
QOWH	Queen's Own Worcestershire Hussars
RAF	Royal Air Force
RAMC	Royal Army Medical Corps
RE	Royal Engineers
Revd	Reverend
RFA	Royal Field Artillery
RFC	Royal Flying Corps
Rfn	Rifleman
RGH	Royal Gloucestershire Hussars
RM	Royal Marines
RN	Royal Navy
RNAS	Royal Naval Air Service
SDGW	Soldiers Died in the Great War
Sgt	Sergeant
Spr	Sapper
SSM	Squadron Sergeant Major
SWB	Silver War Badge
TD	Territorial Diploma
VC	Victoria Cross

Bibliography

Adderley, Hon H A — *History of the Warwickshire Yeomanry Cavalry* (Warwick: W H Smith & Son, 1912)

Adderley, Hon H A — *The Warwickshire Yeomanry in the Great War* (Warwick: W H Smith & Son, 1922)

Anon — *The History of the 1/6th Battalion, Royal Warwickshire Regiment* (Birmingham, Cornish Brothers, 1922)

Ashby, J — *Seek Glory, Now Keep Glory: The Story of the 1st Battalion Royal Warwickshire Regiment 1914-1918* (Solihull: Helion & Co, 2000)

Bill, Major C A — *The 15th Battalion Royal Warwickshire Regiment (2nd Birmingham Battalion) in the Great War* (Birmingham, Cornish Brothers Ltd, 1932)

Caddick-Adams, P — *By God They Can Fight! A History of 143rd Infantry Brigade 1908 to 1995* (Shrewsbury: 143rd Infantry Brigade, 1995)

Carrington, Lt C E — *The War Record of the 1/5th Battalion, The Royal Warwickshire Regiment* (Birmingham: Cornish Brothers, 1922)

Carrington, C — *Soldier From the Wars Returning* (London: Hutchinson & Co, 1965)

Carter, T — *Birmingham Pals: 14th, 15th and 16th Battalions of the Royal Warwickshire Regiment* (Barnsley: Pen & Sword Books Ltd, 1997)

Chidgery, H T — *Black Square Memories: An Account of the 2/8th Battalion Royal Warwickshire Regiment 1914-1918* (Stratford upon Avon: Shakespeare Head Press, 1924)

Cooksey, A & & Griffiths D (ed) — *Harry's War: the Great War Diary of Harry Drinkwater* (Ebury Press, 2013)

Cooper, W — *Henley in Arden: An Ancient Market Town* (Birmingham: Cornish Brothers, 1946).

de Ruvigny, Marquis — *The Roll of Honour: a Biographical Record of Members of His Majesty's Naval and Military Forces Who Fell in the Great War 1914-1918* (2 volumes, Naval and Military Press)

Elliott, Sir I (ed) — *The Balliol College Register 1833-1933* (Oxford: University Press, 1934)

Fairclough, J E B — *The First Birmingham Battalion in the Great War 1914-1919* (Birmingham: Cornish Brothers, 1933)

Heath, C E (ed) — *Service Record of King Edward's School Birmingham During the War 1914-1919* (Birmingham: Cornish Brothers, 1920).

Higginbotham, G — *Rugby School Register 1892-1921* (Rugby: George Over, 1929)

Hudson, J — *Beaudesert Park School: a Centenary History* (The History Press, 2008)

James, Brig E A — *British Regiments, 1914-18* (London: Naval & Military Press, 4th Edition 1993)

Keyte, V J — *Beaudesert Park School: the First 75 years* (Privately printed, 1983)

Spinks, P — *Brooke's Battery: A History of 1/1 Warwickshire Horse Artillery 1908-1919* (Studley: Brewin Books, 2008)

Tennant A J — *British Merchant Ships sunk by U-Boats in the 1914-1918 War* (Chipstead: Tennant, 1990)

Wagner, M — *My Memories: An Autobiography* (Northumberland Press, 1964)

Welham, R C — *Henley in Arden: Life from the Past* (Studley: Brewin Books, 1993)

Westlake, R — *Kitchener's Army* (Tunbridge Wells: Nutshell Publishing Co, 1989)

Winter, J M — *The Great War and the British People* (Basingstoke: Macmillan, 1986)

Vaughan, E C — *Some Desperate Glory* (London: F Warne, 1981)

The War List of the University of Cambridge 1914-1918 (Cambridge: University Press, 1921)

Oxford University Roll of Service (Oxford: Clarendon Press, 1920)

The Malvern College Register 1865-1924 (London: Charles Murray, 1925)

Memorials of Rugbeians who fell in the Great War (7 volumes: printed by the Medici Society for private circulation only, 1916-1923)

Uppingham School Roll 1880-1921 (London: Edward Stanton Ltd, 1922)

The Monumental Inscriptions of St John's Henley in Arden, St Nicholas' Beaudesert and the Henley in Arden Baptist Church (Birmingham & Midland Society for Genealogy and Heraldry, 1995)

Joint War Committee Reports by the Joint War Committee and the Joint War Finance Committee of the British Red Cross Society and the Order of St John of Jerusalem in England on Voluntary Aid rendered to the Sick and Wounded at Home and Abroad and to British Prisoners of War 1914-1919 (London: HMSO, 1921)

Index